THE BURIED CAUSE

THE BURIED CAUSE

Unearthing Hidden History in the Lee Monument Cornerstone

EDITED BY KATHERINE RIDGWAY,
CHRISTINA KEYSER VIDA,
AND ELIZABETH MOORE

University of Virginia Press
Charlottesville and London
PUBLISHED IN ASSOCIATION WITH THE
VIRGINIA DEPARTMENT OF HISTORIC RESOURCES

The University of Virginia Press is situated on the traditional lands of the Monacan Nation, and the Commonwealth of Virginia was and is home to many other Indigenous people. We pay our respect to all of them, past and present. We also honor the enslaved African and African American people who built the University of Virginia, and we recognize their descendants. We commit to fostering voices from these communities through our publications and to deepening our collective understanding of their histories and contributions.

University of Virginia Press

Printed in the United States of America on acid-free paper

First published 2026

9 8 7 6 5 4 3 2 1

LIBRARY OF CONGRESS CATALOGING-IN-PUBLICATION DATA
Names: Ridgway, Katherine (conservator), editor | Vida, Christina Keyser, editor | Moore, Elizabeth A. (Elizabeth Ann), editor | Virginia. Department of Historic Resources issuing body
Title: The buried cause : unearthing hidden history in the Lee Monument cornerstone / edited by Katherine Ridgway, Christina Keyser Vida, and Elizabeth Moore.
Description: Charlottesville : University of Virginia Press | Includes bibliographical references and index.
Identifiers: LCCN 2025018239 (print) | LCCN 2025018240 (ebook) | ISBN 9780813954233 hardback | ISBN 9780813954240 paperback | ISBN 9780813954257 ebook
Subjects: LCSH: Lee, Robert E. (Robert Edward), 1807–1870—Monuments—Virginia—Richmond | Collective memory—Virginia—Richmond | Richmond (Va.)—Antiquities | United States—History—Civil War, 1861–1865—Monuments | Monument Avenue (Richmond, Va.) | BISAC: HISTORY / Americas (North, Central, South, West Indies)
Classification: LCC F234.R547 B87 2025 (print) | LCC F234.R547 (ebook) | DDC 975.5/23—dc23/eng/20250813
LC record available at https://lccn.loc.gov/2025018239
LC ebook record available at https://lccn.loc.gov/2025018240

Unless indicated otherwise, all images courtesy of the Virginia Department of Historic Resources. Photos taken by Leslie Straub, former collections manager.

Cover art: The Lee Monument box in its cornerstone, Monument Avenue, Richmond, Virginia. (Courtesy of the Virginia Department of Historic Resources)
Cover design: David Fassett

To all the people with stories buried under Monument Avenue

CONTENTS

Life and Times

Militariana

ILLUSTRATIONS

ACKNOWLEDGMENTS

The editors would like to acknowledge Devon Henry, Team Henry Enterprises, and their associates, who removed the Robert E. Lee Monument, allowing us to uncover all of the stories in the boxes hidden within. Thank you to Leslie Straub, without whose help we would not have an accurate inventory for the boxes' contents and photographs of the artifacts. Thank you to Sue Donovan, without whose help the artifacts would have suffered. Thanks to all involved with the opening of the box, too many to name, some who want to stay anonymous, you know who you are and y'all are the best. A final thanks to all of the authors who stepped up to tell these stories, first in blog form and then in print.

KCR would like to thank all of her friends and family who had to listen to her talk about monuments for years, her colleagues who supported her throughout this process, and her therapist, who gave her the mental tools to survive the process. Finally, she would like to thank CKV and EM for their friendship and patience while she figured out how to put together a book.

CKV is grateful for her colleagues, friends, and family and all the emotional and intellectual support they have provided, from casual conversations to deep dives in archival material. She is also thankful for KCR for shepherding this project and for her years of friendship.

EAM would like to thank the many colleagues, friends, and family who provided support throughout this entire adventure, from the first calls about Monument Avenue to the last conversations about this volume. She is especially appreciative of KCR for her consummate professionalism and grace under pressure and her willingness to take the lead on this project. CKV's research and insight have been invaluable for both big picture interpretations and small yet critical historical details. It has been an interesting couple of years.

EDITORS' NOTE

The editors have used the *Chicago Manual of Style 18* (CMOS18) when making editorial choices for this manuscript. This includes the capitalization of the words black and white when not used in direct quotes. The CMOS states, "the adjective *Black* is now usually capitalized to refer to people" (Section 8.39) It also says, "Some writers and editors capitalize *White* also, on the principle that the capital letter in both instances signals a person rather than a color" (8.39). For these reasons, the reader will see both black and white capitalized when used in this way.

Similarly, the CMOS18 capitalizes the words south, southern, southerner, north, northern, and northerner when used in the context of a national region (8.48). Otherwise, these terms are not capitalized. This was the decision used throughout this manuscript. These editorial decisions in no way reflect the preferences of the individual authors and were made to create consistent grammar throughout the volume.

Opinions and assertions contained within this volume do not imply, nor represent, the official policies or positions of the Commonwealth of Virginia or the Virginia Department of Historic Resources, nor are they endorsed via this publication. As with any edited volume, the authors may not necessarily agree with writings of other authors.

THE BURIED CAUSE

Figure 1. This drone image of the Robert E. Lee Monument from above shows the base of the monument completely covered in graffiti. (Courtesy of Sanjay Suchak)

Introduction

Adam H. Domby

A BEGINNING

We can begin the story in a variety of ways.

In the summer of 2020, the Confederate monuments along Richmond's Monument Avenue were vandalized.

Put another way, in the summer of 2020, the Confederate monuments along Monument Avenue were spray-painted in an act of protest against the killing of unarmed Black Americans.

Or put a third way, in the summer of 2020, Richmond's citizenry updated the Confederate monuments along Monument Avenue, announcing what modern Richmonders felt these monuments were all about. Their expressions of dislike for the monuments eventually led to their removal.[1]

The spray-painting of monuments, followed by their removal, was a testament to both the changing views among White Richmonders regarding the Confederacy and of the political empowerment of African Americans within the city. The monument to Jefferson Davis, who served as President of the Confederacy, had "Fuck Davis," "Cops Kill," "BLM," "End White Silence," and "we hate this fucking statue!!!" painted on it, as well as numerous other phrases. Each of the monuments bore similar messages, and most had calls to end White supremacy. Those who painted the monuments clearly understood these statues as monuments to White supremacy, and they weren't wrong. Many of those who erected the monuments would have agreed.[2]

After all, monuments teach values far more than they teach history. They teach you who to look up to (literally), not about events of the past. The least

Figure 2. In 2020, protesters spray-painted monuments in Richmond like J. E. B. Stuart with social justice graffiti. (Courtesy of Adam Domby)

prominent Confederate monument provided perhaps the most eloquent example of how little historical knowledge monuments pass on to the citizenry that sees them on a day-to-day basis. On the Matthew Fontaine Maury Monument, dedicated to a relatively obscure naval figure, Richmonders simply wrote, "Fuck This Guy Too," the vagueness being a clear indicator of how little of Maury's life was known to most locals.

In the end, the Confederate monuments were all removed, but discoveries were made during that process. In 1887, when the cornerstone of the Robert E. Lee Monument was laid, a box full of mementos had been placed within the foundation. A second box was placed during the construction midway up the plinth that the Lee statue rested on. As explained more fully in chapters

3 and 4, these were not true time capsules, as there was no intent to dig them up later, but rather were meant to remain within the monument in perpetuity, imbuing it with meaning and significance. The items found provide insight into Richmond in the late nineteenth century and the evolution of how Richmonders remembered the Civil War. This book explores the objects (and in some cases, the objects that were not included) to better understand the monuments' intended function. At times, the artifacts even provide a window into the war itself.

The first four chapters examine how these monuments and "time capsules" came to be, what they were meant to do, and why some artifacts survived. The next two chapters look at who was missing from the time capsules, notably African Americans and women. Combined, these chapters provide crucial context for the rest of the volume, which then turns to the contents of the boxes, providing different forms of analysis on individual objects and the people who donated them to the box.

THE LOST CAUSE

The statues that once lined Monument Avenue were, in many ways, quintessential Confederate monuments. They were part of the rewriting of history known as the "Lost Cause," a shared set of beliefs or narrative tropes about the past used to justify the present. While the Lost Cause is more fully explored in chapters one and six, I will briefly summarize a few of the falsehoods that were central to the mythologizing of the past that shaped the future. First was a denial of slavery as the cause of the war, despite the institution being clearly the root cause. Lost Causers also celebrated slavery as benevolent even as they denied the war was about slavery. This, despite the horrible brutality of slavery, was a system of labor extraction based on violence and the threat of violence. Boosters of this Lost Cause narrative also proclaimed Reconstruction a period of misrule by African Americans and Northerners (ignoring the positive progressive policies of Reconstruction, including public schools). When contrasted with slavery as benevolent, the supposed misrule of Reconstruction presented a justification for returning to White rule in the South. Indeed, one critical motivator for the rewriting of history was justifying Jim Crow and uniting White Southerners with a shared memory of the past—a shared memory not based on historical reality but on post-war needs.

As discussed in several of the following chapters, these monuments were meant to spread this Lost Cause narrative and help reify White control of Southern politics. It is in many ways appropriate that monuments erected by White supremacists in the midst of disfranchisement of African Americans were ultimately removed by a Black-owned construction company hired by an African American mayor. It certainly would have outraged the men who put the monuments up, as it meant African Americans were once again part of the body politic. Indeed, during the dedication of the Davis Monument, Governor Swanson "exalted . . . the principal of local self-government," a statement met with applause.[3] In 1907, "local self-government" was another way of saying "ignore the Fourteenth and Fifteenth Amendments," thereby allowing Jim Crow rule in the South and the disfranchisement of African Americans.

THE REAL ROBERT E. LEE

And what of the monuments' subjects themselves? Who was Robert E. Lee? Would Lee have supported the White supremacist project his monument was part of? As some of these chapters discuss, whether he would have approved of the monument is open to debate, but his devotion to White supremacy seems unequivocal.[4]

Today's neo-Confederates often absurdly cite Lee as an advocate for racial reconciliation and frequently repeat a story about Lee taking communion alongside a Black man after the Civil War. But as Andy Hall has shown, this story is an evolution of an older myth that Lee and other White members of St. Paul's Episcopal Church had taken communion while ignoring a Black man who had knelt alongside them, thus showing their "superiority" to the African American who had the temerity to try and take communion with Whites. The Black man was never given communion. Not only is the story likely entirely fabricated, but it was first used in 1905 to demonstrate Lee's devotion to White supremacy and opposition to Black equality. Only later did it evolve to claim the opposite.[5]

But we don't need made-up tales to know Lee's views on race and reconciliation. After the war, Lee remained convinced of White superiority and openly spoke about his views. Pushing for the return of White rule in the South in 1866, he testified to Congress, "I do not think that [the Black man] is as capable of acquiring knowledge as the white man is." Asked how Whites would respond to Blacks being given the vote, he responded, "I think it would excite unfriendly feelings between the two races," before eerily menacing, "I cannot pretend to say to what extent it would go, but that would be the result." Indeed, Lee preferred that Virginia might have a smaller number of congressmen than give the vote to Black men. And he didn't stop there, going so far as saying, "I think it would be better for Virginia if she could get rid of them," referring to the state's entire Black population.[6] As some scholars have pointed out, Lee was arguing for ethnic cleansing—not something I would personally deem worthy of celebration.[7]

Lee certainly made little to no effort to protect African Americans around him. While he was president of Washington College (now Washington and Lee University), his students sexually assaulted Black girls without consequence and started their own chapter of the Ku Klux Klan. When Lee bothered to address racist harassment, he treated it as a minor transgression, a crime less serious than when students threatened to take a holiday.[8]

Only if you ignore Black Southerners as part of the United States can you imagine that Lee facilitated reconciliation and was a unifying force. As John Salmon aptly points out in the next chapter, perhaps the one thing Lee did say that fostered any sense of reconciliation (besides surrendering) was to oppose the erecting of Confederate monuments. On the surface, Lee seemed to have wished to forget the war, something neo-Confederates now accuse those seeking the removal of monuments of desiring.

While this can legitimately be seen as evidence that Lee opposed statues, there is another interpretation possible that drives home his commitment to White supremacy. An alternate reading of this rejection of monuments is that it was a matter of timing that drove Lee, not an aversion to celebrating the Confederacy or any evolving views on White supremacy. As Salmon hints at, Lee might have changed his mind when the situation—and White control of the South—was cemented. It seems likely he would have. His opposition to monuments in the 1860s can be interpreted as a political calculation made by a man who recognized that attempts to celebrate the Confederacy would lead to outrage in the North and might lengthen Reconstruction. Lee wanted Southern Whites to regain political control of the South and the nation as soon as possible. As Salmon concludes, his views of monuments might have changed had he lived to see Jim Crow firmly established. Indeed in 1866, he wrote in a letter:

> As regards the erection of such a monument [. . .] my conviction is, that however grateful it would be to the feelings of the South, the attempt in the present condition

of the Country, would have the effect of retarding, instead of accelerating its accomplishment; & of continuing, if not adding to, the difficulties under which the Southern people labour. All I think that can now be done, is to aid our noble & generous women in their efforts to protect the graves & mark the last resting places of those who have fallen, & wait for better times.[9]

That last line is especially indicative of his motivations. By "wait for better times," Lee meant that once White Southerners (the only group he included in "the Southern people") were no longer under Reconstruction and occupation by United States Army troops—the "present difficulties"—then monuments might be appropriate.

Lee's opposition to monuments was at least in part about defending White supremacy. At some level, he understood that monuments seek to demonstrate who controls public spaces; erecting them too early would raise the ire of those who opposed the return to power of former Confederates. Ultimately, we cannot know for sure how Lee would have viewed these monuments, as he died in 1870, never seeing the disenfranchisement of Black Southerners or the rise of Jim Crow—Lee's "better times"—which led to the subsequent widespread erection of Confederate monuments across the South.

While in the end, we cannot know how Lee would have responded, we can ask ourselves, should we even care what Lee would have thought? Was his opinion one we are obligated to value?

MONUMENTS VS. HISTORY

As I mentioned at the start, monuments do not teach history. Indeed, monuments celebrating Lee seem to have obscured the past rather than informed the public. They hide the fact that Lee committed treason and took up arms against the United States in an effort to create a slaveholders' republic—and at times, these monuments hide even that he was defeated. They obscure the fact that Lee's army committed war crimes, enslaved free people, and refused to treat Black prisoners as POWs. Lee opposed freeing people he and his family held in bondage, and his family profited from leasing slaves to the Confederate army.[10]

Monuments tell people whom to admire. Until the removal of Lee's statue, viewers were forced to literally look up to a bronze copy of him on Monument Avenue. But was the real man worthy of the monument he received? Did he represent Richmond's values in the twenty-first century? The statue certainly represented the values of those who erected the monument as part of a residential development that banned African Americans from buying houses. The spray-painting, protest, and subsequent removal imply that many Richmond residents no longer wish to be associated with those values. It also implies that they do not believe Americans should be beholden to an interpretation of the past held by self-avowed White supremacists over a century ago.

As discussed in several chapters, Lee's monument sought to silence the voices of those men and women whom Lee enslaved, who recalled him as a cruel and harsh oppressor who separated families.[11] The truth about Lee—that he was a flawed, racist loser—was obscured by monuments that presented him as perfect. It is hardly surprising that defenders of these monuments frequently struggle to identify the root causes of the war they wish to celebrate. Lost Cause supporters long distorted the past in an effort to uphold White societal privilege. But while these monuments were part of a successful PR campaign, for just as long, others have opposed this erasure of the past.

CONTROVERSIAL FROM THE START

While on the surface it seems these monuments only became controversial in the twenty-first century, in reality, they have always been political, and some Americans have objected to them since their erection.[12] As noted in chapter 6, there was not agreement in 1890 that the Lee Monument should be erected. The statue was unveiled the day before Decoration Day (now known as Memorial Day), a day devoted to cleaning and decorating the graves of the men who died fighting against the Confederacy. The timing was seen as insulting by many US Army veterans.

While giving a Decoration Day speech at the Soldiers Home National Cemetery in Washington, DC, Elijah Morse objected to the erection, saying:

> In what other country were traitors ever allowed to erect monuments to glorify treason and traitors? We may forgive the wrong, and a great wrong it was, which shed rivers of blood, filled the land with widows and orphans and wasted billions of treasure, but "let my right hand forget its cunning and my tongue cleave to the roof of my mouth" when I make traitors and patriots equal, or when I fail to discern between the loyal soldiers, who periled and laid down their lives in defense of their country and the traitors who sought to destroy it.[13]

He was not alone. At the Congressional Cemetery across town, William Mason, giving another Decoration Day speech, provided a "note of warning" that he "must earnestly protest against [. . .] the unveiling of Gen. Lee's statue yesterday." He also argued that anyone who waved a Confederate flag was still "as much a traitor as he was thirty years ago."[14] Similar complaints were heard during addresses at Gettysburg and Antietam that day.

African Americans also criticized the monument.[15] The *Richmond Planet* bemoaned the fact that celebrants at the dedication "still clung to theories which were presumed to be buried for all eternity."[16] Indeed, African Americans had not taken part in the dedication; they hadn't been invited, after all. As one African American reporter noted, "Perhaps no celebration ever took place in the history of mankind in which a whole race stood by, silent and unsympathetic, while another race was simply deliriously vociferous and enthusiastic with measureless interest."[17] Tales of a few formerly enslaved people happily attending with their former masters were either made up or, the reporter noted, represented "the arrogance and insolence of the master and the servility and cringing cowardice of the slave" and stood in the way of White Southerners accepting Blacks as "free and equal citizens."[18]

Black Americans were opposed to such celebrations of the Confederacy because they understood the ties between memory and politics. Black Richmonders celebrated a three-day "National Thanksgiving Day for Freedom" in October 1890, and others argued for holding Emancipation celebrations on April 3 and April 9, highlighting the defeat of Lee in their celebration of freedom.[19] Indeed, African Americans in majority Black Mecklenburg County had celebrated Lee's defeat instead just a month earlier during their annual "Surrender Day" ceremony.[20] The primary speaker at that event was John Mercer Langston, the first Black congressman from Virginia, who was actively running for reelection. His speech, nominally serving to celebrate the past, was as much a campaign speech as it was a historical celebration. As seen with Confederate monuments, celebrations of the past are nearly always about the present.

Responding to the Lee Monument dedication, the *New York Age* asked rhetorically, "Wherein does the red flag of anarchy differ from the flag of the stars and bars?" before tying their objection to the monument not only due to Lee being a traitor but also because, "have not the followers of Robert E. Lee undermined the war amendments of the Constitution and reared in defiance of them revolutionary governments, maintained by the repressive methods usually adopted by the beneficiaries of tyranny?" The paper was willing to concede that Lee was "one of the greatest generals of modern times . . . but he was a traitor and gave his magnificent abilities to the infamous task of disrupting the Union and to perpetuating the system of slavery."[21]

In 1929, while reporting on how former Confederates were trying to rewrite history, a Black journalist observed that "the lost cause was not only lost but misguided and God-forsaken."[22] Yet monuments like the Lee statue in Richmond sought to suppress any viewpoints that pushed back against the Lost Cause's narrative of history, a narrative premised upon lies.

Who knows? Perhaps, fewer monuments venerating this Confederate general will lead to a more accurate assessment of Lee and his cause. The removal of monuments does not mean they are forgotten. Quite the opposite. Indeed, this book, which shines light on the history of Confederate monuments and Richmond, would not exist without their removal. In at least this case, the removal of a monument has led to the production of new historical knowledge.

NOTES

1. Parts of this chapter were originally published as a blog post. Adam H. Domby, "Virgil, quick, come see there goes Robert E Lee," *UVA Press*, https://www.upress.virginia.edu/news/virgil-quick-come-see-there-goes-robert-e-lee/.
2. For more on the ties between White supremacy and the Lost Cause, see Adam Domby, *The False Cause: Fraud, Fabrication, and White Supremacy in Confederate Memory* (University of Virginia Press, 2020). Other excellent works on Lost Cause memory include Cynthia Mills and Pamela H. Simpson, eds., *Monuments to the Lost Cause: Women, Art, and the Landscapes of Southern Memory* (Knoxville: University of Tennessee Press, 2003); Karen Lynne Cox, *Dixie's Daughters: The United Daughters of the Confederacy and the Preservation of Confederate Culture* (Gainesville: University Press of Florida, 2003); W. Fitzhugh Brundage, *The Southern Past: A Clash of Race and Memory* (Cambridge, MA.: Belknap, 2005); David W Blight, *Race and Reunion: The Civil War in American Memory* (Cambridge, MA.: Belknap, 2001); Caroline E. Janney, *Remembering the Civil War: Reunion and the Limits of Reconciliation*, Reprint edition (University of North Carolina Press, 2016); Christopher Alan Graham, *Faith, Race, and the Lost Cause: Confessions of a Southern Church* (University of Virginia Press, 2023); Barbara A. Gannon, *Americans Remember Their Civil War* (Santa Barbara, CA: Praeger, 2017).
3. "Hundred Thousand Cheer as Monument Is Unveiled" *Richmond Times-Dispatch*, June 4, 1907, 4.
4. For the best biographies of Lee see Elizabeth Brown Pryor. *Reading the Man: A Portrait of Robert E. Lee Through His Private Letters* and Michael Fellman, *The Making of Robert E. Lee.*

5. Andy Hall, "Fantasizing Lee as a Civil Rights Pioneer" *Civil War Monitor*, July 23, 2012, https://www.civilwarmonitor.com/blog/fantasizing-lee-as-a-civil-rights-pioneer.
6. "Robert E. Lee's Testimony before Congress (February 17, 1866)" *Encyclopedia Virginia*, https://encyclopediavirginia.org/primary-documents/robert-e-lees-testimony-before-congress-february-17-1866/.
7. Ty Seidule, "Trump Praise for Robert E. Lee's Statue in Virginia Shows How Far This 'Hero' Has Fallen" *NBCNews*, September 9, 2021, https://www.nbcnews.com/think/opinion/trump-praise-robert-e-lee-s-statue-virginia-shows-how-ncna1278742.
8. Brandon Hasbrouck, *White Saviors*, 77 Wash. & Lee L. Rev. Online 47 (2020), https://scholarlycommons.law.wlu.edu/wlulr-online/vol77/iss1/4; Adam Serwer, "The Myth of the Kindly General Lee," *The Atlantic*, June 4, 2017, https://www.theatlantic.com/politics/archive/2017/06/the-myth-of-the-kindly-general-lee/529038/; Siedule, *Robert E Lee and Me*.
9. Robert E. Lee to Thomas L. Rosser, 13 December 1866, Lee Papers, University of Virginia Archives https://leefamilyarchive.org/history-papers-letters-transcripts-uva-v076/.
10. Andy Hall, "We Have Received Provocation Enough," *The Atlantic*, August 11, 2010 https://www.theatlantic.com/national/archive/2010/08/we-have-received-provocation-enough/61276/; "Myth: Grant Stopped the Prisoner Exchange," *Andersonville National Historic Site*, November 27, 2017, https://www.nps.gov/ande/learn/historyculture/grant-and-the-prisoner-exchange.htm; Gregory J. W. Urwin, ed. *Black Flag Over Dixie: Racial Atrocities and Reprisals in the Civil War* (Carbondale: Southern Illinois University Press, 2005); "Slave Payroll 3434," Confederate Slave Payrolls, 1874–1899, Record Group 109, National Archives, Washington, DC. Special thanks to Patrick Sheridan for finding this roll.
11. "An Unpleasant Legacy . . ." *Arlington House, The Robert E. Lee Memorial*, July 26, 2021, https://www.nps.gov/arho/learn/historyculture/an-unpleasant-legacy.htm.
12. For more on resistance to monuments see Karen L. Cox, *No Common Ground: Confederate Monuments and the Ongoing Fight for Racial Justice* (Chapel Hill: University of North Carolina Press, 2021); Ethan J. Kytle and Blain Roberts, *Denmark Vesey's Garden: Slavery and Memory in the Cradle of the Confederacy* (New York: The New Press, 2019).
13. "Flowers and Praise" *Baltimore Sun*, May 31, 1901, 6.
14. "Flowers and Praise" *Baltimore Sun*, May 31, 1901, 6.
15. For more on these African American memories of the war see Hilary N. Green, *Unforgettable Sacrifice: How Black Communities Remembered the Civil War* (New York: Fordham University Press, 2025). For more on Lee's memory see Ty Seidule, *Robert E. Lee and Me: A Southerner's Reckoning with the Myth of the Lost Cause* (New York: Macmillan, 2021).
16. "The Lee Monument Unveiling" *Richmond Planet*, May 31, 1890, 1, https://chroniclingamerica.loc.gov/lccn/sn84025841/1890-05-31/ed-1/seq-1/.
17. "An Incident of the Lee Monument Unveiling" *New York Age*, June 7, 1890, 2.
18. "An Incident of the Lee Monument Unveiling" *New York Age*, June 7, 1890, 2.

For more on African Americans being coopted into Confederate celebrations see Domby, *False Cause*, chapters 4–5; Kevin M. Levin, *Searching for Black Confederates: The Civil War's Most Persistent Myth* (Chapel Hill: University of North Carolina Press, 2019).

19. African American resistance in Richmond to the monument is discussed more fully in Green, *Unforgettable Sacrifice*.
20. "A Virginia Celebration" *New York Age*, April 19, 1890, 4.
21. "Robert E. Lee," *New York Age*, May 31, 1890, 2
22. "No Civil War," *Afro-American*, (Baltimore), June 22, 1929, 6. For more on push back see Domby, *False Cause*, 41–43, 69.

General Monument Avenue

1

Creating Monument Avenue

John Salmon

The story of the creation of Monument Avenue consists of several intertwined subplots: how the avenue came to exist, how it became an avenue both of monuments and of houses, and how mythmaking influenced which Confederates deserved monuments. Although this story is closely connected to the Civil War, the street evolved amid efforts to expand the city in the decades after the war. Making it an avenue of Confederate monuments between 1890 and 1929 was part of a deliberate reinterpretation of Southern history half a generation after the conflict ended.

CREATING THE AVENUE OF MONUMENTS

During the Civil War, Richmond and its surroundings, as with many other Southern cities and towns, suffered significant infrastructure damage. Federal troops burned railroad bridges and tore up tracks outside the city to cut Confederate supply lines. Roads and farm lanes were damaged or destroyed when Confederate engineers constructed three lines of earthworks and artillery batteries across them to defend Richmond. Near the end of the war, when the Confederate army burned several warehouses between Capitol Square and the James River on April 3, 1865, and the flames spread, the resulting Richmond Evacuation Fire destroyed much of the downtown business district. Fortunately, most of the residential areas survived unscathed.

As the city quickly rebuilt and businesses reopened, new residential neighborhoods were developed, mostly to the north and west of downtown.

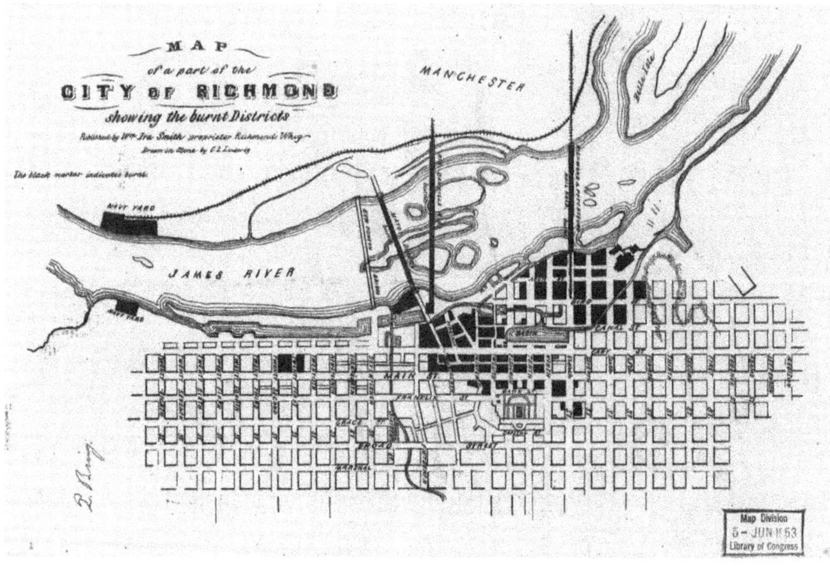

Figure 3. C. L. Ludwig, *Map of a part of the City of Richmond showing the burnt Districts*, 1866. The map, oriented to the south, notes the burned bridges and blocks of buildings in black. Note the block between 8th and 7th Streets; almost the entire block behind the Stewart House was destroyed. (Courtesy Library of Congress)

For decades before the war, after the capital was moved from Williamsburg to Richmond in 1780, many members of Richmond's upper class resided either near the Capitol or on Church Hill, to the east across Shockoe Creek. By the 1840s and 1850s, the area just west of Capitol Square was gaining in popularity, especially several blocks along Franklin Street, which terminated at Monroe Park, just west of Belvidere Street. After the war, Franklin Street and neighboring streets were extended west to present-day Lombardy Street, about one and a half miles from Capitol Square. Richmond's elite (including newly prosperous merchants) continued to build new houses along Franklin Street.

At the war's beginning, Monroe Park was the western edge of the city's web of streets. Farms lay beyond. During the fifteen years following the end of the war in 1865, the streets resumed their westward advance to the vicinity of Lombardy Street and Richmond College. There, the urban streetscape largely ended, and the view toward the setting sun was of farmlands, stretching for miles. Immediately west of the college lay a large tract belonging to the estate of William C. Allen (1794–1874).[1]

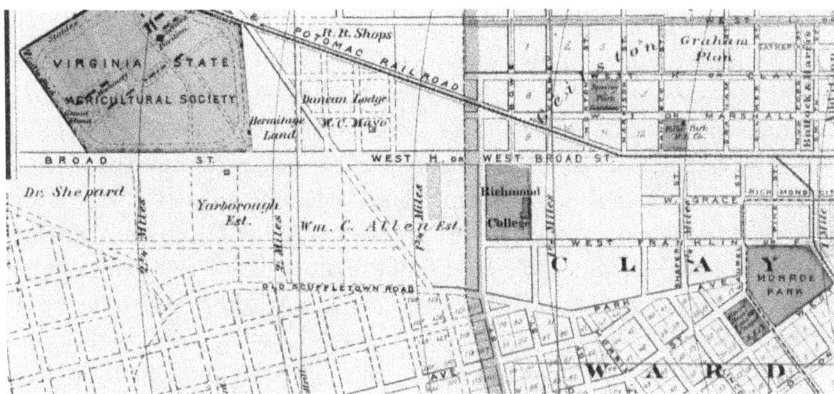

Figure 4. Detail of F. W. Beers, *Illustrated Atlas of the City of Richmond,* 1877, showing the area of present-day Richmond bordered by West Leigh St. to the north, Monroe Park to the east, Grove Avenue to the south and, the edge of the map to the west. (Courtesy Library of Congress)

Allen had come to Richmond about 1810 with his mother and was apprenticed to a bricklayer. Through hard work, he gradually became a successful antebellum contractor and developer, amassing a substantial fortune, tracts of land, and city lots before he died in 1874, aged 81. Among his heirs were his son Otway S. Allen and three daughters (Mary C. Sheppard, Bettie F. Gregory, and Martha A. Wise). They inherited Allen's tract, which he had acquired as a long-term investment, that extended from Lombardy Street three blocks west to present-day Allison Street. In part because of the economic panic of 1873 and its aftermath, Allen's heirs were slow in developing plans for the tract. Finally, in 1887, Otway Allen had the city engineer, Collinson Pierrepont Edwards Burgwyn[2] (commonly and understandably referred to as C. P. E. Burgwyn), draw a plan for an extension of Franklin Street through the tract to its western end at Allison Street. The extension was drawn as a broad avenue intersected by a similarly wide north-south street named Allen Avenue. At the intersection, named Lee Place, was a large circle, and the avenue was named Monument Avenue. The drawing was attached to a plat that accompanied a deed of the circle to the Lee Monument Association; the avenues and streets were deeded to "the public," meaning the city and Henrico County. The Allen heirs retained the rest of the tract for future development.[3]

The Lee Monument Association was formed from two earlier groups—one male, one female—in March 1886. Governor Fitzhugh Lee, a former Confederate general and nephew of Robert E. Lee, headed the new organization. For the site of the monument, the women preferred Hollywood Cemetery, where many Confederate dead were interred, while the men advocated for various locations including Capitol Square, Monroe Square, Gamble's Hill, and Libby Hill. Two factors turned the tide in favor of the future Monument Avenue. First, it was on open and undeveloped land located in an area of impending growth, and second, it was just north of Robert E. Lee Camp Number One, the home established in 1883–1884 for destitute Confederate veterans. So, in 1887, Burgwyn endorsed the location, and Otway Allen deeded the circle to the association.[4]

Although it took three more years to create the Lee Monument, by June 1887 the association had selected a design and a sculptor, the renowned French artist Marius-Jean-Antonin Mercié. On October 27, 1887, the association held a parade of Confederate veterans who marched west from downtown Richmond to the circle to dedicate the cornerstone. Speeches were given, the cornerstone was laid, and the site was readied for the monument. In 1888, the Allen heirs in cooperation with Burgwyn produced a map of the area that showed Monument and Allen Avenues with their medians and the lots laid out along the streets from Broad Street south to Park Avenue. Monument Avenue was now ready for development.[5]

The development, however, was slow to come. No houses had been constructed there by the time the completed Lee Monument was at last unveiled and dedicated on May 29, 1890. And then, in 1893, the financial panic of that year was followed by about a decade of slow growth. The first house, located at 1601 Monument Avenue, was completed in 1894 (it was demolished in 1978 for a parking garage). By the time Otway Allen died in February 1911, however, about sixty houses had either been built or were under construction. Monument Avenue had finally become the neighborhood for Richmond's elite, living in houses designed by such notable architects as William Lawrence Bottomley, W. Duncan Lee, Carl Lindner, and Max E. Ruehrmund, among others. The avenue was extended west over sixty years following the Lee Monument dedication, stretching to Roseneath Road and beyond; house construction on the street between those two points was largely complete by the 1940s.[6]

More monuments followed Lee's as prosperity returned and funds were raised. The next one erected, for Major General J. E. B. Stuart, was dedicated on May 30, 1907. It was located in a circle a block east of Lee's, at the intersection of Lombardy Street and Monument Avenue. Originally, the Stuart

Figure 5. Lee Monument assembled, 1890, with remnants of crates in the foreground, looking northwest toward the state fairgrounds at left rear, giving an idea of the rural surroundings west of Lombardy Avenue. (Courtesy Library of Congress)

Monument Association had hoped to place it in Capitol Square, but the city's board of aldermen insisted that it go elsewhere. The design, executed by Frederick Moynihan, was based on a concept drawn by Captain M. J. Dimmock, in turn based on the 1874 statue of General Sir James Outram in Calcutta, India. Both statues showed the riders reining in spirited horses with one front leg in the air, as the rider twisted in the saddle to look at the action to the rear. The Stuart statue was in marked contrast to that of Lee, calm and unperturbed on a steady mount.[7]

Four days after the Stuart Monument unveiling, the Jefferson Davis Monument was dedicated on June 3, 1907. The Jefferson Davis Monument Association had been formed in December 1889 ten days after the former Confederate president died in Mississippi. Various proposals were put forth but died for lack of funds, including a massive domed temple and a huge arch, to be placed in Monroe Park and at Broad and 12th Streets, respectively. Finally, in 1903, the United Daughters of the Confederacy (UDC) approached the Richmond city council to suggest a Monument Avenue site four blocks west of the Lee Monument at a street renamed Davis Avenue. The council approved, and the UDC engaged local talent—architect William C. Noland and sculptor Edward V. Valentine—to design the monument. The final product, oriented east toward Capitol Square, depicted Davis giving a speech with a tall column immediately behind the figure, topped with a female statue of Vindicatrix. To the rear of both was a semicircular "screen" of thirteen smaller columns. The monument presents the Lost Cause (discussed in detail below) in full flower, with inscriptions in both Latin and English referencing "the Rights of States." The speeches delivered at the dedication likewise pounded the message home.[8]

During the war, Confederate authorities had erected three defensive lines to protect the city: the Outer, Intermediate, and Inner Lines. All but the Inner Line consisted of miles of earthworks with intermittent artillery emplacements; the Inner Line featured large earthen forts or batteries for multiple cannons but no earthworks to connect the batteries. Battery No. 10 was constructed astride the future route of Monument Avenue. Like almost all of the other batteries and earthworks surrounding the city, it gradually disappeared as farmers re-leveled their torn-up fields and pastures. By the time Monument Avenue came into being, only a hump of earth remained on the street's south side, and soon it was gone, too. In 1915, the Confederate Memorial Literary Society and the city erected a miniature monument (in comparison to the others) to mark the site, half a block east of the Davis Monument in the median at about 2319 Monument Avenue. The small memorial consisted of a cannon aimed west and mounted on a short pier of stone and concrete, with a plaque.[9]

The next monument, which commemorated Lieutenant General Thomas J. "Stonewall" Jackson, was dedicated on October 11, 1919. One might wonder why it took so long for the first major hero of the Confederacy during the war to claim a place on Monument Avenue at Boulevard (now Arthur Ashe Boulevard). Several statues of Jackson had already been erected, including one in Capitol Square; however, all presented him standing, while this was the first to show him mounted. The Jackson Monument Corporation was founded at the Lee Camp on November 29, 1911. Sculptor F. William Sievers, known for his ability to create exact likenesses, was chosen in 1915 to create the monument. Instead of Little Sorrel, Jackson's favorite horse, Sievers used a Thoroughbred named Superior as his horse model, probably because its proportions worked better on the twenty-two-foot-high pedestal. Appearing as calm as Lee, the statue of Jackson faced north, seemingly awaiting the battle to come.[10]

The last of the Confederate monuments installed on Monument Avenue was dedicated to Matthew Fontaine Maury, "The Pathfinder of the Seas." Born in Virginia in 1806, Maury joined the US Navy in 1825, sailed around the world, and wrote a treatise on navigation. A knee injury suffered in 1839 disabled him from further sailing; he was appointed first head of the US Naval Observatory in Washington, DC, in 1842. Far from the sea, he undertook the mapping of stars and oceans, seabeds and land masses. He is considered the father of scientific oceanography and hurricane forecasting, the focus of the future US Weather Bureau. After Virginia seceded, he served in the Confederate States Navy, invented an electric "torpedo" or mine to protect Southern harbors, and traveled abroad as a Confederate government agent. Returning to Virginia after the war, he taught at Virginia Military Institute until he died in 1873. Ironically, although Maury's oceanographic discoveries gained him worldwide fame, he was almost unknown in America outside the naval and scientific spheres. Maury enthusiasts raised money for a monument, F. William Sievers sculpted it, and it was unveiled three blocks west of the Jackson Monument, at the intersection with North Belmont Street, on November 11, 1929. The monument, like the man himself, was very different from those dedicated to Confederates known for their political or military accomplishments. The statue of Maury was seated, deep in thought, while behind and above the figure several storm-battered allegorical figures strain beneath the weight of a globe. As depicted in the monument, Maury's scientific accomplishments rendered his Confederate associations almost incidental, although the United Daughters of the Confederacy contributed to the monument fund and helped raise money for it.[11]

The Confederacy and its heroes, then, were well-represented on Monument Avenue, beginning with the Lee Monument in 1890 and continuing with the memorialization of Stuart (1907), Davis (1907), Jackson (1919), and Maury (1929). Each monument presented an idealized image of its subject; and each was erected during a period when the war and its causes, like the Confederate defeat and the utter destruction of the antebellum way of life, were receding into history along with the dwindling number of Confederate veterans. During the same period, however, just as the heroes gained mythic status in Southern memories, so too did a new way of "remembering" the causes, course, and conclusion of the war, as well as its aftermath. It was known as the myth—or cult—of the Lost Cause.

THE PATH FROM STATES' RIGHTS TO SECESSION AND WAR TO THE LOST CAUSE

The pedestals and statues erected on the avenue have been called monuments to the myth of the Lost Cause in part because the street and its monuments evolved simultaneously with the myth. To understand the Lost Cause, it is first necessary to understand what led up to it. In other words, to understand the progression, especially in the South, from states' rights to secession and war, and finally to the end of enslavement and the postwar period of Reconstruction.

When the Republicans, endorsing an antislavery platform, nominated Abraham Lincoln for president in 1860, and Lincoln won, the Southern enslaving states rejected the result. Embracing their interpretation of states' rights, they began to secede from the Union. But why, specifically, were they seceding?

As historian Charles R. Dew explains in his book *Apostles of Disunion: Southern Secession Commissioners and the Causes of the Civil War* (Charlottesville: University of Virginia Press, 2001), the reason was simple and clearly stated: to preserve enslavement from the threat of abolition. South Carolina, the first state to secede (December 20, 1860), explained its rationale succinctly in a pamphlet published by the secession convention (*Declaration of the Immediate Causes Which Induce and Justify the Secession of South Carolina*). Secession was necessary, it explained, because "an increasing hostility on the part of the non-slaveholding States to the Institution of Slavery has led to a disregard of their obligations" to capture and return "fugitive slaves" to their owners.[12]

The secession commissioners, sent from Deep South states to persuade the Upper South and border states to secede, likewise were clear as to the states' motivation. On February 18, 1861, for example, two commissioners addressed the Secession Convention in Richmond, held at the Mechanics' Institute Hall at Nineth and Bank Streets. Commissioner Fulton Anderson of Mississippi proclaimed that the Lincoln administration's goal would be "the ultimate extinction of slavery."[13] Commissioner Henry L. Benning of Georgia made his state's reason for Southern secession as plain as the South Carolina declaration: "a separation from the North was the only thing that could prevent the abolition of her slavery."[14] The message was delivered clearly, both in Virginia and in other Southern states, that secession was the only way to preserve enslavement.

One reason to preserve it was economic: enslaved men, women, and children were the second-largest capital investment in the South, next to the land itself. But a second reason was, in the opinion of Confederate Vice President Alexander H. Stephens and many other White Southerners, even more important: the enslavement of Black Africans by White men was God's will. Stephens made this point clear in his Cornerstone Speech on March 21, 1861, in Savannah, Georgia. He asserted that Thomas Jefferson and the other Founders of the United States had fundamentally erred in assuming "that the enslavement of the African was in violation of the laws of nature; that it was wrong in principle, socially, morally, and politically," and eventually would fade away. In fact, Stephens said, "Our new [Confederate] government is founded upon exactly the opposite idea; its foundations are laid, its cornerstone rests, upon the great truth that the negro is not equal to the White man; that slavery subordination to the superior race is his natural and normal condition. This, our new government, is the first, in the history of the world, based upon this great physical, philosophical, and moral truth."

Earlier, on December 28, 1860, Alabama congressman Jabez L. M. Curry wrote in a letter to Maryland Governor Thomas Hicks that the Northern conception of slavery as sinful and demanding abolition was "an infidel theory." If it became the law of the land, Curry claimed, then "instead of the culture and development of the boundless capacities and productive resources of [the White Southern] social system, it is to be assaulted, humbled, dwarfed, degraded, and finally crushed out." Disunion was the only way to preserve the purity and accomplishments of the White race.

Virginia did not agree with the most ardent secessionists, at least not at first. On January 7, 1861, the General Assembly convened in a special session that Governor John Letcher had called. The assembly in turn called for an election on February 4 of delegates to a state convention to consider the question of whether to join the torrent of seceding Southern states. When the convention met on February 13, the majority of members were opposed. Former US president John Tyler attended a "peace conference" in Washington that tried to resolve the crisis but failed. On April 4, despite all of the efforts by the secession commissioners and other supporters, the convention soundly defeated by a vote of eighty-eight to forty-five a motion to recommend secession to Virginia voters.[15]

Any hope for a peaceful conclusion to the secession crisis ended with the Confederate bombardment of Fort Sumter, South Carolina, and the fort's surrender on April 14, 1861. Lincoln called for volunteers to suppress the insurrection, and the tide turned in the convention. A motion to secede passed, eighty-eight to fifty-five, on April 17, and Virginia joined the Confederate States of America. Soon the war began in earnest. Over the next four years, the Confederate States followed a strategy that they hoped would end in victory for their side. Not a military victory in which their armies would crush their opponents, for the Northern states were too superior in numbers of men and quantities of war matériel, but a political victory that would result in the Southerners being left to go their own way, with enslavement intact.

For this strategy to succeed, the Confederates needed to avoid a crushing defeat while inflicting enough damage on Union forces to wear down the North's will to fight. This strategy, it was hoped, would attract support and the recognition by one or more foreign powers of Southern viability and independence. Under Lee's generalship, his army waged a largely defensive war in the South while conducting audacious campaigns into Northern territory in 1863 and 1864. Both campaigns ended in defeat and the lack of recognition abroad. In 1864 and 1865, General Ulysses S. Grant's campaigns in Virginia produced decisive Union victories.

After four years of war, both militarily and politically, the Confederates lost the war to preserve enslavement. Soon after the fighting started, Lincoln had realized that even if the North won the war to reunite the Union, little would have been gained if the institution still existed in the United States. Abolition became a military as well as a political necessity. After the Union victory at Antietam in September 1862, Lincoln issued a carefully worded preliminary Emancipation Proclamation (to take effect January 1, 1863) that announced the liberation of enslaved persons in states or parts of states still fighting for the Confederacy. The Proclamation in effect eliminated enslavement in areas outside of Union military control but left it intact in areas that it did control. But it put the United States on the side of abolition, which further dissuaded England and other foreign countries from recognizing the Confederacy; it directly attacked the Confederacy's principal reason for secession; and it authorized Black men to serve in the United States Army and Navy, further inducing them to flee to Union lines in increasing numbers to deprive the Confederates of their labor.

By the end of the war, swaths of the South, especially those parts of Virginia where the armies had fought and camped, lay in ruins—buildings burned, railroads and bridges destroyed, equipment damaged, farms deserted, and loved ones dead, injured, and missing. Most important to the support of White supremacy, at least for the moment, the enslavement-based Southern way of life, its social and economic system, and White authority were destroyed, damaged, or deeply threatened. Instead of merely ordering the enslaved around, White Southerners were reduced to what most saw as the "indignity" of having to negotiate with the freedmen for their labor. Whites were further crushed as United States Army troops occupied the South, in large part to protect the formerly enslaved persons as they transitioned to freedom. Military and political Reconstruction further upended the social and political system, offering education to Black people, extending suffrage to Black men, and even encouraging them to campaign for elective offices. In almost every way imaginable, the "nightmare world" that the secession commissioners had predicted had arrived. The Confederacy had failed on every front with a vast cost in lives and fortunes.

For many White Southerners, it was far too much to bear. Counter-Reconstruction efforts, including the rise of the Ku Klux Klan, widespread lynching, and segregationist Jim Crow laws, quickly emerged. The Whites endured the new political and social order during the brief postwar period when the United States armed forces and the federal Freedmen's Bureau enforced and supported the liberties that Black people gained through their own efforts and the laws and constitutional amendments that codified them. With the end of the military occupation of Virginia in 1870 and the withdrawal of federal enforcement in the interest of "reconciliation" between North and South, however, a new era began as White Southerners regained control. To further compensate for their losses, White Southerners also began to create and subscribe to a myth that rewrote the history of secession and the war and assuaged to a degree the catastrophic failure of the Confederacy. It was called the Lost Cause.

The phrase originated as the title of a book about the war from the Southern point of view, Edward A. Pollard's tome *The Lost Cause: A New Southern History of the War of the Confederates*, published in Richmond in 1866. The book began a reinterpretation of the war and its causes that produced six tenets or assertions. First, that secession and Northern aggression caused the war, not enslavement. Second, that enslaved persons were faithful to their masters and the Confederacy and unprepared for freedom. Third, that the

Confederacy lost the war only because of the overwhelming superiority of the North in men and resources. Fourth, that Confederate soldiers were universally brave and saintly. Fifth, that Robert E. Lee was the saintliest of them all, the epitome of Southern manhood. And sixth, that Southern women were all loyal to the Confederacy and sanctified by the sacrifices of their men. Each of the assertions contained at least a few grains of truth, but taken as a whole, the myth or theory was contrary to the facts of history.[16]

First, the preservation of enslavement in the face of a perceived abolitionist threat prompted Southern secession, as the secession commissioners candidly stated; the war began when the secessionists attacked Fort Sumter and Lincoln called for volunteers to suppress the rebellion. Second, soon after the war began, enslaved persons fled in droves to the Union lines and freedom, as federal officials refused to return them to their owners, and after the Emancipation Proclamation took effect, approximately 200,000 Black men enlisted. At least 60 percent of Virginia's enslaved adult males escaped from bondage during the war. Third and fourth, although Union superiority in men and resources obviously played a role in grinding down the Southern armies, so too did desertions, soldiers failing to return from furloughs, and illness. Every army has its problems with cowardice and desertion, and the Confederate armies were no exception. Fifth, Lee himself would have declined the label of "saint," or of the perfect general (several modern historians have offered mixed reviews of his generalship). He did, however, maintain his army as a fighting force until the end, and earned the admiration and devotion of his soldiers. Finally, although it was claimed that during the war all White Southern women as well as men supported the Confederacy, this in fact was not the case. Unionists were plentiful, although many were quiet about it depending on their local situations. In the Upper South especially, there was a bloody but often overlooked "war within the war" featuring divided families, guerrilla attacks, and civilian bushwhackers. Some of the fighting had less to do with secession or unification and more to do with the settling of old scores. Generally, support for secession was lower in mountainous areas, which had smaller populations of enslaved persons.[17]

During the war, women on both sides of the conflict formed organizations to support their men in several ways. Women raised money, sent food and clothing to the troops, nursed the sick and wounded, accompanied the armies as cooks and seamstresses, and in some cases disguised themselves as men and served in the ranks. After the war, women again led movements to support veterans, especially in the South. The US government funded and created national cemeteries to inter the Union dead; pensions and soldiers' homes for Union veterans; and a program for giving amputees artificial limbs. Former Confederates, of course, were not eligible for such benefits at federal taxpayer expense, so Southern women formed societies to promote and support cemeteries, state pensions and homes, and artificial limb programs. They also formed organizations that encouraged and advanced the memorialization of the Lost Cause and Confederate heroes such as Lee, Stuart, Jackson, Davis, and Maury.

Further enhancing the rise of the Lost Cause was the return of former Confederates to political power in the 1880s. Virginia had accrued a large public debt in the decades preceding the war and had suspended payments on the debt during the war. Payments resumed at about the time that public education was mandated by the new 1870 state constitution, but the payments reduced the public school funding to almost nothing. Two groups soon emerged on each side of the issue: Funders, mostly White conservative Democrats, who wanted tax money devoted to paying off the debt to improve the state's credit rating even at the sacrifice of public schools (which they disliked anyway); and Readjusters, a coalition of more moderate Whites, Blacks, and Republicans, who wanted to repudiate roughly a third of the debt and pay enough on the remainder to fund schools and other projects. Ironically, the leader of the second group was former Confederate Major General William Mahone. The contest between the groups began after the General Assembly passed the full Funding Act of 1871. It gained momentum during and after the Panic of 1873. In 1881, the Readjusters attained control not only of the General Assembly but also the governor's office. They enacted their fiscal policies into law, abolished the poll tax that kept many Blacks and poor Whites from voting, and formed an alliance with the Republican Party. The conservatives and Funders countered by forming a new Democratic Party and regained control of the legislature in 1883; they elected former Confederate Major General Fitzhugh Lee, Robert E. Lee's nephew, as governor two years later. Before those elections, they had abandoned the public debt issue to stoke fear of Black domination if the biracial Readjusters continued in power. The Readjusters disbanded after their defeat and joined the Republican Party. The Democrats continued their program of White superiority into the next century, when they effectively disfranchised Blacks and poor Whites with the adoption of the state constitution of 1902.[18]

The return of former secessionists to political dominance, the avenue, the monuments, and the Lost Cause, then, all developed and evolved at the same time over several decades. First came the veneration of Lee and the construction of his statue in 1890, when many Confederate veterans still lived and the organizations that supported them during the war continued to do so. And then, as the numbers of old soldiers dwindled, the descendant organizations—the Sons of Confederate Veterans and the United Daughters of the Confederacy—aggressively supported and encouraged the Lost Cause myth, securing its place in history books, public celebrations, and (with the help of sympathetic lawmakers) in laws and the new Virginia Constitution of 1902. The latter document, combined with Jim Crow laws, effectively removed Black men from Virginia's political life, driving them from the polls and ensuring White dominance. The monuments epitomized this victory and the myth that supported it.

A FINAL QUESTION

What would Lee himself have thought of his monument and the cult of hero worship and mythology that it initiated? A year before he died in 1870, Lee wrote a letter regarding a proposal to erect granite monuments on the Gettysburg battlefield, to illustrate the movements of the armies. Asked to participate in the effort, Lee declined, with the following comment: "I think it wiser moreover not to keep open the sores of war, but to follow the example of those nations who endeavored to obliterate the marks of civil strife and to commit to oblivion the feelings it engendered."[19]

Lee died twenty years before his statue was erected and the other physical representations of the Lost Cause began appearing on Monument Avenue. It is interesting and ironic that—although he may have changed his mind had he lived—Lee's opinions between 1865 and 1870 were in opposition to what occurred, and why it occurred, on this grand avenue.

NOTES

1. Kathy Edwards, Esme Howard, and Toni Prawl, *Monument Avenue: History and Architecture* (Washington, DC: U.S. Department of the Interior, Historic American Buildings Survey, 1992), 26–27.
2. For more information about Collinson Pierrepont Edwards Burgwyn read about the book he wrote that was placed in a lead box under the Lee Monument here: https://www.dhr.virginia.gov/news/virginia-is-for-huguenot-lovers/.

3. Edwards, Howard, and Prawl, *Monument Avenue: History and Architecture*, 14. Sarah Shields Driggs, Richard Guy Wilson, and Robert P. Winthrop, *Richmond's Monument Avenue* (Chapel Hill: University of North Carolina Press, 2001), 99–101.
4. Driggs, Wilson, and Winthrop, *Monument Avenue*, 29–31.
5. Driggs, et al., *Monument Avenue*, 34–35.
6. Driggs, et al., *Monument Avenue*, 100–101.
7. Driggs, et al., *Monument Avenue*, 55–63.
8. Driggs, et al., *Monument Avenue*, 64–74.
9. Driggs, et al. , *Monument Avenue*, 67–68.
10. Driggs, et al., *Monument Avenue*, 74–79.
11. Driggs, et al., *Monument Avenue*, 79–87.
12. *Declaration of the Immediate Causes Which Induce and Justify the Secession of South Carolina*, Archives.org, https://web.archive.org/web/20170808015740 /http://teachingushistory.org/pdfs/DecImmCauses.pdf.
13. Charles R. Dew, *Apostles of Disunion: Southern Secession Commissioners and the Causes of the Civil War* (Charlottesville: University of Virginia Press, 2001), 62.
14. Dew, *Apostles of Disunion: Southern Secession Commissioners and the Causes of the Civil War*, 65.
15. Emily J. Salmon and Edward D. C. Campbell, Jr., eds., *The Hornbook of Virginia History*, 4th ed. (Richmond: Library of Virginia, 1994), 45–46.
16. Caroline E. Janney, "The Lost Cause," *Encyclopedia Virginia*, last modified December 7, 2020, https://encyclopediavirginia.org/entries/lost-cause-the/.
17. Janney, "The Lost Cause," For the United Daughters of the Confederacy's summary of the Lost Cause myth, see "U.D.C. Catechism for Children (1904)" *Encyclopedia Virginia*, website, https://encyclopediavirginia.org/entries/u-d-c-catechism -for-children-1904/; For analysis of the numbers of enslaved persons who self-emancipated to Union lines during the war see "Slavery during the Civil War" *Encyclopedia Virginia*, https://encyclopediavirginia.org/entries/slavery-during -the-civil-war/; see "Unionism in Virginia During the Civil War," *Encyclopedia Virginia,* https://encyclopediavirginia.org/entries/unionism-in-virginia-during -the-civil-war/.
18. Brent Tarter, "The Readjuster Party," *Encyclopedia Virginia*, Last modified September 22, 2023, https://encyclopediavirginia.org/entries/readjuster-party-the/.
19. Emory M. Thomas, *Robert E. Lee: A Biography* (New York: W. W. Norton, 1995), 383, 392; Lee wrote the letter about the battlefield monuments to Hon. D. McConaughy, Lexington, Aug. 9, 1869, Lee Papers, Washington & Lee University.

2

Richmond's Other Confederate Cornerstones

Christina Keyser Vida

On October 27, 1887, the Lee Monument joined a long line of buildings and memorials in Richmond to have cornerstones dedicated by Masons and filled with commemorative boxes. Although these boxes were never intended to be uncovered, the location and presence of cornerstone boxes became important when the Commonwealth of Virginia hired Team Henry Enterprises to remove the pedestal of the Lee Monument in 2021. Conservators with the Department of Historic Resources took center stage for the unpacking of the 1887 cornerstone box and the 1889 contractor box from the then-state-owned Lee Monument.[1] But when the City of Richmond ordered the removal of the pedestals of the city-owned Confederate monuments, historians and Team Henry considered the cornerstone boxes for those monuments as well.

Groups and associations had to request the Masons to perform a ceremony, but it is unclear why not all Confederate monuments in Richmond had Masonic cornerstone ceremonies. Some, like the Williams Carter Wickham statue in Monroe Park, did not need a cornerstone ceremony to fundraise or build momentum for its construction. However, the J. E. B. Stuart Monument and Confederate Soldiers' and Sailors' Monument, both decades in the making, also did not receive the Masonic cornerstone rites.

Along Monument Avenue, the Jefferson Davis Monument, Thomas "Stonewall" Jackson Monument, and Matthew Fontaine Maury Monument did have cornerstone ceremonies complete with cornerstone boxes.[2] But, as Team Henry carefully dismantled the pedestals of the Jackson and Maury monuments in 2022, those two cornerstones and the boxes were not found.[3]

The June 3, 1915, cornerstone ceremony for the Jackson Monument, which was located at Monument Avenue and North Arthur Ashe Boulevard, included depositing "a box 12x12x8 inches" filled with "relics" into the cornerstone made by Richmond stonemason William R. Mason.[4] (See Appendix A for a full list of contents.) The monument was finally unveiled October 11, 1919.[5] On June 22, 1922, the Matthew Fontaine Maury Association and the United Daughters of the Confederacy (UDC) organized a cornerstone ceremony along Monument Avenue culminating at Belmont Avenue. The UDC streamlined the contents of the cornerstone box down to "a tiny Confederate flag and a list of its officers" of each UDC division.[6] After seven years, the UDC unveiled the completed monument on November 11, 1929.[7]

Although the Jackson and Maury boxes were not recovered during deconstruction, on February 16, 2022, Team Henry workers found the cornerstone box in the Jefferson Davis Monument pedestal. The box itself predates the construction of the 1907 monument along Monument Avenue. It was originally placed with great fanfare on July 2, 1896, in Monroe Park. At that time, the Jefferson Davis Monument Association (JDMA) had hoped to build a temple-like structure to honor Davis. Within three years, fundraising had stalled and the JDMA turned the project over to the UDC.[8] Members organized fundraising events and solicited funds from across the country. The plan for the monument continued to be in flux until 1903 when the UDC and JDMA commissioned Richmond sculptor Edward Valentine (1838–1930) and Richmond architect William Noland (1865–1961) to design a monument to be constructed along Monument Avenue at Cedar Street (now Davis Street). The monument was ready for construction in 1907 with Valentine's sculptural elements cast by Gorham Company's foundry in Providence, Rhode Island.[9] On April 10, 1907, committee members unearthed the 1896 cornerstone box from Monroe Park. "Yesterday it was exhumed and this morning will be placed in its final position just under the great square of granite that will be the pedestal of the Davis figure at the Jefferson Davis Monument." The JDMA and UDC added some additional items to the box prior to its placement on April 11 but did not host any formal Masonic exercises.[10] Newspapers published the contents of the 1896 Davis cornerstone box as well as the additional items added in 1907. (Appendix B details the full list.) But the box's recovery in 2022 made it possible to learn what had survived the unearthing and reburial.

X-rays taken prior to the box's opening alluded to some round metal items and bound materials. But an old hole in the top of the copper box caused concern that water intruded into the box while it was still underground. On August 10, 2022, conservators with the Department of Historic Resources as

CEREMONY
of
LAYING *the* CORNER STONE
for the
EQUESTRIAN
STATUE
of
Lieutenant-General
Thomas Jonathan (Stonewall) Jackson
C. S. A.

Richmond, Va., June 3, 1915
One O'clock P. M.
Intersection *of* Monument Avenue
and Boulevard

MITCHELL & HOTCHKISS, PRINTERS, RICHMOND, VA.

Figure 6. Program from the cornerstone ceremony for the Jackson Monument, 1915. (Courtesy of the Valentine Museum)

well as staff from the Black History Museum & Cultural Center of Virginia, the Valentine Museum, and the Virginia Museum of History & Culture assisted with the opening of the third box found by Team Henry Enterprises. DHR conservator Katherine Ridgway cut away the top of the copper box, revealing a copper envelope sitting on top of a pile of soggy papers and books.

Figure 7. Paperweight donated to the Jefferson Davis cornerstone box that was made from remnant bronze from the Confederate Soldiers' and Sailors' Monument. (Courtesy of the Valentine Museum)

Unlike the tidy boxes from the Lee Monument, the Davis cornerstone box had suffered the very typical fate of water intrusion, essentially destroying the majority of the paper items. One book, Carlton's McCarthy's *Soldier Life in the Army of Northern Virginia, 1861–1865*, survived intact, while the other newspapers, programs, and books had melded together into waterlogged bundles. Some relics survived. A chip of marble taken from the steps of Jefferson Davis's home during the Civil War, today known as the White House of the Confederacy, was tucked into the bottom as was a paperweight made from bronze left over from the casting of Richmond's 1894 Confederate Soldiers' and Sailors' Monument.

After emptying the 1896 box entirely, Ridgway turned her attention back to the copper envelope. Careful work with a Dremel tool allowed her to slice open one edge of the packet. Inside were all the additions from 1907, perfectly preserved in their airtight, metal envelope. Designs for the monument, an updated history of the JDMA, programs from fundraising events, and even the first and last ten-cent pieces raised at a 1903 bazaar in Richmond looked as if they were merely days—not 115 years—old.

With Richmond's Confederate monuments removed from the city's landscape, the contents of the cornerstone boxes are important reminders for students of history about why they were erected in the first place. Leaders of the organizations that raised the money for these pieces of public art were not trying to retell the biographical details of the men they glorified in bronze. In these boxes they sought to glorify the Confederacy on the whole. They wanted future generations to believe the lie that the Civil War was about states' rights and not the preservation of slavery. They hoped to reframe the battles of the

Civil War and all Confederate soldiers as righteous and worthy of praise even if their cause had lost. And they left out the voices of those who disagreed with them, ignoring the perspectives of Black Richmonders who did not want figures from the Confederacy looming over them as they worked in and around the homes on Monument Avenue. The Jefferson Davis cornerstone box and its content are now owned by the Valentine Museum, which will continue to explore the legacy of Richmond's Confederate monuments and help foster conversation about the impacts of the Lost Cause mythology and Jim Crow policies on the Richmond region.

NOTES

1. The Commonwealth of Virginia transferred the statue and pedestal of the Lee Monument, and the land on which it sat, to the City of Richmond in 2022.
2. *Proceedings of the Grand Lodge of Virginia* (Richmond, VA: James Goode, 1896), 9–23; *Proceedings of the Virginia Grand Lodge* (Richmond, VA: Ware & Duke, 1916), 14; *Proceedings of the Virginia Grand Lodge* (Richmond, VA: Everett Waddey, 1923), 32.
3. While cornerstones are traditionally placed in the northeast corner of a structure, these monuments were not standard buildings, and the exact placement was never detailed in primary sources. Also, in the years since the monuments' cornerstones were laid, the City of Richmond has adjusted the curbing and road surface many times. Team Henry was given leeway to dig a bit below their contractually obligated depth in order to recover the Jackson and Maury cornerstone boxes, but even then, the boxes were still not found. It is possible that the cornerstones and boxes are still buried in those locations.
4. "Stonewall Jackson Monument Cornerstone to Be Laid Thursday," *Richmond Times-Dispatch* (Richmond, VA), May 30, 1915; *Greater Richmond City Directory* (Richmond, VA: Hill Directory, Inc. Publishers, 1910), 655.
5. *Richmond Times-Dispatch* (Richmond, VA), October 12, 1919.
6. *Richmond Times-Dispatch* (Richmond, VA), June 20 and 22, 1922.
7. *Richmond Times-Dispatch* (Richmond, VA), November 11, 1929.
8. *Richmond Times* (Richmond, VA), September 4, 1899.
9. Davis Monument folders, Edward Valentine Papers, The Valentine Museum, Richmond, VA.
10. *Richmond Times-Dispatch* (Richmond, VA), April 11, 1907.

3

"For a Far Remote Posterity"

Cornerstone Boxes and Masonic Ceremonies

Sir Knight Peter Spring and Christina Keyser Vida

Freemasonry is the oldest and largest fraternal organization in the world. Its origins can be traced to medieval stonemasons and cathedral builders, and in 1634, the first speculative Masons (men who have no actual masonry experience) joined the group. These men did not practice stonemasonry and expanded the charitable mission of the organization as it transitioned from a guild to a fraternal order.[1] Today, millions of men around the globe belong to Masonic lodges. They participate in a series of degrees and ceremonies centered on the values of brotherly love, relief, and truth while fundraising for various charities.

One of the traditional Masonic ceremonies performed in public by Freemasons is the cornerstone laying ceremony. The first Masonic cornerstone ceremony is documented to 1738 when Freemasons dedicated the cornerstone of the New Royal Infirmary in Edinburgh, Scotland.[2] On September 18, 1793, President George Washington laid the cornerstone of the United States Capitol building with full Masonic rites.[3] By 1808, the ceremonies were ritualized and prescribed in Thomas Smith Webb's 1808 publication, *The Freemason's Monitor*, which dictated that under the stone should be placed "various sorts of coin and medals of the present age."[4] And while no box is known to have been deposited in the US Capitol cornerstone, by 1848, Freemasons included a zinc box in the cornerstone of the Washington Monument in Washington, DC. That box contained "books, speeches, a medal, and seventy-one newspapers from across the country."[5] When an international audience gathered in Yorktown in 1881 to commemorate the centennial of the battle there of 1781 and lay the cornerstone for a monument, Masons deposited in

Figure 8. Program of the Acca Temple of the Ancient Arabic Order Nobles of the Mystic Shrine, Thursday, October 27, 1887, following the laying cornerstone of Lee Monument. Given to W.B. Isaacs by W. H. Sands for inclusion in the Lee Monument cornerstone box.

it "a silver-lined copper box, made in Richmond, Va., two and a-half feet long, two feet wide and eighteen inches deep" containing books, coins, programs, and documents.[6] And even in Richmond in 1887, the cornerstone of the Lee Monument was not the only cornerstone laid with great fanfare. In April of that year, the public gathered for the Masonic ceremonies dedicating the cornerstone of Richmond's city hall.[7]

William Bryan Isaacs (1818–1895) became the Grand Secretary for the Grand Lodge of Virginia in 1876, and, in that role, was intimately involved in Virginia's cornerstone ceremonies of the 1880s. Born in Norwalk, Connecticut, Isaacs moved to Richmond as a young man. During the Civil War, he belonged to the Richmond Ambulance Corps, which served the Confederate wounded and dead from around the Richmond region. In 1842, he married Julia Lee Dove, daughter of Dr. John Dove who was then the Grand Secretary of the Grand Lodge of Virginia. In that same year, Isaacs also became a Mason

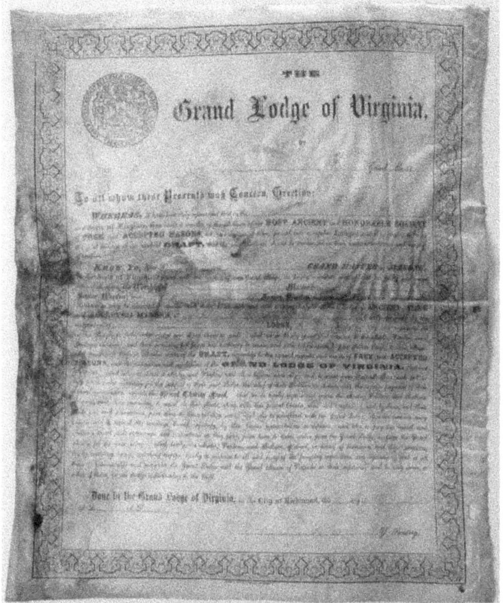

THE

Grand Lodge of Virginia.

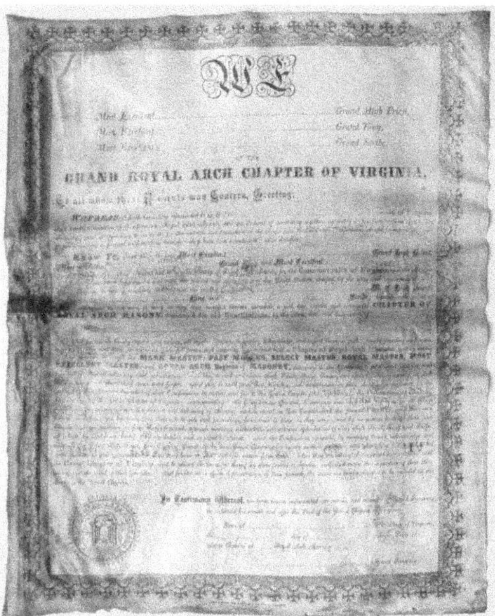

WE

GRAND ROYAL ARCH CHAPTER OF VIRGINIA.

Figure 9. Copies of the charters of the Grand Lodge of Virginia and the Grand Royal Arch Chapter of Virginia, included by W.B. Isaacs in the Lee Monument cornerstone box.

at the Masons' Hall on Franklin Street. Following in his father-in-law's footsteps, he was very active in Freemasonry not only in Virginia but around the country, eventually serving as the Grand Recorder of the Grand Encampment of Knights Templar of the United States. One obituary noted that the financial panic of 1873 "ruined him," but also allowed him to dedicate even more time to his community through Freemasonry. He earned the title "Right Worshipful Brother" with the Grand Lodge of Virginia but also was a member of the Richmond Royal Arch Chapter and a member of Richmond Commandery No.2, Knights Templar. [8]

In his role as Grand Secretary, Isaacs oversaw the compilation of items going into the cornerstone boxes. In many instances, he advertised in local newspapers for contributions and then gave the final list of items to reporters prior to the official public ceremonies.

It is important to note that Isaacs and his contemporaries would not have thought of these cornerstone boxes as "time capsules." That term was not popularized until the 1930s when Westinghouse Corporation created a "time

Figure 10. "Laying of the Corner Stone" of the Lee Monument depicted in *Frank Leslie's Illustrated Newspaper*, November 2, 1887. (Courtesy of the Valentine Museum)

capsule" for the World's Fair of 1939 to be opened 500 years later.[9] Also, cornerstones and cornerstone boxes were inherently foundational, embedded in the structure and not easily accessible. The items inside were meant for a "far remote posterity" and were not intended to be readily accessed and explored on a certain date in the future. [10]

For the Lee Monument cornerstone box, "far remote posterity" came in 2021. As Team Henry Enterprises deconstructed the monument's pedestal, the Department of Historic Resources' staff and other historians sought to preserve the box and its contents. Team Henry first uncovered an 1889 lead box, placed up in the pedestal by the contractors who built and filled it with items highlighting their role in the construction of the Lee Monument. But in December 2021, they located the cornerstone and cornerstone box, which had sat under the pedestal at just below ground level since October 27, 1887.

The inventory of items recorded in the cornerstone box is listed in Appendix C. Of the over 100 items in the copper cornerstone box, Isaacs placed over twenty separate Masonic items. This tracks with the Masonic role in the cornerstone ceremonies and is also similar to other published listings of cornerstone contents from the time period. The majority of the items in the Lee Monument cornerstone box relate to the Confederacy. This fact speaks to the sentiments of the donors and the major cause of the monument—favorably shaping the public's memory of the Civil War and Robert E. Lee. The rest of this volume explores the stories of some of the items recovered as well as the stories of those purposefully left out of the box.

NOTES

1. Robert Feke Gould, *The History of Freemasonry, Volume II* (Oxford: T. C. Jack, 1883), 405.
2. Documented in Alexander Lawrie, *The History of Freemasonry* (Edinburgh: A. Lawrie, 1804), 174.
3. Mark Tabbert, "Freemasonry," *George Washington's Mount Vernon*, https://www.mountvernon.org/library/digitalhistory/digital-encyclopedia/article/freemasonry/.
4. Thomas Smith Webb, *The Freemason's Monitor* (Boston: Cushing & Appleton, 1808), 129; S. Brent Morris, Cornerstones of Freedom: A Masonic Tradition (Washington, DC: The Supreme Council, 33° S.J., 1993).
5. John Lockwood, "The Men and Women Who Built the Washington Monument," *National Archives*, Spring 2016. https://www.archives.gov/files/publications/prologue/2016/spring/monument.pdf.
6. *Stephens City Star* (Stevens City, VA), October 29, 1881.
7. *Richmond Dispatch* (Richmond, VA), April 5, 1887.
8. *Norfolk Virginian* (Norfolk, VA) June 11, 1895; *Clinch Valley News* (Tazewell, VA), June 14, 1895; *Richmond Dispatch* (Richmond, VA), June 11, 1895.
9. "Building the World's Fair of Tomorrow," *New York Times*, https://archive.nytimes.com/www.nytimes.com/specials/magazine3/1939.html.
10. *Richmond Dispatch* (Richmond, VA), April 5, 1887.

4

How to Make a Time Capsule

Lessons Learned While Opening and Preserving the Lee Monument Cornerstone Boxes

Katherine Ridgway and Sue Donovan

In the years immediately following the summer of 2020 and the global protests against the killing of George Floyd, conservators Sue Donovan (Conservator for Special Collections at University of Virginia Library) and Kate Ridgway (Virginia Archaeological Conservator at the Department of Historic Resources) were involved in the preservation and salvage of three cornerstone boxes. Unearthing these cornerstone boxes from the pedestals of Confederate monuments enhanced the conservators' understanding of the complex dynamics of the boxes with their burial environment and the *literal* monumental pressures surrounding them. This experience, along with Ridgway's and Donovan's knowledge of the composition and degradation of the materials in their specialty, can inform and prepare other conservators, museum professionals, and regular citizens who might find themselves faced with a newly unearthed box or the dilemma of how to prevent damage to a future time capsule.

The following sections explain the issues that arose when cornerstone boxes placed underneath Confederate monuments were unearthed, salvaged, opened, and preserved between September 2020 and January 2022. More information on these boxes can be found in several chapters in this book, especially those authored by Christina Vida, Professor Ervin L. Jordan Jr., and Dr. Caroline Janney. For more on the history of the *At Ready* Monument, please see Dr. Janney in the UVA Clubs and UVA Library's *When the Monuments Went Up* on UVA Engagement on YouTube.[1]

A vital part of the journey of preserving and conserving the cornerstone boxes unearthed by Donovan and Ridgway was understanding their original

Figure 11. Lee cornerstone box next to the hole it came out of full of water.

purpose. Cornerstone boxes are often confused with or grouped into the category of time capsules. Time capsules are filled with items carefully selected by an interested individual or group to tell a specific story upon the opening of the container in the future. The burying of a time capsule often corresponds with a certain event, such as an anniversary or building dedication, and the contributors plan to open the container at a set date, usually 50, 100, or 200 years later. A cornerstone box, on the other hand, is buried as part of the monument itself, and they have no set opening date because they are not meant to come out of the ground. These containers are deposited in an early course of the foundation during a ceremony that dedicates a building, monument, or other construction project.

Cornerstone boxes may contain many of the same types of objects that a time capsule contains, but there may also be ritual items that are placed as a part of the larger ceremony. These are frequently placed as part of a Masonic tradition, as was the case of the Lee Monument, or as a way of blessing the building. Because a cornerstone box is situated inside the foundation, there is no expectation that this type of container will be opened again in the future. Indeed, the burial of the cornerstone box underneath the *At Ready* statue in front of the Albemarle County Courthouse in Charlottesville, Virginia, was accompanied by a notice in the local newspaper declaring that the box and its contents would not be opened until judgment day when the "angel Gabriel would declare the earth no more."[2] This declaration was fitting for the benefactors of this monument because it spoke to their support of the vanquished Confederacy and of the Lost Cause propaganda popular in the years after Reconstruction.

Because cornerstone boxes are essentially part of the monument or building itself, their immediate burial environment is often made of the exact same materials that hold up the monument above. This creates issues for cornerstone boxes that are quite unique and intricate, even for archaeological conservators who have experience with objects that are buried in the ground or water for centuries. Similarly, the exterior conditions of buried containers impact the microclimate in which the containers' objects are held, so that the agents of deterioration, or the factors that negatively impact the preservation of cultural heritage, can be heightened in the sense of time and intensity. The agents of deterioration are as follows: physical forces, thieves and vandals, dissociation, fire, water, pests, pollution, light, incorrect temperature, and incorrect humidity; and the authors will refer to certain of these agents when discussing how the cornerstone boxes they preserved were damaged. Not all of the agents of deterioration are pertinent in these examples, but the authors will address all ten in the second half of this chapter to better help those who are preparing to create their own time capsule.

Cornerstone boxes have traditional locations for placement that are often linked to Masonic traditions. As the name suggests, cornerstone boxes are placed in or underneath the cornerstone of a building, monument, or memorial. This means they are at or below ground level, making them vulnerable to submersion in water, damage due to issues with the building's foundation or settling, earthquakes, and other damage that may happen to the building structure. This does afford a level of security as it makes them almost impossible to access until the building is demolished. It also means that the temperature will likely remain stable as the entire building acts as a thermal buffer. However, this also means that the container is at risk of water infiltration, is usually surrounded by concrete, and may possibly even be mortared in place with cement, which are all inherently problematic.

Containers that are placed as a part of a building are frequently surrounded by cement or concrete, or they may be put in a special concrete alcove or possibly secured within a layer of cement.[3] While concrete may appear to be a stable material, its high pH, its capacity to produce heat as it cures, and its ability to expand and contract in response to the environment makes it an incredibly poor preservation substrate. Concrete expands and contracts as the temperature and humidity in the immediate environment rise and fall. While this normally would not be significant enough to observe, this property is germane to historical buried containers because the strength of the expanding concrete can damage the weaker material of the containers themselves. A twelve-inch square container made of metal might fit easily into a 12.5-inch square cavity left in concrete upon burial, but after over one hundred years, the cavity can become significantly narrower. Depending on the amount of space left in the cavity, the result can resemble the situation of the *At Ready* monument. In this example, the hole into which the container was placed was so snug that the box was crushed as the concrete expanded and contracted every winter and summer, causing the lid to pop open and the solder to crack over time. The box was then compromised, which led to the destruction of much of the material inside as it was exposed to the elements and pests.[4] The first container unearthed from underneath the Lee Monument in Richmond, VA, had also been put into a very tightly fitting cavity, but it was mortared in place into stone, which created other problems for the conservators. An entire piece of stone, weighing hundreds of pounds, had to be transferred to the conservation lab in Richmond for the box to be removed safely.

A potentially surprising property of concrete is that it gives off heat as it cures. When water is added to cement, the resulting chemical reactions are exothermic, meaning that they produce heat as a byproduct. The heat that is generated is called the heat of hydration. The amount of heat greatly depends on the amount of cement, the temperature outside when the concrete is poured and the thickness of the concrete. A poured-concrete slab for an entire building can create a significant amount of heat, as high as 100 degrees Fahrenheit, and while much of that heat can be radiated out into the surrounding soil and air, a container buried in the concrete will no doubt be affected by the temperature increase. Additionally, concrete expands when temperatures get too high during curing, which may also explain the damage to the *At Ready* container.[5] This heat of hydration is mostly dissipated within the first week of the concrete being poured, but heat acts as an accelerant for most chemical reactions, including those that degrade artifacts, books, paper, and photographs, all common things to find in a time capsule or cornerstone box.[6]

Another feature of concrete that affects the burial environment of a historical container is concrete's pH. Many materials have pH, which is a mea-

Figure 12. Lead container from the Lee Monument trapped in stone by mortar.

sure of how acidic or basic that material is on a scale of 1 to 14, with 1 being the most acidic and 14 being the most basic. The pH is inherently linked to water, since it measures the number of hydrogen ions in a material.[7] With an average pH of twelve, concrete is very basic, and its effect on cultural heritage can be extreme. Cement can initially create a protective layer on iron and steel as the calcium hydroxide reacts with the iron to create iron oxide. However, if the concrete also contains chlorine, this element causes severe corrosion in iron over time.[8] From the authors' experience, copper containers fare well in the long term, even when exposed to cement, as long as their walls are thick enough. The *At Ready* cornerstone box was made of very thin copper walls soldered with lead, as was the historically documented container found in the Lee Monument. The undocumented, but first-discovered, Lee container had been made of lead that was significantly thicker than the walls of the copper boxes. Over time, chemical interactions with the materials and pH of the mortar changed the physical attributes of the lead walls: instead of being pliable and relatively soft, the lead was extremely hard and easily broken.

While the *At Ready* box had collapsed due to the expansion of the concrete, the thin copper walls withstood over a century of the assault from the concrete. Indeed, according to the Portland Cement Association "copper and copper alloys are practically immune to action from fresh concrete and mortar."[9] The walls of the copper Lee box were also quite thin but were similarly intact despite inclusion in a basic burial environment. Nevertheless, the conservators noted that the inside of the *At Ready* copper box had been affected by the acidity of the damaged paper inside: the low pH stripped away the protective outer layer, known as patina, of the copper, causing a distinct tideline showing shiny bare metal where water mixed with degraded paper had touched.

Prior to locating the cornerstone boxes, much less opening them, the conservators were most concerned about water infiltration. Water is an extremely potent solvent, conductor, and catalyst for certain reactions and materials, and burial under tons of concrete, marble, and bronze put the boxes at risk of damage that could lead to moisture accumulating. Water can cause corrosion, encourage pest and mold activity, cause paper to turn back into paper pulp, and make inks bleed and become illegible. Before the *At Ready* copper box was found, mold growth was also a huge worry. Humid air or actual water droplets caused by the box being broken underground could lead to conditions favorable for mold growth, which could then systematically destroy all organic material in the boxes. Damage to the boxes seemed likely, given previous boxes found underneath monuments, such as the box underneath the Raleigh, NC, Lee statue which had been crushed.[10] Both Virginia and North Carolina are in the South and known for hot and humid weather in the summer, with storms that bring heavy rains and risk of impact from coastal hurricanes.

Indeed, the *At Ready* cornerstone box had been squeezed by the pressure of the concrete, as described above, and groundwater had soaked the contents. It was quickly apparent that mold was not something the conservators had to worry about for the *At Ready* box, because the location of the box underground and the groundwater essentially created an anoxic (oxygen-free) environment, meaning mold could not thrive. Instead, the action of the water in contact with paper from the early 1900s made from acidic wood pulp destroyed the integrity of individual sheets of paper over time, returning the paper to pulp itself.

Since the *At Ready* box was the first uncovered, the conservators feared the worst, but were prepared for it with the Lee boxes in Richmond. Luckily, both the lead and copper boxes were intact when they were unearthed. However, because the cornerstone boxes were a closed system, seasonal changes in temperature—the heat of the Virginia summer and the relative cold of the winter—resulted in condensation of water inside the box itself. In the example of the Lee copper box, when three sides of the lid were cut, a blotter was inserted underneath the lid before opening completely because water droplets had been seen. At the time, protecting the contents from water droplets seemed very important, but when the lid was completely removed and the materials were examined, it became abundantly clear that the contents were thoroughly soaked. No standing water had been visible in an x-ray of the box, but since paper is a hygroscopic material and can absorb a lot of water, the books and pamphlets stored in the cornerstone box for over a century had drawn up a substantial amount of moisture.

A less obvious destructive process that water can help to hasten is galvanic corrosion. The Canadian Conservation Institute describes it as "When two wet metals are in contact, one of them usually corrodes faster than when the metals are separated. The increase in corrosion rate is called galvanic corrosion."[11] Generally speaking, the less noble metals degrade more quickly, so if gold is touching copper, the copper will corrode more quickly, but if copper is touching iron, then the iron will corrode faster. Both the *At Ready* and Lee copper boxes were made of copper sheets fastened together with a lead-based solder. Lead is the less noble metal, and since both of these boxes were in wet environments, the solder was more degraded than the copper walls. The lead of the *At Ready* solder was especially deteriorated where it was thinner, along the edges, and in some cases the solder failed all together (one side of the box was completely open). Galvanic corrosion will also lead to damage of any metal artifacts that touch each other or a metal container. With the examples of silver coins touching a bronze medal, a gilded medal next to a copper penny, or an iron container touching the metal artifacts in the box, all of these interactions will create galvanic corrosion cells that will cause damage.

When the last stone was removed from the *At Ready* pedestal, revealing the hole in the cement foundation, a handful of beetles came scurrying out. While it isn't clear what impact these pests had on the *At Ready* box, their presence was the first indicator that something had gone horribly wrong. Indeed, pests are another of the ten agents of deterioration that conservators must reckon with, and their impact can be huge. Pests can come in many different shapes and sizes, from small bookworms and carpet beetles to large rats, and they can wreak havoc on cultural heritage. Whether by eating the substrate of manuscripts because they are attracted to the glue or other organic matter, or by shredding paper and textiles to make nests or urinating and defecating on items, pests can cause changes in pH, texture, legibility, format, and all manner of deteriorations.

Because there was no discernible evidence of a full life cycle of insects in the *At Ready* cornerstone box, the conservators assumed that the beetles observed emerging from the hole were adults that had sought temporary shelter in the dark, as opposed to feeding on any of the organic matter in the cornerstone box. The water was also so acidic because of the wood pulp paper that it is likely to have been completely inhospitable to insects as well. Nevertheless, even the movement of the insects' feet could have disrupted the extremely damaged paper, so the potential risk of pests on cultural heritage and on buried containers cannot be overstated.

Because time capsules are meant to be opened at a particular date in the future, their enclosures may also have a way for them to be opened to make them more easily accessible when that time comes. These purpose-built openings are vulnerable to attack by the agents of deterioration, especially if they are a different material than the rest of the enclosure. Metals can corrode and cause surrounding concrete to crack, water can find a way in through these openings, and so can vandals. Making these alcoves less accessible means that the time capsule may be damaged when well-meaning future people try to remove it from its enclosure. This potentiality for time capsules has unfortunately been the reality for the cornerstone boxes that the conservators have preserved. As mentioned before, cornerstone boxes are *part* of the monument itself, and they are not meant to be removed. Removing and opening the boxes caused damage to all three, although in different ways. While the *At Ready* box was already open because of the conditions of the hole and the effects of curing cement and galvanic corrosion, damage occurred to the contents when the box was physically transferred to the conservation lab. The box was tipped on an angle during transit, causing the wet papers and books to slosh to one side, irreversibly crushing them. The Lee lead box was mortared into stone, as mentioned above, requiring a forklift to transfer it. Both Lee boxes had to be cut open because of the solder that had hardened over more than a century. All of this damage was done by well-intentioned people involved in sanctioned removal efforts by local and state entities who were trying their best to minimize harm.

An unexpected result of the environment created within the *At Ready* cornerstone box was that the Confederate medals that had been placed between layers of books and pamphlets at the time of the burial were unlike any archaeological metal treated by the conservators before. Bathed in the same acidic water that had stripped the walls of the copper box, the medals, too, were shiny and appeared pristine when first uncovered. Quickly, though, the oxygen, carbon dioxide, water, and other chemicals in the air the medals had been suddenly exposed to, caused the copper metal to tarnish and darken.[12] This lesson learned with *At Ready*, the conservators were prepared for the metal objects found within the Lee cornerstone boxes and exposed them to the air for as short a time as possible when they were extracted from their boxes.

When the conservators envisioned working with time capsules, as much of the world called them when the Confederate monuments were being taken down, it is safe to say that neither Ridgway nor Donovan expected them to be as wet as they ended up being. As mentioned above, water, in its form of "incorrect humidity" is a well-known catalyst for many adverse reactions that can damage cultural heritage, but the extent of the damage, the quantities of water, and the way moisture infiltrated were surprising. Prepared for the worst after experiencing how water had solubilized the acidity of early-twentieth-century paper in the *At Ready* box, the conservators were relieved to find documents that did not disintegrate upon the slightest touch in the Lee Monument boxes. The relief quickly turned to action as books were frozen to prevent mold growth and speed drying, and metal objects (including the boxes themselves) were placed in bags with silica gel to dry them quickly and reduce the risk of tarnishing. Paper-based items that were able to be flattened into a single layer were dried under blotter or air dried. The coordination of conservators across specialties was extremely helpful and was truly key to the success of the preservation of the Lee Monument boxes. Having professionals working as a team who are confident in their specific knowledge base reduces stress and improves speed and positive outcomes for the contents of the containers. The authors acknowledge that all who need help preserving a time capsule or cornerstone box might not have access to or funding for conservators of cultural heritage, so they have compiled suggestions from their experiences with the cornerstone boxes and in their years of professional experience in the hopes that those who read them may find them useful.

CARING FOR YOUR TIME CAPSULE: AVOIDING THE TEN AGENTS OF DETERIORATION

Despite having seen, salvaged, and preserved the contents of cornerstone boxes, and being thoroughly opposed to burying cultural heritage underground, the authors understand that commemorating a special building or event by creating a time capsule or cornerstone box is something that will continue to happen. For those pursuing this endeavor, there are resources available to help ensure that the items within, and the enclosure itself are protected and preserved. Information about the ten agents of deterioration that threaten cultural heritage is extremely useful in this situation and can be found at the end of this chapter. The agents of deterioration are as follows: physical forces, thieves and vandals, dissociation, fire, water, pests, pollution, light, incorrect temperature, and incorrect humidity. For those seeking information and guidance based on the authors' specific expertise, the below list of considerations for your time capsule is a good starting point. Contacting a conservator of cultural heritage in your area is one of the best ways to find specific, tailored information for your project and your goals. The "Find a Professional" tool on the website www.culturalheritage.org will narrow the field of conservators down based on location and specialty.

Physical Forces

If the artifacts in your container are shaken up, kicked, hit, or physically and violently affected in some way, then they can be damaged. This includes damage from earthquakes, tornadoes, or a building collapse. Seek advice from building engineers and other experts if your locality is subject to this kind of event. Of course, once the box is laid in its location, physical forces may be out of your control, but packing a container tightly may mitigate some of this kind of damage by not allowing the artifacts to move around. Keep in mind that the best chance of physical damage to a time capsule is when it is recovered and opened. Digging it out of a foundation and cutting it open is an issue for the safety of the materials inside.

Thieves and Vandals

Because the laying of these types of containers is frequently well advertised and the contents of the container may be subject to public knowledge, there is a risk of theft and vandalizing the container. If the container is to be placed above ground in a public location, cameras, motion sensors, and guards will help mitigate and monitor this issue, as will ensuring that there is nothing of real value to attract a thief to these kinds of boxes. With the Lee cornerstone container, there was persistent rumor that a valuable photograph of Abraham Lincoln lying in state was inside the box. Most historians doubted this fact, and it did prove to be untrue, but that rumor did compromise the safety of the box.

Dissociation

Dissociation is the loss of the physical object or the information, provenance, and context for the item. To avoid dissociation, ensure there is appropriate documentation regarding the box, its contents, its location, and how to open the box, that is stored safely in a location separate from the burial location. Keeping copies at a state library, institutional archives, and a story in the paper can all be helpful.

Fire

Whether it is a fire that destroys a building or a memorial flame that eventually stains and cracks the stone around it, fire is an ever-present danger. Protecting a time capsule from fire is more about protecting the building or monument in which it is contained from fire. A less obvious source that could cause the contents of the container to catch alight is the method used to open it. If the box is made of metal and is cut open, then depending on the metal, sparks could form and damage the material inside. Keep this in mind both when choosing the materials the container is made from and when leaving instructions on how to open it in the future.

Water

Where there is fire, there is frequently water, but fire suppression is not the only way a time capsule might be exposed to water. As previously explained in detail regarding the cornerstone boxes opened by Ridgway and Donovan, water can facilitate galvanic corrosion and mold growth, wash away soluble media, turn certain paper types back into pulp, and much more. Water is so good at infiltrating through any crack it can find that waterproof containers are a must when the artifacts inside must be protected from it, especially for decades. Burying a container in high ground, far from a water table, or better yet, keeping the container out of the ground and inside a building protected from areas with high risk for hurricanes and other strong storm systems and from the sea level rise due to climate change can all help prevent this destructive agent of deterioration from damaging a time capsule.

Pests

Pests are any animals that can cause damage to cultural heritage, including rodents that might chew through a time capsule to get at the paper which they see as good nesting material. The most common pests found, however, are insects that love dark places with food to eat. In this case the food is the artifacts that you are trying to preserve for the future. Not only do insects eat many kinds of materials (mostly paper, leather, and textiles in the case of time capsules), they also leave behind their feces (frass) and can urinate on artifacts, all of which can cause damage.

Pollutants/Pollution

Conservators call pollutants volatile organic compounds (VOCs), and the process of creating polluting gases is known as off-gassing. When creating a time capsule, it is best to choose materials that emit the least amount of VOCs possible. Some of the most common pollutant-emitting materials are plastics, wood, paper, and textiles. This is one of the many reasons that containers should not be constructed of plastic or wood, and most are made of metal, which is inert, meaning it does not off-gas. VOCs in general are not as much of an issue if there is appropriate ventilation. Unfortunately, the nature of time capsules is that there is almost never any ventilation, either for the box or its contents. Most time capsules are well sealed, and this traps any pollutants inside with the artifacts, which themselves are often the source of VOCs. Paper notes, wooden artifacts, woolen keepsakes and more will cause all of the artifacts in a container to deteriorate over time. This is why it is recommended that any time capsule also includes a pollutant absorber like activated charcoal to help to reduce damage to the artifacts by pollutants.[13]

If the container chosen for the time capsule is sufficiently airtight, it may be possible to create a special environment inside that will help the artifacts last longer. One of the best options is the placement of an oxygen scavenger inside the time capsule. These materials remove all of the oxygen from a given amount of air. Oxygen is very damaging to artifacts and is a key player in many decay processes, so making sure it is removed from a time capsule can exponentially help the chances of survival of the artifacts inside. As mentioned above, oxygen scavengers give off heat as they bind oxygen, but the benefits far outweigh the consequences.

If an oxygen scavenger is not an option, then it is also possible to replace the atmosphere inside a time capsule with an inert gas. Inert gases like argon or nitrogen will not react with the artifacts and can be used to replace the oxygen-containing air that is in the time capsule. This process can be trickier and requires an expert to help make sure it is done properly.

All of these environmental regulators rely on the container being difficult to breach and having no air exchange. If the container is compromised or is leaky, then the specialized environment created will not last until the time capsule is to be opened, and the agents of deterioration would be free to wreak their brand of havoc.

Light

In the case of buried historical containers, light as an agent of deterioration is mitigated by placing artifacts in a sealed container and burying them for decades. Visible, ultraviolet, and infrared light can all cause damage to artifacts, especially those made of organic materials like paper and textiles. These are blocked once the artifacts are sealed in a container. Damage because of light exposure can cause fading, brittleness, acid production, and deformation of materials. If the time capsule being prepared is to be stored in a prominent location, it is highly recommended that it be made of a light-blocking material like metal.

Incorrect Temperature

Incorrect temperature can be very detrimental to the cultural heritage within cornerstone boxes and time capsules, as well. The chemical processes that decay and corrode artifacts are spurred on by heat, and fluctuations of temperature can cause issues with humidity, which we will explain below. When talking about a time capsule, heat can come from a variety of sources. As we have mentioned, concrete can give off heat as it sets. The processes of soldering the container shut may also cause a rise in temperature inside the box. Leaving the container in the sun during a ceremony to place it can also cause the container to heat up.

Less obvious heat sources are oxygen scavengers, such as Ageless®, Fresh-Pax®, or Hanwell AnoxiBug® that are frequently used to help preserve artifacts in containers in more recent years. These products are great because oxygen can be a catalyst for many detrimental deterioration processes and eliminating that from a time capsules can help preserve what is inside them, but the process they use to remove the oxygen gives off heat. Ultimately, the detrimental heat that they emit is offset by the benefits of removing oxygen from the container.

Incorrect Relative Humidity

Relative humidity issues can seem both logical and illogical to most people. High relative humidity environments promote mold growth. Low relative humidity environments cause materials to dry out and become brittle. When talking about time capsules, the internal relative humidity is changed by the temperature (if the container remains sealed). It seems illogical, but if the temperature rises inside a sealed container, the relative humidity drops and if the container gets colder, the relative humidity increases.

One of the reasons this seems illogical is because people are used to thinking of humidity in terms of the weather. In Virginia, where the authors live, when the temperature goes up, it usually means it is also very humid. In the winter, the temperatures fall and the humidity in our houses and outside drops too. This causes confusion when the conversation turns to relative humidity and conservation, where the opposite is true.

This means that if a time capsule is removed from a cold, stone or concrete chamber and brought into a much warmer climate inside a building, the paper and textiles become brittle, wood cracks, and the delicate emulsion on photographs and film crack, flake, and can cause the photo to roll onto itself. Leather-bound books also suffer in these conditions, as the shrinking of the leather can be so powerful that it can deform the textblock within the covers. Metal artifacts are actually more stable in dry environments. The opposite situation also can happen, causing too much humidity. When the temperature drops, the relative humidity in the container will rise, and depending on how high the humidity is, there may be condensation, mold growth, and an increase in corrosion of metals. The goal is to maintain a moderate humidity, maybe a little low, around 45 percent relative humidity, and to keep the temperature stable. This is very difficult depending on where the time capsule is, but buried under a building is not a bad way to maintain temperature control, although for reasons listed above, it is not ideal, either.

Silica gel and other humidity controlling materials can also be placed inside a time capsule. Water in the air is a catalyst for many processes that will corrode and decay artifacts. Silica gel can help to maintain a stable humidity during the placement, removal, and opening processes when the likelihood of condensation and large changes in humidity are most likely to take place. Keep in mind that while metals would like the air to be as dry as possible, this is not always the best for organic materials such as paper, photographs, and textiles. It is therefore best to find a middle ground in terms of humidity for the diverse items going into a time capsule.

Agents of Deterioration Working Together

While the agents of deterioration were just explained as individual factors, it is important to know that they frequently work together. For example, the pouring of concrete can cause physical damage, increased temperature, and add pollutants to the surrounding area. For those planning to bury a time capsule, it is important to ask the people in charge of concrete what the pH of the concrete is, what they are doing to mitigate heat production and what kind of heat increase they are expecting. Will the box material protect what is inside in the long term when exposed to that pH? Will the material react with the pH and cause rapid degradation of the container? These are all things to consider. It is well known that, like iron, copper will also corrode when exposed to chlorine. It is important to make sure with the contractors that non-chlorine containing sources are used for all the materials in your concrete if you are placing a metal box in it.

These complex interactions among the agents of deterioration create a situation where it is impossible to predict the outcomes of all the different ways they can combine. This is why it is important to limit these interactions as much as possible to create a path forward that will allow a time capsule the best chance of survival.

SELECTING AND MANAGING THE CONTENTS FOR YOUR TIME CAPSULE

Those who, like the authors, open time capsules and advise people and institutions on how to create them, very much prefer that they are not buried underground. Placement above any potential water ingress from flooding and water pipes is a great start. Having a safe, climate-controlled area where the container can live out its days with minimal damage from the agents of deterioration is best. Making it a part of a display so people do not forget it exists and when it should be opened can also be helpful. Nevertheless, if your time capsule must be placed below ground or at ground level, the authors have compiled suggestions below, arranged by type of material, as to how to avoid the agents of deterioration. In terms of location, making an alcove that is lined with stone or even bricks to reduce the amount of exposure to cement and concrete is ideal. This allows the box to be more easily removed at a later date, limits exposure to the alkaline cement, and may reduce the expansion and contraction of the building materials around the container. A very non-porous stone will also help to limit the ability of water to infiltrate the space.

Even with the pervasiveness of digital information in the last few decades, language written on paper is our primary method of communication and how humans represent their thoughts, opinions, priorities, and dreams. Books and documents on paper are the most simple forms of communication, and they do not require playback methods that become obsolete, so they are good candidates for inclusion in a time capsule. That said, it is important that these books and paper-based items be printed on good quality paper. The word "archival" is often used in stationary shops and craft stores to indicate that a paper or material is good quality. However, this does not always mean the same thing across manufacturers. That's why it is best to look for paper that is not only "acid-free" but that has an alkaline buffer in it. Since the mass-produced paper of today is made from tree pulp and can become acidic over time, it is important for there to be a buffer of an alkaline product such as calcium carbonate. In this way, the alkaline additive tempers the effect of the wood pulp's acidity as it ages and deteriorates.

If photographs are to be included, they should be printed on artist quality paper as well and ideally separated into acid-free folders or envelopes. If books or pamphlets are to be included, these should also be assembled with the best quality materials, such as linen thread and adhesives that won't off-gas. Time will always cause some degradation of materials, but by making sure the components of paper-based items are good quality, the effects of exterior agents of deterioration will be lessened.

Coins, medals, and other similar keepsakes are commonly placed inside of time capsules. They are robust, have a good chance of survival, convey information about the society and its economics, and frequently are dated. They also don't take up a lot of space. They are subject to corrosion, especially galvanic corrosion if they are touching another metal object. The key here is to keep them dry and separated. Cleaning coins with alcohol or acetone to remove dirt and oils from handling before placing them in the container will also help reduce the chance of corrosion. Gold and silver coins will last the longest, but they increase the chance of theft if it is public knowledge that there are precious metals inside the time capsule.

Medals will frequently have issues where the textile ribbon is attached to the medal. Textiles are acidic and will cause corrosion of the metal. The metal fasteners that attach a medal to the clothing of the wearer will also be corroded by the textile and can have issues with galvanic corrosion depending on how they are constructed. The textile can be adversely affected by the medal as well. The medal is heavy and over time can stretch, tear, or crease the fabric of the ribbon. Metal corrosion can stain and cause damage to textiles. Some of this damage may be unavoidable and is just the nature of this type of artifact.

Because human beings are still a fairly martial species, there is a chance that weapons will be placed in a time capsule. Edged weapons should be rendered as safe as possible by making sure they are dull, in a scabbard, or otherwise wrapped for safety. Scabbards and wrapping may cause the blade to corrode, but human safety always outweighs the safety of artifacts. The authors do not recommend any firearms be placed into a time capsule. If this is absolutely necessary, make sure the weapon is unloaded and otherwise safe to handle. Also make sure that it will not get oil onto other artifacts, causing staining. Please warn the future openers if there are any weapons inside a time capsule.[14]

Keeping in mind the agents of deterioration, there are some things that should be left out of a time capsule if at all possible. This list includes the following: plastics (including CDs), fasteners, playback media, and batteries. There are other things that may not be good to put into a time capsule, but these are the most common ones that the authors have been asked to review before they were put into a time capsule.

Whenever possible, plastics should be avoided. Most plastics are not made to last and give off VOCs that will damage the plastics themselves and artifacts around them if those gases are not allowed to dissipate quickly. They can also stain and make artifacts sticky as the plasticizers leak out of them. If they have to be used, try to use the most stable, chloride-free plastics such as polyethylene bags and polyester film enclosures.[15]

Fasteners are items such as paper clips, binder clips, staples and pins that are used to keep documents together. These are typically made of metal that will eventually corrode because it is in association with paper or due to oxidation from the environment. Corrosion products will eventually eat through the paper, causing potential loss of content.

Current media and electronic devices are not good candidates for a time capsule. Most of the technology that holds records of our daily lives, like CDs, DVDs, thumb drives, tablets, and smartphones contain plastic, which as discussed above, can off-gas and become sticky, endangering other materials. They also contain metals, flammable batteries, and may be subject to corrosion. Worse still, the battery in any battery-powered device could leak acid into the time capsule which will destroy everything inside and might even destroy the container.

Furthermore, because of the rapid evolution of technology and media, it is almost guaranteed that today's technology will be difficult to decipher by a society 50 to 100 years in the future. Even if the media makes it until the time capsule is opened, will the battery be dead? Will the future be able to decipher it? Museums today struggle to find playback methods for art pieces created thirty years ago. One hundred years in the future, this problem will be compounded.

CONCLUSION

There is no way for the authors to predict what might be included in a time capsule, which is why understanding the agents of deterioration and how they affect artifacts is so important. Hopefully, those who read this will be better prepared to assess their own materials that are going into a time capsule by understanding what can cause harm to the objects and their container. That being said, there are some very common items that go into many time capsules and there is advice that may help in these instances.

The authors cannot possibly cover everything about time capsules in one article, and the goal of this article is primarily to help people make better, more educated choices when assembling them. There is a list of resources to help those making time capsules learn more and access professionals who might be able to help and give advice. The better the plan for creating and placing a time capsule is, the better chance of survival the capsule and its contents have. When in doubt, contact a conservator if you have questions about opening or creating a time capsule. The American Institute for Conservation has a webpage where the public can find conservators in their area who can help.

After reading this chapter one might think it is impossible to create a time capsule that is guaranteed to last. That is correct. No one can predict everything that might happen, and the agents of deterioration cannot be stopped. Hopefully, this information will give those who might be creating a time capsule some ideas and tips to give their container and its contents the best chance of survival using the resources that are available. As the saying goes, plan for the worst and hope for the best.

As accomplished conservators and experts in the field, the authors have had the opportunity to open more time capsules and cornerstone boxes than most people. The combination of the specialties of book and paper conservation and archaeological conservation proved key to the successful preservation of materials from the historic boxes opened in the years following 2020 and the societal reckoning with Confederate monuments. Subsequently, the authors' diverse backgrounds and hands-on experience with these boxes provide insight into and what might have helped the boxes and their contents endure the onslaught of environmental and man-made ordeals. The authors hope that their expertise and experiences will help more time capsules survive to their opening dates in the best condition possible.

RESOURCES

Time capsules and their contents are too diverse a topic for the authors to possibly include everything. This list will hopefully provide resources and further reading to help those making time capsules make informed decisions about their messages to the future. New things and materials are created every day. Eventually even this article will become a relic of the past and a time capsule for the future.

American Institute for Conservation, Conservation-Wiki on the Ten Agents of Deterioration, https://www.conservation-wiki.com/wiki/Ten_Agents_of_Deterioration/.

American Institute for Conservation, Find a Professional, https://www.culturalheritage.org/about-conservation/find-a-conservator/.

Canadian Conservation Institute, *Agents of Deterioration*, https://www.canada.ca/en/conservation-institute/services/agents-deterioration.html.

Canadian Conservation Institute (CCI), *Notes*, https://www.canada.ca/en/conservation-institute/services/conservation-preservation-publications/canadian-conservation-institute-notes.html.

Library of Congress, *Making a Time Capsule*, https://www.loc.gov/preservation/resources/educational/timecapsule/index.html.

Minnesota Historical Society, *Guidelines for Selecting and Preserving Items in a Time Capsule* by Paul Storch, https://www.mnhs.org/preserve/conservation/docs_pdfs/GUIDELINESFORSELECTINGANDPRESERVINGITEMSINATIMECAPSULE090710.pdf.

Smithsonian—Museum Conservation Institute, *Time Capsules*, https://mci.si.edu/time-capsules/.

NOTES

1. Dr. Caroline Janney, "When the Monuments Went Up," UVA Clubs & UVA Library, UVA Engagement channel, November 20, 2020, YouTube video, 58:17, https://youtu.be/H6zzUd86Xq4?si=XqdtlLxuix1wQJLZ.
2. Author Unknown, "May Fifth the Date Selected for Unveiling Confederate Monument: Anniversary of Organization of Monticello Guard," *The Daily Progress*. March 15, 1909.
3. Cement, when mixed with water, creates mortar which is used to adhere bricks and stones to one another. This mortar when mixed with an aggregate like sand or stones becomes concrete.
4. A. M. Neville and J. J. Brooks, "Deformation and Cracking Independent of Load" in *Concrete Technology* (Essex, England: Pearson Education, 2010), 242–49.
5. Portland Cement Association, "Concrete, and Heat of Hydration," *Concrete Technology Today* 18, no. 2 (1997): 1.
6. A. M. Neville and J. J. Brooks, "Cement" in *Concrete Technology* (Essex, England: Pearson Education, 2010), 13.
7. Helen Wilks and Graham Weaver, eds. *Science for Conservators*, (London: Routledge, 1992), 91.
8. A. M. Neville and J. J. Brooks, "Permeability and Durability," in *Concrete Technology* (Essex, England: Pearson Education, 2010), 269–71.
9. Portland Cement Association paper, *Corrosion of Nonferrous Metals in Contact with Concrete*, 1.
10. Christina Morales, "What's at the Bottom of a Confederate Monument? It Could Be a Time Capsule," *The New York Times*, July 8, 2020.
11. "Understanding Galvanic Corrosion," Government of Canada, last modified March, 16, 2021, https://www.canada.ca/en/conservation-institute/services/training-learning/in-person-workshops/galvanic-corrosion.html.
12. David A. Scott, "Corrosion and Environment," in *Copper and Bronze in Art: Corrosion, Colorants, Conservation* (Los Angeles: The Getty Conservation Institute, 2002).
13. Alexandra Schieweck, "Adsorbent Media for the Sustainable Removal of Organic Air Pollutants from Museum Display Cases," *Heritage Science* 8, no. 12 (2020): 17, doi: 10.1186/s40494-020-0357-8.
14. Paul S. Storch, "Guidelines for Selecting and Preserving Items in a Time Capsule," *Minnesota Historical Society*, 2, 2010, https://www.mnhs.org/preserve/conservation/docs_pdfs/GUIDELINESFORSELECTINGANDPRESERVINGITEMSINATIMECAPSULE090710.pdf.
15. Storch, "Guidelines for Selecting and Preserving Items in a Time Capsule," 2.

Life and Times

5

Where Are the Women?

Caroline E. Janney

Among the myriad objects placed in the cornerstone box, it is curious that none reflects the central role Confederate women played in the Lee Monument's creation. The only items related to women are a report of the Mount Vernon Ladies' Association (a group never involved in the Lee Monument) and several items women donated, all of which focused on veterans. Despite Confederate veterans' near constant adulation of Confederate women at Memorial Day speeches and other occasions, perhaps the two-decade long battle they had endured with Richmond's women over the monument had driven them to conveniently forget the critical role White women had served in the planning, fundraising, and designing of the Lee Monument.

Following Robert E. Lee's death in October 1870, a group of ex-Confederates met in Lexington, Virginia, forming the Lee Memorial Association, with the expressed purpose of erecting an equestrian statue on the Washington College grounds (where Lee had served as president until his death), a bust in the chapel, and a recumbent statue on his tomb.[1] But other Virginians, namely those in Richmond, believed Lee should be laid to rest in Hollywood Cemetery where so many of his men now reposed. Mary Custis Lee, the general's widow, temporarily put an end to disputes over his burial by agreeing to have him interred in a vault beneath the college chapel in Lexington. Disputes over a monument to the general, however, were only beginning.

The women of Richmond's Hollywood Memorial Association (HMA) wasted no time in initiating their own organization to memorialize Lee. In 1866, the HMA along with other Ladies' Memorial Associations (LMAs) had led the creation of Confederate cemeteries and established the practice of

Memorial Day. In their role as mourners, women had been the key figures in these early Lost Cause ceremonies, and in the wake of Lee's death, they claimed to be the guardians of Confederate memory. Rejecting the Lexington plan, the Ladies established a committee tasked with placing a bronze equestrian monument to the general in Hollywood Cemetery. In accord with their previous fundraising activities, they published a list of more than a hundred prominent Confederate leaders and soldiers, including nearly every member of the Lexington association, they wished would "*act as assistants*" to their committee. Notably present on the list of "assistants" was former Confederate general Jubal A. Early.

While women might be especially well-suited for organizing Memorial Days and honoring the common soldier, Early did not consider them fit to lead the most important Lost Cause task, that of honoring Lee. Instead, within a few weeks, he had established the Lee Monument Association (not to be confused with the Lexington-based Lee *Memorial* Association). In rhetoric no doubt aimed at the women of the HMA committee, Early believed that any effort to honor Lee should emanate from those who had fought under the general. "A sacred duty devolves upon those whom . . . he led so often in battle," Early claimed, although he had no intentions of confining the contributions to veterans alone, encouraging all those who "admire[d] and revere[d] true greatness" to donate. Early thoroughly resented any other effort to memorialize Lee, especially the Lee Memorial Association's efforts to enshrine Lexington as a memorial to the Confederate leader and similar projects underway in New Orleans and Atlanta. Rather than encouraging White Southerners to dot their landscapes with memorials to the famed general, Early insisted there be only "one grand Confederate Monument" situated in the heart of Richmond—one that was under his control.[2]

To gain a monopoly over the memorial movement to the late chieftain, by mid-November, Early had invited the HMA to "lend . . . their assistance" in collecting contributions. The women promptly agreed and formed auxiliary committees throughout the South—on the condition that they were to be considered equal partners in the endeavor. But Early and his associates had other plans. If the men could keep the women close enough, the women could not best the veterans' efforts to honor Lee. Early and the Lee Monument Association certainly knew how successful the HMA and other LMAs had been in raising funds for their cemeteries and other projects; their networks and money-generating capabilities must have been attractive to the men. The HMA women, however, were not nearly so naïve and passive as the men expected. Even though the women agreed with Early on several counts, including that the monument belonged in the former capital, they proved an especially troubling thorn in Early's side, demanding full recognition and cooperation throughout the process.[3]

By 1871, a bitter and often cantankerous rivalry arose between the HMA (recasting its committee as the Ladies' Lee Monument Committee [LLMC] to be led by Sarah Randolph) and Early's Lee Monument Association, a rivalry enduring for nearly two decades.[4] Both competed to raise funding, with the veterans falling far short of the money flowing into the women's coffers. Feeling bested by the women, Early embarked on a smear campaign, warning White Southerners that some of the women's agents were impostors and denying affiliation with the Ladies Committee.[5] For nearly fifteen years, the fires of hostility between Early and the women burned intensely as the agents for competing associations flooded towns and cities throughout the South trying to raise money for the Lee Monument.

The divisiveness between Early's veterans and the women of the LLMC, combined with the confusion of multiple groups canvassing the region for contributions, managed to slow the Lee Monument's progress to a near standstill within just a few years. In 1875, Virginia Governor James L. Kemper, a Confederate veteran, stepped forward to take the reins of the listless Lee memorial campaign. With Early's collaboration, Kemper commissioned a Board of Managers consisting of himself, ex-officers of the Confederate army, the state auditor of public accounts, and the state treasurer whose purpose would be the erection of a "Colossal Equestrian" statue of Lee on the Capitol Square. Early thus relinquished control of the movement and handed over his insufficient funds to the governor's board. There are some indications that the Ladies were approached to unite with the men, but it appears that the men never intended to give the women a position on the executive board. The women would not bequeath full control to the men. Not surprisingly, like Early's monument association, the governor's group remained exclusively male.[6]

Despite the very public solicitations of the men's group, throughout the 1870s the LLMC continued its own fundraising ventures. But disputes over who might collect the most money proved to be only a skirmish in the male/female war over Lee's monument; the real battles unfolded over the statue's design. Early and the men preferred the selection of Edward Valentine, a Virginia sculptor who had crafted the recumbent Lee statue at Lexington. Sarah Randolph and the women, on the other hand, favored French artist Marius-

Jean-Antonin Mercié as they desired that the monument be construed as a masterpiece of art, reflecting the greatness of White Southern culture. The women insisted, yet again, that *they* were the true and undisputed leaders of the memorial effort, and would submit to no man, including the governor. "Better no monument at all than an inferior one," Randolph quipped.[7]

Even as Confederate veterans in New Orleans managed to complete and dedicate a memorial to Lee in 1884, the LLMC continued to forestall the Richmond project. Rejecting nearly every design model and refusing to relinquish their funds, the women spurned calls to cede their authority over the public representations of the Lost Cause.

Finally, in 1886, newly elected governor and nephew of Robert E. Lee, Fitzhugh Lee worked out a compromise association that included a new board of directors with representatives from the state government and LLMC, including Randolph and Elizabeth Nicholas. With fundraising nearing completion, the new association selected the women's sculptor of choice, Mercié. Early balked at the decision, describing Mercié's design as "General Lee on a 'bob tail horse,' looking like an English jockey" and implying that if it were erected, he would rouse "the survivors of the 2d Corps" to demolish the statue.[8] The women prevailed, however, and the Freemasons laid the statue's cornerstone amid a cold, drizzling rain on October 27, 1887.

Yet the women proved conspicuously absent from the cornerstone dedication.

In his remarks, Governor Lee mentioned the Hollywood Memorial Association's (notably *not* the Ladies Lee Monument Committee's) initial efforts to raise money in passing, but he lavished praise on Early's association of veterans before introducing the general. Nineteenth-century Southern, White gender norms precluded women from addressing the crowd, yet it is striking that the women had no objects included in the cornerstone. Of those women who donated objects (Mrs. H. A. Marshall, Nettie Lee Brown, Emma R. Ball, and Patti Leake), none appears to have had a direct connection to the LLMC or HMA. This is especially notable considering that some of the men who donated items, such as J.W. Randolph, were married to members of the Hollywood association. Likewise, one might have expected to find documents such as the *Register of the Dead, Interred in Hollywood Cemetery* published in 1869, which highlighted the women's efforts to enshrine the Lost Cause in Confederate cemeteries. Finally, newspaper accounts suggest that although women attended the event, they did not participate in the procession to the cornerstone laying. In most Memorial Day and monument-unveiling processions throughout the 1860s–1890s, LMA women rode in carriages at either the beginning or end of the line. In contrast, this event appears to have been exclusively a male affair, with 3,000 Confederate veterans marching in-step to the dedication site.

The LMAs and their successors the United Daughters of the Confederacy (est. 1894) proved largely responsible not only for the Confederate memorial landscape that flourished in the first three decades of the twentieth century, but indeed the very success and longevity of the Lost Cause through their textbook campaigns, scholarships for Confederate descendants, and other efforts. Yet an examination of the objects found in the cornerstone would suggest women played little to no role in Richmond's—indeed Virginia's—most notable Lost Cause symbol. A recounting of the monument's history, especially the contentious role of Confederate women in its establishment, serves as a reminder that silences often speak volumes.

For more about the role of the Ladies Memorial Associations in Richmond and Virginia, see Caroline E. Janney, *Burying the Dead but Not the Past: Ladies Memorial Associations and the Lost Cause*.

NOTES

1. *Richmond Daily Dispatch*, October 20, 1870; Gaines Foster, *Ghosts of the Confederacy: Defeat, the Lost Cause, and the Emergence of the New South, 1865 to 1913* (New York: Oxford University Press, 1987), 51.
2. Jubal A. Early to Dabney H. Maury, December 14, 1870, item #50, Goodspeed's Catalogue 592 (Boston, MA: Goodspeed's Book Shop, n.d.), 11; "To the Survivors of the Army and Navy of the Confederate States and to all the admirers of the Character of the late General Robert E. Lee, wherever they may reside," November 1870, Lee Monument Association Records, Library of Virginia; *Richmond Daily Dispatch*, November 15, 1870; *New York Times*, October 28, 1870; Thomas Connelly, *The Marble Man: Robert E. Lee and His Image in American Society* (Baton Rouge, LA: Louisiana State University Press, 1977), 43–45.
3. *Richmond Daily Dispatch*, November 15, 1870; Sarah N. Randolph to General Jubal A. Early, Richmond, March 13, 1871, Lee Monument Association Records, Library of Virginia.
4. *Richmond Daily Dispatch*, November 15, 1870; Sarah N. Randolph to General Jubal A. Early, Richmond, March 13, 1871, Lee Monument Association Records, Library of Virginia.
5. *Richmond Daily Dispatch*, November 15, 1870; Sarah N. Randolph to General Jubal A. Early, March 13, 1871, Lee Monument Association Records, Library of Virginia.

6. Minutes of the Lee Monument Association, September 28, October 30, 1875, Lee Monument Association Records, Library of Virginia; "The Monument to General Robert E. Lee, Part 1," Southern, January—December 1889, APS Online, 187.
7. Ladies' Lee Monument Association to his Excellency the Governor of Virginia and the members of the Lee Monument Association, Richmond, March 3, 1877, Minutes of the Lee Monument Association, February 2, 1877 to May 4, 1877, Lee Monument Association Records, Library of Virginia.
8. "The Monument to General Robert E. Lee: History of the Movement for Its Erection," *Southern Historical Society Papers* 17:185–205; Connelly, *Marble Man*, 45; Early quoted in Foster, *Ghosts*, 98–100; Kirk Savage, *Standing Soldiers: Race, War, and Monument in Nineteenth-Century America* (Princeton, NJ: Princeton University Press, 1997), 146–50.

6

Mitchell's Prophecy

Black Richmonders, the Lee Monument, and the Lost Cause Redux, 1890–2021

Ervin L. Jordan Jr.

Throughout America's long history, someone's heroes are often someone else's villains. This chapter is a historical overview of Black Richmonders' reactions to the Lee Monument's 1890 dedication ceremonies in the context of the racial times and the Lost Cause mythology as a sociopolitical force. Although in attendance at the unveiling, the event's organizers sought to exclude Black people from the historical record represented by 100 select artifacts placed in the monument's cornerstone box—or so they thought. But in Shakespeare's words, "The truth will come to light . . . truth will out."

Later that year the African American community held an Emancipation Day parade, an audacious counterprotest during "the Nadir," a tragic era of Jim Crowism, lynchings, and racial terrorism as the grimmest post-emancipation period in African American history (1870s–1890s). At the intersection of the nineteenth and twenty-first centuries, as communities reassess who and what they memorialize, Confederate monuments require meaningful forms of redress to old grievances. Such considerations are deep-rooted conundrums. Efforts to banish such monuments from public spaces reflect conflicted memories of what some historians characterize as "The War That Never Ended."

"THE SOUTHERN WHITE FOLKS IS ON TOP"

On Confederate Decoration (Memorial) Day, May 29, 1890, twenty-five years after the Confederacy's defeat, during the unveiling of a gigantic equestrian

Figure 13. Draped Lee statue just prior to its May 1890 unveiling, with four Black male laborers who helped hoist the statue into place barely visible in the background. (Courtesy of Robert A. Lancaster, Jr. Collection, The Valentine)

statue of General Robert E. Lee (1807–1870) in what was then empty farmland on the outskirts of Richmond, Virginia, "an old colored man, after seeing the mammoth parade of the ex-Confederates . . . and gazing at the rebel flags, exclaimed, 'The Southern white folks is on top—the Southern white folks is on top!'" Others expressed disdain instead of despair. *Richmond Planet* editor and ex-slave John Mitchell Jr. (1863–1929), was one of three Black city council members who voted against a $7,500 city appropriation ($209,000 in 2025 dollars) for the ceremonies. Among the few Richmond Black men who publicly ridiculed "Rebel flags," Mitchell's scathing front-page editorial reminded readers "these emblems of the 'Lost Cause' . . . had been perforated by Union bullets." He continued: "The South may revere the memory of its chieftains. It takes the wrong steps in so doing, and . . . serves to retard its progress in the country."[1]

The *Planet*, founded in 1882 and published Saturdays, was among America's foremost Black weekly newspapers. Its "Strong Arm" editorial page logo (and later masthead) depicted a muscular Black male arm's torch-like fist radiating lightning bolts—an exemplar of racial pride. Mitchell's first biographer lauded him as "a man who would walk into the jaws of death to serve his race." The then-twenty-seven-year-old "Fighting Editor" was at the beginning of his distinguished half-century career as an anti-lynching crusader, banker, civil rights activist, journalist, and politician. He grimly prophesied: "The Negro . . . put up the Lee Monument, and should the time come, will be there to take it down." Mitchell's prophesy proved true 131 years later when, in the wake of national protests of the 2020 murder of George Floyd (1973–2020), Team Henry Enterprises, a Black-owned contracting firm, removed the monument in September and December 2021. The Commonwealth transferred it to the City of Richmond, which later gave it to the Black History Museum & Cultural Center of Virginia.[2]

MITCHELL'S MARCH: "WE ARE AMERICAN CITIZENS"

Five months after the Lee Monument's unveiling, and unintimidated by Confederate veterans "from New York to Texas," *Planet* editor John Mitchell countered with a massive two-mile long Emancipation Proclamation parade in Richmond on Thursday, October 16, 1890, which he proudly led on horseback as chief marshal. Five thousand Black marchers represented forty civic, business, and fraternal organizations accompanied by bands and militia. Mitchell was "King this Week . . . and looked as if he were governor of Virginia," opined the *Washington Bee's* editor. The parade concluded with a public meeting and speeches before an audience of ten thousand. "We are American citizens," declared renowned orator Reverend Joseph Charles Price (1854–1893), president of Livingston College, North Carolina, a Black Christian school. "When the white people go back to Europe then we will go back to Africa." John Mercer Langston (1829–1897), less than a month in office as Virginia's only Black congressman, urged political participation in the post-Reconstruction South: "They say this is a white man's government [but] I am here to tell you that it is a Black man's government as well."[3]

The October 16 date (part of three days of celebrations including the fifteenth and the seventeenth) had been the subject of "quite a difference of opinion" among Black Richmonders. After soliciting views "among our

Figure 14. John Mitchell Jr. (1863–1929) at the time of the Lee Monument unveiling. *The Afro-American Press and Its Editors*, 1891, page 185. (Courtesy of the Internet Archive)

people" (seventeen prominent men), a sixteen-member "Executive Committee of the Emancipation Celebration" elected Mitchell "Chief Marshal of the entire Celebration" and reported four favored dates, in order of local preference: April 9 (Lee's 1865 Appomattox surrender), April 3 (Richmond's capture and "because that was the day I shook hands with the Yankees" recalled one respondent), January 1 (1863 Emancipation Proclamation), and September 22 (1862 preliminary Proclamation). Three of these seventeen respondents were executive committee members who preferred January 1 or April 9. Mitchell's preferences, and why October was chosen, is unknown but planning had not begun until July 1890—too late for January or April that year.

Another internal issue concerned Edwin Archer Randolph (1850–1919), Yale Law School's first Black graduate (1880) and one of the city's leading Black lawyers. He and Mitchell, though *Planet* co-founders, had a litigious relationship concerning stock profits but as city council members set aside their differences for the greater good of the race. Randolph was elected executive committee chair for the Emancipation Day celebrations and Mitchell its chief marshal. (Mitchell later confided to an Alexandria journalist: "I win over the colored people by coming in personal contact with them and bringing them over to my way of thinking.")[4]

Determined to exercise their right to equal access to public spaces, parade organizers took out front-page advertisements in Black newspapers promising "great days of the colored people . . . none should fail to come." Unable to prevent the parade, Whites' intransigence thwarted plans for an artillery salute at Capitol Square by the Richmond Howitzers. A "citizens of African descent" mass meeting authorized a delegation led by 'Captain' Benjamin Scott (who in 1866 organized a Black self-defense militia in Jackson Ward, the "Navy Hill Irrepressibles") to petition Governor Philip Watkins McKinney (1832–1899) on their behalf as "commemorative of our emancipation," but McKinney denied their request as "it has not been the custom for the executive to order salutes." The organizers' executive committee retorted they did not need Whites "to fire any salutes for them, they would fire their own." Other Whites, not questioning the color of African American dollars, saw entrepreneurial opportunities. Reduced-rate round-trip tickets offered by the Richmond, Fredericksburg, and Potomac Railroad Company assured prospective passengers they could attend and return home the same day.[5]

THE LOST CAUSE DEFINED

Early postwar public commemorations of the American Civil War occurred in a backdrop of social and racial tensions. Black Richmonders' Tuesday, April 3, 1866, Emancipation Day parade marking the first anniversary of the city's capture by Union troops prudently dissociated the South from slavery. Nevertheless, event organizers and potential attendees were threatened. "Those who participate in this most ill-advised affair," warned the *Daily Richmond Whig*, "may be sure that they will be observed and remembered." Some Whites alleged the Confederate flag would be dragged through the streets "tied at the tail of a horse" and Lee and other Confederate 'heroes' burned in effigy. The "work of an incendiary" on the afternoon of Saturday, March 31, destroyed the Second African Baptist Church on Byrd Street four days before the parade; undiscouraged, its congregation laid the cornerstone for a new building in May. (Surprisingly, the conservative *Richmond Daily Dispatch* praised Second African Baptist as embracing many of the worthiest of "our colored population" and meriting the "aid of our community" in rebuilding efforts.)[6]

The day before the parade, responding to rumors by nervous Whites, a five-member "Colored League" issued broadsides explaining the commemoration as "the day on which God was pleased to Liberate their Long-oppressed race" and denying Blacks were celebrating the "failure of the Southern Confederacy as it has been stated in the papers of this City." Preceded by "Peace, Friendship, and Liberty with all mankind" and "Union Liberties Protective Society" banners, the parade of 2,000 marchers peacefully concluded at the State Capitol grounds where an audience of 15,000 were addressed by Black and White speakers. One city newspaper derisively reported the bronze equestrian statue of George Washington at the public square "fairly trembled" in disgust upon seeing the "many-headed emancipated." (This was not the earliest Afro-Virginian event at Capitol Square; the Fourth of July 1865 witnessed Black Richmonders' first public celebration of their "Independence" Day.) Richmond's Black residents publicly celebrated Emancipation Day and similar freedom festivals the remainder of the nineteenth century (January, April, or October) and into the twenty-first century until these were generally surpassed by Juneteenth, an official statewide holiday as of 2022.[7]

The April 3 celebration coincided with the beginnings of the Lost Cause ideology as conceptualized in Edward Pollard's (1832–1872) *The Lost Cause: A New Southern History of the War of the Confederates* (1866), a sixty-word-titled tome of nearly eight hundred pages, and *The Lost Cause Regained* (1868). The Richmond *Examiner's* wartime editor and a critic of Confederate president Jefferson Davis (1808–1889), Pollard had been imprisoned at Fort Monroe, Virginia, after his 1864 capture while attempting to reach Great Britain by running a Union naval blockade. Curiously, for all his championing of the South, several of Pollard's books were published in Philadelphia and New York City. He was not universally admired among White postwar Southerners. In April 1866 Louisiana's wartime ex-governor Henry Watkins Adams (1820–1866), writing from self-exile in Mexico, publicly ridiculed Pollard as a shirker during the war who "like Job's war horse . . . snuffed the battle from afar." Adams added that Pollard "dips his pen in the gall of New England hatred" while "hob-nobbing" with Yankees like newspaper editor Horace Greeley (1811–1872).

Unlike many embittered ex-Confederates, Pollard conceded secession as unconstitutional, but he insisted slavery had made the South a "noble type of civilization." He endorsed White supremacy, asserted Black racial inferiority, denounced their suffrage and citizenship, and opposed federalized Reconstruction. Some Southerners questioned whether slavery and secession were ever divinely sanctioned as the cornerstones of their cause; Jefferson Davis (whose memoirs concluded with "the Union, *Esto perpetua*" or "may it endure forever") told a clergyman "the failure of our righteous cause rendered doubtful the government of the world by an overruling providence."[8]

White postwar ex-Confederates and Southerners have long downplayed slavery as the war's cause and lynching and legalized racism as its horrific twentieth-century perpetuations. The Lost Cause ideology is the mother of all cultural wars, spawning holidays, commemorations, pseudo-nationalistic organizations, publications, racial violence, radio and television programming, and movies. Its false nostalgia and distorted mythology rationalized Confederate defeat and White supremacy. Its zenith (1880s–1920s) accompanied enactment of racist laws in the Jim Crow South, followed by a resurgence during the Civil War Centennial (1957–1965) and the American civil rights movement (1950s-1960s).

Among the Lost Cause's tenets: the Confederate South did not win the war but should have because it fought for what it believed were noble reasons; the failure to establish a slavery-based nationhood was regrettable because the South was better with slavery; veneration of Confederate "heroes" was justified because they fought with honor; Reconstruction was federal oppression, thus vindicating the reestablishment of White-supremacist state governments (often at the expense of citizens of color). The Library of Congress defined it as an "idealization of a society and culture perceived as noble and civilized but doomed by overwhelming forces—an enduring myth to ameliorate defeat" with "nostalgia for Southern gallantry and the prewar status quo." One Pulitzer Prize-winning historian belittled it as "a cult of the dead"; a twenty-first-century historian cheekily remarked "white Southerners were more unified in looking back at the Civil War than they had been during it."[9]

DEAD CONFEDERATES ON HORSEBACK

Monuments were unifying cultural and political factors for White Southerners during the Jim Crow era. The difference between monuments and memorials is that monuments are commemorative statuary or buildings while memorials comprise everything else (historical markers, parks, ships, streets, place names) of events and persons deemed worthy of honored remembrance. Confederate monuments valorize and summarize what I define as 'the seven S's of Southern history': sanitizing of Confederate history; sanctity of White womanhood; secession; segregation; slavery; States' Rights extremism; and White supremacy.

The violent August 2017 Unite the Right rally against the removal of Charlottesville statues of generals Robert E. Lee (1924) and Thomas J. "Stonewall"

Jackson (1921) resulted in their White supremacist defenders inadvertently provoking their subsequent removal. Were it not for this twenty-first century "Battle of Charlottesville" these and similar statues would still be in their public spaces. The rally resulted in the death of one anti-racism protestor, dozens injured, an accidental crash of a Virginia State Police helicopter that killed two Virginia state troopers, and subsequent removal of thirty-seven similar monuments around the nation by year's end. According to the Southern Poverty Law Center, Virginia has the most such monuments and as of 2021—for the second year in a row—has removed the most such monuments of any state, followed by Texas and Florida.[10]

A study of Virginia's Confederate statuary noted that of its then-360 monuments (a hundredfold increase since the Civil War Centennial), none denounced slavery. A Charlottesville cemetery monument epitomizes the Lost Cause mindset: "Fate Denied Them Victory But Crowned Them With Glorious Immortality." Confederate statuary in bronze, granite or marble are Lost Cause idolizations and, like battlefields, favored destinations of neo-Confederate pilgrimage. Union/Northern military monuments are triumphalist; Confederate/Southern statues symbolize unapologetic defiance and typically face north, ready to hurl back their foes 160 years after the Civil War.[11]

SLAVERY'S SWORD: GENERAL LEE AND AFRICAN AMERICANS

Robert E. Lee is the subject of more Confederate monuments than anyone else; "as America's most honored traitor, his image is indelibly etched across the landscape and his reputation is based largely on national gratitude for what he did not do: win Confederate independence and his refusal to endorse guerrilla resistance against restored federal authority." A product of his region (the Slave South), social class (First Families of Virginia), gender (White male patriarchy) and race (White supremacy), Lee's loyalists consider "Marse Robert" a benevolent, reluctant slaveholder and too much of a gentleman to have been a racist.

One quirky legal matter ironically made him a reluctant emancipator. During 1858 and 1862 Lee unsuccessfully petitioned the Alexandria County circuit court and the Supreme Court of Appeals of Virginia to delay his compliance as executor of his father-in-law George Washington Parke Custis's (1781–1857) last will and testament which stipulated his slaves be freed within five years (1862) of his death. Lee contended he needed more time to pay off the estate's debts; had he legally prevailed (and won the Civil War), the enslaved would have remained in bondage until 1867—a decade after their owner's death.

Three days before Abraham Lincoln's January 1863 Emancipation Proclamation, Lee reluctantly complied with court rulings reaffirming the will's manumission provisions to "hereby manumit, emancipate and forever set free" 194 slaves at three Custis plantations (Arlington House, Arlington County; Romancoke, King William County; White House, New Kent County). None took "Lee" or "Custis" as their new surnames.

There are a few surviving first-hand accounts by African Americans personally acquainted with Lee. An 1866 newspaper interview of ex-slave Wesley Norris (b. 1850) recalled the "real character of the man." Lee ordered him, his sister Mary and their cousin George Parks whipped fifty lashes each for their 1859 failed escape attempt. They were sent to Alabama and afterward to Richmond, from where Norris escaped in 1863. Employed by the federal government at Arlington National Cemetery (Lee's former estate), Norris offered to arrange for Black and White witnesses, including his sister Mary (an employee of the French ambassador in Washington), to verify his statements; no doubt he was struck by the irony of again laboring in Lee's symbolic shadow.

Lee never reconciled his defeat. The historical fact is the antebellum Lee supported slavery and the postwar Lee publicly reembraced White supremacy and recommended Black Americans' forced deportation to Africa. At an August 1868 meeting of twenty-seven ex-Confederate leaders at The Greenbrier resort, White Sulphur Springs, West Virginia, he endorsed what became known as the White Sulphur Springs Manifesto that called for Whites' national reconciliation but opposed African American suffrage and political equality.

During a private conversation with fellow attendee and former Texas governor Fletcher Summerfield Stockdale (1823–1890), Lee remarked: "If I had foreseen the use those people designed to make for their victory, there would have been no surrender at Appomattox Courthouse; no, sir, not by me. Had I foreseen these results of subjugation, I would have preferred to die at Appomattox with my brave men, my sword in this right hand." Greenbrier welcomed Lee as an esteemed guest during his vacations, hosted annual Lee Monument Balls as fundraisers for his Richmond equestrian monument after his 1870 death, and observed Robert E. Lee Week well into the 1940s.[12]

Frederick Douglass (1817–1895), the nineteenth century's most influential African American, shed no tears at his passing: "General Lee . . . is dead, and so is Benedict Arnold . . . The one great fact of Lee's life [is] namely, his treason." Douglass criticized Lee statue proposals: "Monuments to the 'lost cause' will prove monuments of folly . . . of a wicked rebellion . . . It is a needless record of stupidity and wrong." It took twenty years of fundraising after Lee's death (1870–1890) for his equestrian monument ("the greatest monument to the Confederacy") to be erected during the "Confederate revival" era of the 1880s-1890s with its self-important sense of historical consciousness, ancestor obsession and filial piety. "The fact that these are hard times no one will doubt," one Richmond newspaper morosely commented. Cultural historians Michael Kammen (1936–2013), Edward Ayers (b. 1953) and Kirk Savage (b. 1958) attributed this delay to the postwar South's "lack of funds," the depressions and panics of the 1870s and 1890s, and would-be donors' "crop failures, yellow fever and poverty." A generation later African American intellectual W. E. B. Du Bois (1868–1963), a co-founder of the National Association for the Advancement of Colored People (NAACP), castigated Lee as a fool and a traitor because "he led a bloody war to perpetuate human slavery . . . [and] helped maim and murder thousands in its defense."[13]

BLACKS IN THE BOX?

In the year of the Lee Monument dedication, the 1890 federal census enumerated Black Virginians as comprising 38 percent of the state's 1,655,980 population and 44 percent of "gainful occupations." Richmond's 32,555 Black residents comprised 40 percent of the city's 81,388 inhabitants. They owned $968,736 in real estate ($27 million in 2025 dollars) and accounted for 30 percent of Black property ownership among sixteen major Virginia cities. But all did not bode well; between 1870 and 1892, three thousand Black men were disenfranchised after felony or larceny convictions in Richmond courts. In 1890, three Black men were lynched in the counties of Russell, Charlotte, and Mecklenburg; thirty-four Black males, six White males, and one White female were lynched during the 1890s.[14]

Of approximately one hundred items discovered in the monument's copper cornerstone box in 2021, at least three are publications referencing Black Richmonders. Chronologically, the first is *History and Reminiscences of the Monumental Church* (1880). It contains fourteen mentions of "colored"

Figure 15. *History and Reminiscences of the Monumental Church* from the Lee cornerstone box.

Figure 16. *Chataigne's Directory of Richmond, Virginia 1885* from Lee cornerstone box.

and slavery/slaves and Whites' postwar forebodings of them as indigenous threats: "By the action of the Federal government, several millions of slaves have suddenly been set free, and left amongst us a potent power for good or evil, in connection with the destinies of this country."[15]

A second publication, *Chataigne's Directory of Richmond, Va., to Which is Added a Street and Number Directory* (1885), originally priced at four dollars ($102 in 2025 dollars), identifies Black churches, cemeteries ("Colored Persons' Burying Ground"), city councilmen, organizations, occupations and places of business (for example, John Mitchell's *Richmond Planet* and Planet Publishing Company) by means of asterisks preceding their names ("Names marked with * are of colored persons"). Similar nineteenth- and twentieth-century directories employed the racial abbreviation "col." [colored] after Black residents' names or listed them in segregated sections in the rear of these volumes.[16]

A third publication, *The Warrock-Richardson Maryland, Virginia, and North Carolina Almanack* (1887), contains miscellaneous information and a

CHATAIGNE'S

RICHMOND CITY DIRECTORY,

1883-'84.

ABBREVIATIONS.

ab.	above	com mer.	commission merchant	paperhgr.	paperhanger
agt.	agent	cor.	corner	pres.	president
asst.	assistant	dep.	deputy	propr.	proprietor
ave.	avenue	dept.	department	r.	rear
bds.	boards	e.	east	rd.	road
bet.	between	ins. agt.	insurance agent	rms.	rooms
bkkpr.	bookkeeper	int. rev.	internal revenue	Rev.	Reverend
bldg.	building	lab.	laborer	s.	south
blksmith.	blacksmith	mkr.	maker	sec.	secretary
bdg. h.	boarding house	mnfr.	manufacturer	supt.	superintendent
capt.	captain	mngr.	manager	treas.	treasurer
confr.	confectioner	mkt.	market	w.	west
carpr.	carpenter	nr.	near	wid.	widow
clk.	clerk	n.	north	wkr.	worker
co.	county	opp.	opposite	wks.	works
		P. O.	post-office		

☞The classification by business will be found after the alphabetical arrangement of names. For full indices to the contents of the work, and names too late for regular insertion, see preceding pages. **Names marked * are Colored.**

Figure 17. Abbreviations page from *Chataigne's Directory of Richmond, Virginia 1885*, with a note indicating that names marked with an asterisk "are Colored." (Courtesy of The Internet Archive)

monthly chronology of noteworthy events. Among these is the Emancipation Proclamation (January), Black members of the General Assembly ("Italics, colored"), and "Virginia Congressional Votes" by race ("White" and "Colored"). The almanac mentions Lee's January 1807 birthday, of April as when the "Civil War begun 1861," and of the 1865 Appomattox surrender, and Lee's October 1870 death.[17]

Unsurprisingly, items representative of Black civic, fraternal, and business institutions such as John Mitchell's *Richmond Planet*, William Washington Browne's (1849–1897) the Grand Fountain, United Order of True Reformers, the First African Baptist Church and similar exemplars were excluded. As far as Whites were concerned, Black Richmonders were Unionist collaborators during the war, postwar "racial agitators" for Republican "radical political agendas," and social inferiors.[18]

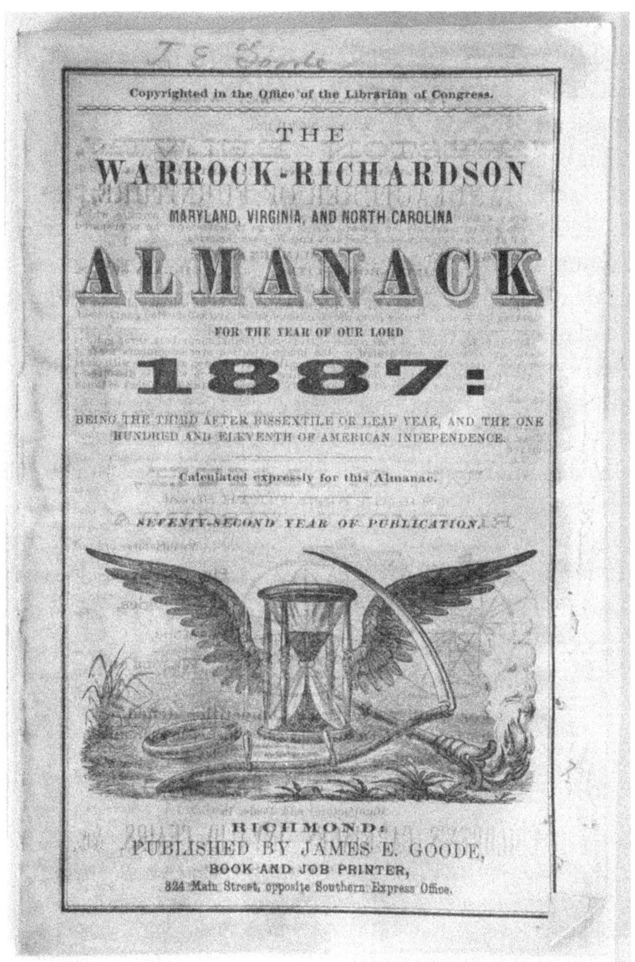

Copyrighted in the Office of the Librarian of Congress.

THE

WARROCK-RICHARDSON

MARYLAND, VIRGINIA, AND NORTH CAROLINA

ALMANACK

FOR THE YEAR OF OUR LORD

1887:

BEING THE THIRD AFTER BISSEXTILE OR LEAP YEAR, AND THE ONE HUNDRED AND ELEVENTH OF AMERICAN INDEPENDENCE.

Calculated expressly for this Almanac.

SEVENTY-SECOND YEAR OF PUBLICATION.

RICHMOND:

PUBLISHED BY JAMES E. GOODE,

BOOK AND JOB PRINTER,

824 Main Street, opposite Southern Express Office.

Figure 18. *The Warrock-Richardson Maryland, Virginia, North Carolina Almanack* from the Lee cornerstone box.

"WHOSE HISTORY? WHO DECIDES?"

Today's escalating war of words between neo-Confederates and descendants of the enslaved awaits a hopefully more equitable next chapter. Robert E. Lee, "Virginia's Gentleman Warrior," remains Dixie's foremost demigod. In the postmodern reshaping of public memory, Lee and other Confederates, demoted and demythologized from the pantheon of American heroes, are increasingly regarded as anti-Black proslavery secessionists and unrepentant racist traitors seemingly shackled to the Lost Cause. Their modern-day apologists resent what they perceive as demonization of their cultural icons and "heritage" (which inherently include racism).

A century after his death, John Mitchell Jr., "one of the best kept secrets in Virginia history," has been progressively restored to public consciousness: an award by Virginia journalists and a Library of Virginia exhibition (1996); a scholarly biography (2007); and enshrinement in Richmond's Emancipation and Freedom Monument (2021). The federally supported Virginia Newspaper Program's digitization of *Richmond Planet* issues rekindled interest in his career and that of other Black newspapers. A fitting monument (2012) was placed on Mitchell's previously unmarked grave by the Richmond Black History Project: "Editor, Banker, Alderman and Pioneer of Civil Rights."[19]

Monuments matter. The centrality of historical amnesia is evinced by public spaces' ritualized statuary and sanitized nostalgia across a polarized cultural landscape. Is there a middle ground for *recontextualization* of history and memory in a pluralistic society? In an essay commemorating the 400th anniversary of the first enslaved African arrival in Virginia, I posed three questions: "How much history is too much? Whose history? Who decides?"[20] These are still compellingly and profoundly relevant across the Old Dominion's history—and perhaps always will.

NOTES

1. Monument Association, *Official Souvenir of the Dedication of the Monument to General Robert E. Lee: Containing a Full and Lee Monument Association, Complete History of the Monument Association, Together with the Order of Exercises and Other Matter* (Richmond, VA: R. Newton Moon, 1890); [John Mitchell Jr.], "The Moving of the Lee Statue: Confederate Flags on Every Hand—The Stars and Stripes Entirely Ignored," *Richmond Planet*, May 10, 1890, p. 1, col. 3, https://chroniclingamerica.loc.gov/lccn/sn84025841/1890-05-10/ed-1/seq-1/; [John Mitchell Jr.], "The Lee Monument Unveiling: Thousands Present—Confederate Flags Everywhere Displayed," *Richmond Planet*, May 31, 1890, p. 1, col. 2, https://chroniclingamerica.loc.gov/lccn/sn84025841/1890-05-31/ed-1/seq-1/ ("Rebel flags," "The South may revere"); [John Mitchell Jr.], untitled article, *Richmond Planet*, June 7, 1890, p. 2, col. 2, https://chroniclingamerica.loc.gov/lccn/sn84025841/1890-06-07/ed-1/seq-2/ ("an old colored man," "Southern white folks"); Kirk Savage, *Standing Soldiers, Kneeling Slaves: Race, War, and Monument in Nineteenth-Century America* (Princeton: Princeton University Press, 1997), 148, 151–54 ("an old colored man"), 245n64–67, 246n71; William Shakespeare, *The Merchant of Venice*, act 2, scene 2, lines 77–79 ("The truth").

2. Chronicling America: Historic American Newspapers, "About Richmond Planet, (Richmond, Va.), 1883–1938," *Library of Congress*, https://chroniclingamerica.loc.gov/lccn/sn84025841/; *Richmond Planet*, May 31, 1890, p. 2, col. 1, https://chroniclingamerica.loc.gov/lccn/sn84025841/1890-05-31/ed-1/seq-2/ ("Strong Arm" logo); Anne McCrery, Errol Somay & *Dictionary of Virginia Biography*, "John Mitchell (July 11, 1863-December 3, 1929)," *Encyclopedia Virginia, November 18, 2022*, https://encyclopediavirginia.org/entries/mitchell-john-jr-1863-1929/; [John Mitchell Jr.], untitled article, *Richmond Planet*, June 7, 1890, p. 2, col. 2, https://chroniclingamerica.loc.gov/lccn/sn84025841/1890-06-07/ed-1/seq-2/ ("The Negro. . . . put up the Lee Monument"); Rev. William J. Simmons, *Men of Mark: Eminent, Progressive and Rising, with an Introductory Sketch of the Author by Rev. Henry M. Turner* (Cleveland, OH: G. M. Rewell, 1887), 20 ("a man who would"); I. Garland Penn, *The Afro-American Press and Its Editors* (Springfield, MA: Wiley, 1891), 183–87; Rayford W. Logan and Michael R. Winston, *Dictionary of Negro Biography* (New York: W. W. Norton, 1982), 444–45 ("John R. Mitchell, Jr."); Ann Field Alexander, *Race Man: The Rise and Fall of the "Fighting Editor," John Mitchell Jr.* (Charlottesville and London: University of Virginia Press, 2002), 34 and 48 (masthead), 36–37 (*Planet's* influence), 39, 74, 208, 220n36, 248n8; Virginia Writers' Project, *The Negro in Virginia* (New York: Hastings House, 1940; reprint, Winston-Salem, NC: John F. Blair, 1994), 314 (*Planet's* circulation); Emma North, "ABC 8 News," *Richmond WRIC*, January 24, 2022, https://www.wric.com/news/local-news/richmond/unanimous-vote-richmond-confederate-monuments-going-to-black-history-museum/; Marvin T. Chiles, "Reenvisioning Richmond's Past: Race, Reconciliation, and Public History in the Modern South, 1990–Present," *The Journal of Southern History* volume 88, no. 4 (November 2022): 707–52. The "Strong Arm" logo became the *Planet's* front-page masthead five years after Mitchell's march, *Richmond Planet*, March 30, 1895, p. 1, https://chroniclingamerica.loc.gov/lccn/sn84025841/1895-03-30/ed-1/seq-1/. On Mitchell's prophecy fulfilled in the context of recent Confederate monument removals, see Kirk Savage, *Standing Soldiers, Kneeling Slaves: Race, War, and Monument in Nineteenth-Century America*, new edition (Princeton: Princeton University Press, 2018), ix–x.
3. [John Mitchell Jr.], "The Lee Monument Unveiling: Thousands Present—Confederate Flags Everywhere Displayed," *Richmond Planet*, May 31, 1890, p. 1, col. 2, https://chroniclingamerica.loc.gov/lccn/sn84025841/1890-05-31/ed-1/seq-1/ ("from New York"); [John Mitchell Jr.], "A Gala Day: The Parade a Success," *Richmond Planet*, October 18, 1890, p. 1, cols. 1–2, https://chroniclingamerica.loc.gov/lccn/sn84025841/1890-10-18/ed-1/seq-1/) and p. 4, col. 5, https://chroniclingamerica.loc.gov/lccn/sn84025841/1890-10-18/ed-1/seq-4/ ("They say"); "Thanks," *Richmond Planet*, October 25, 1890, p. 1, col. 2, https://chroniclingamerica.loc.gov/lccn/sn84025841/1890-10-25/ed-1/seq-1/ (Mitchell's parade staff); [William Calvin Chase], "The Emancipation Celebration in Richmond," What I Saw and Heard, *Washington Bee*, October 18, 1890, p. 3, col. 3, https://chroniclingamerica.loc.gov/lccn/sn84025891/1890-10-18/ed-1/seq-3/ ("King this Week").
4. Alexander, *Race Man*, 28, 32, 34, 38–39, 45, 76, 108; Luther Porter Jackson, *Negro*

Office-Holders in Virginia, 1865–1895 (Norfolk: Guide Quality Press, 1945), 58 (Mitchell and Randolph as councilmen); J. H. Chataigne, *Chataigne's Directory of Richmond, Va., to Which is Added a Street and Number Directory, Giving Names of Occupants After the Numbers; A List of the Post Offices of the State Of Virginia and Appendix Pertaining to State and City Governments* (Richmond, J. H. Chataigne, compiler and publisher, 1889), 429. ("Randolph,*Edwin A., lawyer [office] 812 Broad [East], home 711 Baker [East]"; asterisk identifies him as "colored"); Ann W. Campbell, "Celebrating Freedom: Juneteenth and Emancipation Day Commemorations, Richmond, Va.," *Virginia Commonwealth University Social Welfare History Project*, https://socialwelfare.library.vcu.edu/issues/discrimination/celebrating-freedom-juneteenth-and-emancipation-day-commemorations-richmond-va/; "Edwin Archer Randolph," *Wikipedia*, https://en.wikipedia.org/w/index.php?title=Edwin_Archer_Randolph&oldid=1114708553; [John Mitchell Jr.], "The Emancipation Celebration. Line of March—Opinion of our Citizens," *Richmond Planet*, October 11, 1890, p. 1, col. 1 ("Chief Marshal," "quite a difference," "among our people," "because that was the day"); [John Mitchell Jr.], "The Thanksgiving Celebration. Address to the Public and All Whom It May Concern," *Richmond Planet*, October 11, 1890, p. 1, col. 3, https://chroniclingamerica.loc.gov/lccn/sn84025841/1890-10-11/ed-1/seq-1/ (July 1890 planning meeting and executive committee membership); [John Mitchell Jr.], "Hons. J. C. Price, [John M.] Langston and John [H. Smyth] to Speak. Alderman John Mitchell Jr. Chosen Chief Marshal," *Richmond Planet*, October 11, 1890 p. 1, col. 4, https://chroniclingamerica.loc.gov/lccn/sn84025841/1890-10-11/ed-1/seq-1/ (E. A. [Edwin Archer] Randolph, "Executive Committee of the Emancipation Celebration" chairperson, Mitchell as chief marshal); John Mitchell Jr., "Editor & Manager, *The Planet*," Richmond, to Magnus L. Robinson, "Editor, *The Leader*" [Alexandria *Leader*], March 12, 1892 ("I win over"), Letters of Magnus L. Robinson, Accession 1499, Albert and Shirley Small Special Collections Library, University of Virginia, Charlottesville (UVA). According to my research, this is apparently among the few surviving Mitchell letters in Virginia, notwithstanding his long public career. His biographer cites a dozen; others doubtless await discovery. Alexander, *Race Man*, 218, 221–22, 224, 231, 241–46, 248.

5. George Williams Jr., General Superintendent, "1863–1890 Grand National Celebration! of the 27th Anniversary of the Emancipation Proclamation at Exposition Grounds, Richmond, Va., October 15, 16th, 17th, '90," *Washington Bee*, October 11, 1890, p. 1, col. 2, https://chroniclingamerica.loc.gov/lccn/sn84025891/1890-10-11/ed-1/seq-1/ ("great days of the colored people"); [C. A. Taylor, Traffic Manager, Richmond, Fredericksburg & Potomac Rail Road Company], *Colored People's Celebration at Richmond, Va., October 15th, 16th, and 17th. . . . to establish a National Thanksgiving Day for Freedom, to be Annually Observed by the Negro Race . . . Speakers from All over the Country* (Richmond, VA: 1890), Broadside 189-. C7FF, Library of Virginia, Richmond; "The Governor Refused: The Committee's Explanation in Re-Request for the Howitzers to Fire," *Richmond Planet*, October 18, 1890, https://chroniclingamerica.loc.gov/lccn/sn84025841/1890-10-18/ed-1/seq-4/, p. 4, col. 3 (Scott's delegation, "citizens of African descent," "commemorative of our emancipation," "it has not been the custom," "to fire any salutes for them");

Peter Wallenstein, *Cradle of America: Four Centuries of Virginia History* (Lawrence: University Press of Kansas, 2007), 275–77 (public spaces); Peter J. Rachleff, *Black Labor in the South: Richmond, Virginia, 1865–1890* (Philadelphia: Temple University Press, 1984), 40, 49, 53–54 (Scott's military career); Michael B. Chesson, *Richmond After the War, 1865–1890* (Richmond: Virginia State Library, 1981), 159, 227n25, 229n41 (Scott's career); J. H. Chataigne, *Chataigne's Directory of Richmond, Va., to Which is Added a Street and Number Directory, Giving Names of Occupants After the Numbers; A List of the Post Offices of the State Of Virginia and Appendix Pertaining to State and City Governments* (Richmond, J. H. Chataigne, compiler and publisher, 1891), 587 ("*Scott, Benjamin, plasterer, home 618 Judah"; the asterisk identifies him as "colored").

6. "At a Mass Meeting Held March 27th," City and Suburban, *Daily Richmond Whig*, March 30, 1866, p. 3, col. 1, https://chroniclingamerica.loc.gov/lccn/sn84024738/1866-12-28/ed-1/seq-1/ ("Those who participate"); Jim [pseudonym], "Special Correspondence of the Day Book, April 1, 1866," *Norfolk Day Book*, April 3, 1866, p. 2, col. 3, https://chroniclingamerica.loc.gov/lccn/sn85025697/1866-04-03/ed-1/seq-2/#date1=1866&index=19&rows=20&words=fire+Fire&searchType=basic&sequence=0&state=Virginia&date2=1866&proxtext=fire+&y=16&x=12&dateFilterType=yearRange&page=1 ("tied at the tail," Baptist African Church fire); "Fires," City Intelligence, *Daily Richmond Enquirer*, April 9, 1866, p. 3, col. 4 ("work of an incendiary"); S. Dow Mills and H. W. Starke, *The City of Richmond Business Directory and City Guide, Complied and Published by Mills & Starke* (Richmond, VA: Gary & Clemmitt, [1866]), 104 (Second Baptist on Byrd Street); Rachleff, *Black Labor in the South*, 40, 222n20 (Second African Baptist arson); "Laying of the Corner-Stone of the Second African Church," Local Matters, *Richmond Daily Dispatch*, May 22, 1866, p. 1, col. 7, https://chroniclingamerica.loc.gov/lccn/sn84024738/1866-05-22/ed-1/seq-1/; "Colored Fair," Local Matters, *Richmond Daily Dispatch*, December 28, 1866, p. 1, col. 4, https://chroniclingamerica.loc.gov/lccn/sn84024738/1866-12-28/ed-1/seq-1/ ("our colored population," "aid of our community").

7. "Notice!: The coloured people of the city of Richmond would most respectfully inform the public, that they do not intend to celebrate the failure of the Southern Confederacy, as it has been stated in the papers of this city, but simply as the day on which God was pleased to liberate their long-oppressed race/C. Harris, J. Cocks, J. Edmunds, F. J. Smith, N. Williams, Committee," "Broadside, from the Committee, 2 April 1866," Virginia Museum of History & Culture, Richmond, Virginia, https://virginiahistory.org/broadside-committee-2-april-1866; Ervin L. Jordan Jr., "'Traitors shall not dictate to us': Afro-Virginians and the Unfinished Emancipation of 1865" in William C. Davis and James I. Robertson Jr., eds., *Virginia at War, 1865* (Lexington: University Press of Kentucky, 2012), 121, 131–32n49 ("Colored League"); "The Negro Celebration on the of 3rd April," Local Matters, *Richmond Daily Dispatch*, April 9, 1866, p. 1, cols. 3, 4, https://chroniclingamerica.loc.gov/lccn/sn84024738/1866-04-09/ed-1/seq-1/ (parade banners, "fairly trembled," "many-headed"); "American Union Commission," *Harper's Weekly* (October 21, 1865): 657, 661 (Fourth of July); "Freedom of Assembly: Online exhibit showcases

little-known Emancipation Day marches and celebrations," *Virginia Commonwealth University Libraries*, March 14, 2013, https://www.library.vcu.edu/about/news/2013-news/freedom-of-assembly-online-exhibit-showcases-little-known-emancipation-day-marches-and-celebrations.html; Sam Fowler, "Virginia lawmakers make Juneteenth a state holiday," *Virginia Business*, October 19, 2020, https://www.virginiabusiness.com/article/virginia-lawmakers-make-juneteenth-a-state-holiday/.

See also William H. Wiggins, Jr., *O Freedom!: Afro-American Emancipation Celebrations* (Knoxville: University of Tennessee Press, 1987), and Mitch Kachun, "Celebrating Freedom: Juneteenth and the Emancipation Festival Tradition" in *Remixing the Civil War: Meditations on the Sesquicentennial,* ed. Thomas J. Brown (Baltimore: Johns Hopkins University Press, 2011), 71–91. For one historian's reminiscences about Juneteenth and its Texas birthplace, see Annette Gordon-Reed, *On Juneteenth* (New York and London: Liveright, 2021), 12–14, 122–25, 134–37.

8. Edward A. Pollard, *The Lost Cause: A New Southern History of the War of the Confederates. Comprising a Full and Authentic Account of the Rise and Progress of the Late Southern Confederacy—the Campaigns, Battles, Incidents, and Adventures of the Most Gigantic Struggle of the World's History, Drawn from Official Sources, and Approved by the Most Distinguished Confederates, with Numerous Steel Portraits* (New York: E. B. Treat, 1866), 50 ("noble type of civilization"), 750, 752; Edward A. Pollard, *The Lost Cause Regained* (New York: G. W. Carleton, London: S. Low, Son, 1868); Jefferson Davis, *The Rise and Fall of the Confederate Government*, 2 vols. (New York: D. Appleton, 1881), 2: 764 ("*Esto perpetua*"); Jefferson Davis, Beauvoir, Harrison County, Mississippi, to Rev. F. Stringfellow, June 4, 1878 (photostat) ("the failure"), folder "1893, n.d. Letters, 1878–1880, from Jefferson Davis to Franklin Stringfellow: copies and transcripts; miscellaneous related," Jefferson Davis Letters to Frank Stringfellow, Accession 5162, UVA; "Beaten at His Own Game," *Norfolk Post*, April 5, 1866, p. 2, col. 4, https://virginiachronicle.com/?a=d&d=NP18660405.1.2&e=---en-20—1—txt-txIN--— ("Job's war horse," "dips his pen," "hob-nobbing"). Why Adams equated Pollard and "Job's war horse" with cowardice is unclear; Job 39: 19–25 (King James Version) extolls horses as fearless in battle: "Hast thou given the horse strength? . . . he goeth forth to meet the armed men . . . he mocketh at fear . . . he smelleth the battle."

9. Margaret E. Wagner, Gary W. Gallagher, and Paul Finkelman, eds., *The Library of Congress Civil War Desk Reference* (New York: Simon & Schuster, 2002), 743 ("idealization of a society"), 805 ("nostalgia for Southern gallantry and the prewar status quo"); Michael Kammen, *Mystic Chords of Memory: The Transformation of Tradition in American Culture* (New York: Alfred A. Knopf, 1991), 217 ("cult of the dead"); David Ulbrich, "Lost Cause," in *Encyclopedia of the American Civil War: A Political, Social, and Military History*, David Heidler and Jeanne Heidler, eds. (New York: W. W. Norton & Company, 2000), 1222 ("white Southerners").

10. Kimberly Probolus, "Whose Heritage? Public Symbols of the Confederacy (3rd Edition)," *Southern Poverty Law Center*, February 1, 2022, https://www.splcenter.org/20220201/whose-heritage-public-symbols-confederacy-third-edition; Seth C. Bruggeman, "Memorials and Monuments," *The Inclusive Historian's Handbook*,

July 18, 2019, https://inclusivehistorian.com/memorials-and-monuments/; Anna Ivanov, Karyn Pugliese, Lucy Yip and Meesh Zucker, "Monumental Memory in Space," *Massachusetts Institute of Technology*, Fall 2019, https://lyip12.github.io/memorial/.

11. Timothy S. Sedore, *An Illustrated Guide to Virginia's Confederate Monuments* (Carbondale: Southern Illinois University Press, 2011), 1,10 and dust jacket (360 count); Benjamin J. Hillman, *Monuments to Memories: Virginia's Civil War Heritage in Bronze and Stone* (Richmond: Virginia Civil War Commission, 1965), 33–48; Tony Horwitz, *Confederates in the Attic: Dispatches from the Unfinished Civil War* (New York: Pantheon Books, 1998), 152, 171–72; Ervin L. Jordan Jr., *Charlottesville and the University of Virginia in the Civil War*, second edition, The Virginia Battles and Leaders Series (Lynchburg: H. E. Howard, Inc., 1988), 109 ("Fate").
12. Ervin L. Jordan Jr., "Monument Man: Robert E. Lee: America's Most Honored Traitor," symposium "Lightning Rods for Controversy: Civil War Monuments Past, Present & Future," Library of Virginia, February 25, 2017, https://www.c-span.org/video/?423748-101/controversy-general-robert-e-lee-monuments ("America's most honored traitor"); Wesley Norris interview, "Robert E. Lee—His Brutality to His Slaves," *National Anti-Slavery Standard*, April 14, 1866, p. 4, col. 4; John W. Blassingame, *Slave Testimony: Two Centuries of Letters, Speeches, Interviews, and Autobiographies* (Baton Rouge: Louisiana State University Press, 1977), 467–68 (Norris interview); Ervin L. Jordan Jr., *Black Confederates and Afro-Yankees in Civil War Virginia* (Charlottesville and London: University Press of Virginia, 1995), 258–59, 324–25 (Custis slaves, "hereby manumit"); Elizabeth Brown Pryor, *Reading the Man: A Portrait of Robert E. Lee Through His Private Letters* (New York: Viking, 2007), 144–46, 149–51, 154, 265–67, 274 (court orders Lee to free Custis slaves), 286, 378, 431, 446, 451–54, 456 (Lee's racism), 561n21; Alan T. Nolan, *Lee Considered: General Robert E. Lee and Civil War History* (Chapel Hill and London: University of North Carolina Press, 1991), 139, 141–50; Robert S. Conte, *The History of the Greenbrier: America's Resort* (Charleston, WV: Pictorial Histories, 1998), 66–73, 67–68, 84–85, 118–19; Thomas Cary Johnson, *The Life and Letters of Robert Lewis Dabney* (Richmond, VA: Presbyterian Committee of Publication, 1903), 499–501 ("If I had foreseen"); Allen Guelzo, "Robert E. Lee and Slavery," *Encyclopedia Virginia*, February 9, 2023, https://encyclopediavirginia.org/entries/lee-robert-e-and-slavery/ (sections "As an Enslaver" and "Disunion").
13. Frederick Douglass, "Monuments to Folly," *The New National Era* (Washington, D. C.), December 1, 1870, p. 3, col. 2; [W. E. B. Du Bois], "Robert E. Lee," *The Crisis*, vol. 1, no. 3 (March 1928): 97 ("he led a bloody war"); Kammen, *Mystic Chords of Memory*, 111 ("lack of funds"), 112 ("Confederate revival"), 217–18, 858 (Southerners' ancestor obsession, filiopiety, historical consciousness); Edward L. Ayers, *The Promise of the New South: Life After Reconstruction* (New York and Oxford: Oxford University Press, 1992), 81, 215, 252–53, 283–84, 334 ("the greatest monument"); Savage, *Standing Soldiers*, 136–37 ("crop failures"); "Hard Times," *Richmond Daily Dispatch*, December 28, 1866, p. 1, col. 4, https://chroniclingamerica.loc.gov/lccn/sn84024738/1866-12-28/ed-1/seq-1/.
14. [U. S. Census Bureau], "Twelfth Census of the United States/Census Bulletin,"

Director of the Census, February 6, 1901, https://www2.census.gov/library/publications/decennial/1900/bulletins/demographic/51-population-va.pdf, Table 1, p. 1; Virginia Writers' Project, *The Negro in Virginia*, 338–39 (1890 Virginia; "gainful occupations"); Alrutheus Ambush Taylor, *The Negro in the Reconstruction of Virginia* (Washington, DC: The Association for the Study of Negro Life and History, 1926), 135 (real estate); Alexander, *Race Man*, 79 (1890 Richmond); Richmond Hustings Court, *Official List of Colored Persons Convicted of Felony or Petit Larceny in the Hustings Court of the City of Richmond and Thereby Disfranchised, From 1870, to October 1892* (Richmond, 1892), 3–13; Richmond Police Court, *Official List of Colored Persons Convicted of Petit Larceny in the Police Court of the City of Richmond and Thereby Disfranchised, From April 2d, 1877, to January 12th, 1892* (Richmond, 1892), 3–14; Gianluca De Fazio, "Racial Terror: Lynching in Virginia," *Department of Justice Studies, James Madison University*, 2020, https://sites.lib.jmu.edu/valynchings/view-by-decade/.

15. Christina Keyser Vida, "Cornerstone Contributions: Unboxing the Lee Monument," *Virginia Department of Historic Resources*, January 12, 2022, https://www.dhr.virginia.gov/news/corner-stone-contributions-unboxing-the-lee-monument/ and "Contents of Richmond Robert E. Lee Monument Copper Cornerstone Box," *Virginia Department of Historic Resources*, July 15, 2022, https://www.dhr.virginia.gov/wp-content/uploads/2022/01/Contents-of-the-Richmond-Robert-E-Lee-Monument-Copper-Cornerstone-Box.pdf; George D. Fisher, *History and Reminiscences of the Monumental Church, Richmond, from 1814 to 1878* (Richmond, VA: Whittet & Shepperson, 1880): 3–4, 121, 133–34, 209, 259 (12 references of "colored"); 234 (2 references "slave/slaves"); 311 ("By the action of the Federal"); Jordan, "'Traitors shall not dictate to us,'" 119–20.
16. J. H. Chataigne, *Chataigne's Directory of Richmond, Va., to Which is Added a Street and Number Directory, Giving Names of Occupants After the Numbers; A List of the Post Offices of the State Of Virginia and Appendix Pertaining to State and City Governments* (Richmond, VA: J. H. Chataigne, 1885), 67–68 (Black Richmond city councilmen), 83 ("Colored Churches"), 96 ("Colored Persons' Burying Ground"), 101 ("Names marked"), 313 (John Mitchell Jr., editor), 342 and 492 (*Richmond Planet* and Planet Publishing Company).
17. David Richardson, John Warrock, R. K. Bowles, *The Warrock-Richardson Maryland, Virginia, and North Carolina Almanack* (Richmond, VA: James E. Goode, 1887), mentions of General Robert E. Lee: 9 (January 1807 birth), 12 (April 1861 "Civil War begun 1861"), 12 (April 1865 Appomattox surrender), 18 (Lee's October 1870 death); Black-related events: 9 (January 1865 Emancipation Proclamation), 26–27 (Black members of the General Assembly), 30–35 "Virginia Congressional Votes" ("White" and "Colored").
18. Alexander, *Race Man*, 34–38, James D. Watkinson, "William Washington Browne and the True Reformers of Richmond, Virginia," *The Virginia Magazine of History and Biography* vol. 97, no. 2 (July 1989): 375–98; Michael B. Chesson, *Richmond After the War, 1865–1890* (Richmond: Virginia State Library, 1981); Ervin L. Jordan Jr., "Lies & Legacies: Cultural Spaces, Public Places, Reparations," Albemarle-

Charlottesville NAACP Branch Annual Freedom Fund Banquet, September 16, 2016 ("racial agitators," "radical political agendas").

19. "Race Chieftain Sheds Armor: The Planet's Editor Succumbs After Half Century in Journalistic Field," *Richmond Planet*, December 7, 1929, front page, https://chroniclingamerica.loc.gov/lccn/sn84025841/1929-12-07/ed-1/seq-1/; Alexander, *Race Man*, ix-xi, 208; "Past George Mason Award Winners," *Society of Professional Journalists VA*, https://spjva.com/george-mason-award/past-george-mason-award-winners/ (Mitchell, 1996); Donna M. Lucey, "The 'Fighting Editor' of the *Richmond Planet*," *Humanities: The Magazine of the National Endowment for the Humanities* 31, no. 4 (July/August 2010), https://www.neh.gov/article/fighting-editor-richmond-planet ("one of the best"); "Born in the Wake of Freedom: John Mitchell, Jr., and the *Richmond Planet*," *Virginia Newspaper Project, Library of Virginia*, https://www.lva.virginia.gov/exhibits/mitchell/ajax.htm and https://www.lva.virginia.gov/exhibits/mitchell/index.htm; Virginia Newspaper Directory, "Richmond Afro-American and the Richmond Planet," *Virginia Newspaper Program, Library of Virginia* https://www.lva.virginia.gov/public/vnd/results.php?searchText=planet&submit=Search; "U.S. Newspaper Program," *National Endowment for the Humanities*, https://www.neh.gov/us-newspaper-program (Virginia); Wallenstein, *Cradle of America*, 275–77, 286–87; Virginia General Assembly, Dr. Martin Luther King Jr. Memorial Commission, "Emancipation and Freedom Monument," *Commonwealth of Virginia*, http://mlkcommission.dls.virginia.gov/lincoln/monument.html; Bob Hufford, "John Mitchell Jr.," *Find a Grave*, https://www.findagrave.com/memorial/32366955/john-mitchell (Richmond Black History Project, "Editor, Banker").

Some sources erroneously provide Mitchell a middle name: Virginia Writers' Project and Hampton Institute, *The Negro in Virginia* (New York: Hastings House, 1940), 284, ("John W. Mitchell" and the *Planet*'s founding as "1884," not 1882); Charles W. Wynes, *Race Relations in Virginia, 1870–1902* (Charlottesville: University of Virginia Press, 1961), 111 ("John W. Mitchell" and *Planet*'s founding as "1883," not 1882); Logan and Winston, *Dictionary of Negro Biography*, 444–45 ("John R. Mitchell, Jr."); Jessie Carney Smith, *Black Firsts: 2,000 Years of Extraordinary Achievement* (Detroit: Visible Ink Press, 1994), 275 ("John R. Mitchell, Jr."). See Mitchell's death certificate (Richmond, Henrico County, December 5, 1929), "Virginia, U.S., Death Records, 1912–2014 for John Mitchell [Jr.]," *Ancestry.com*, https://www.ancestrylibrary.com/imageviewer/collections/9278/images/43004_162028006053_0146-00107?treeid=&personid=&hintid=&queryId=d2386bafbaf5e19fcd9877db8541f965&usePUB=true&_phsrc=vXy63&_phstart=successSource&usePUBJs=true&pId=276832.

20. Ervin L. Jordan Jr., "Jamestown Shuffle: Foundations of American Racism and Slavery in Virginia, 1619–1830," in *Voices from Within the Veil: African Americans and the Experience of Democracy*, eds. William H. Alexander, Cassandra Newby-Alexander and Charles Ford (Newcastle upon Tyne: Cambridge Scholars Publishing, 2008), 46–67 ("How much history").

7

In Other News . . .

Stories from The Daily Times, October 23, 1887

Sam Florer

Organizers of the Lee Monument cornerstone laying ceremony included several newspapers featuring stories related to the dedication inside the cornerstone box. One such paper was the October 23, 1887, issue of Richmond's *The Daily Times*. One half-page article of the eight-page paper discussed the upcoming dedication of the Lee Monument's cornerstone. By exploring the other seven and a half pages of the paper, we can shine a light on trends and oddities of local, state, and national politics and culture.

THE DAILY TIMES

The Civil War caused a huge demand for information across the nation. Even after the war ended, demand remained high, and cities all over the US saw an explosion of new publications. High circulation numbers also led to political influence and large profits for publishers, encouraging even more opportunistic entrepreneurs into the print media business. As Virginia's capital, Richmond was an especially rich newspaper market. Post-war demand resulted in *The Daily Times* being one of more than twenty papers published in the city by 1887.[1]

The Daily Times was an organ of the White, conservative elite of Virginia, which at this time manifested itself politically through the Democratic Party. Originally owned and operated by Richmond tobacco magnate Lewis Ginter (1824–1873), industrialist Joseph Bryan (1845–1908) purchased the paper in 1887. Bryan used the paper to advance his business and Democratic Party in-

The Daily Times.

VOL. 2. NUMBER 315. RICHMOND, VA., SUNDAY, OCTOBER 23, 1887. PRICE, TWO CENTS

Figure 19. Masthead, *The Daily Times* October 23, 1887.

terests, eventually becoming one of the most influential men in the state. By the turn of the century, Bryan had purchased several other Richmond papers, merging *The Daily Times* with the Richmond *Dispatch* to form the *Times-Dispatch*, the predecessor of the city's modern *Richmond Times-Dispatch*.[2]

The Daily Times' publisher in 1887, W. Page McCarty (1839–1900), was well known in his own right. Born to a prominent Virginia family, McCarty studied law at UVA and fought in the Confederate Army. Following the war, McCarty entered Richmond's newspaper industry. In 1873, McCarty and, former friend and classmate, John Mordecai competed for the attention of one of the city's most eligible bachelorettes, Mary Tripplett. Following a possible snub at a local dance, McCarty published a poem rebuffing Mary's enchantments. When Mordecai confronted McCarty about the poem at a local club, the two came to blows. In response, McCarty challenged Mordecai to a duel, which his friend-turned-enemy readily accepted. The two met at Oakwood Cemetery on May 9, 1873. Exchanging revolver shots at a dozen paces, Mordecai fell mortally wounded, while McCarty received a crippling wound to the leg. Authorities charged McCarty with first-degree murder, but he ultimately limped away with only an involuntary manslaughter conviction, a $500 fine, and a stained reputation. The 1870s and 1880s were the last gasps for dueling in Virginia, with the McCarty-Mordecai affair the final deadly duel in Richmond.[3]

POLITICS AND MEMORY

By examining *The Daily Times'* stories involving politics and race, one can better understand the cultural environment in which the Lee Monument cornerstone was dedicated. The paper's articles discussing the dedication of the cornerstone focus on Lee's character and the decorations planned for the city. Supporters avoided negative language related to politics or race. However, the memory of the Civil War remained fresh in White conservative elites' minds, the same people planning the upcoming festivities. This can be seen through *The Daily Times'* report on a Henrico County Democratic Party meeting, at which speaker Colonel R.F. Beirne (1856–1891) announced, "Our foe is the same one that we have had to confront ever since the war. There are many people who have forgotten the injuries done us by the Radical party . . . It is the party which has kept alive the war feeling and persisted in stirring up strife and bitterness in the North in order to perpetuate its power." Accusing his opponents of 'waving the bloody shirt' and provoking partisan resentment, Beirne does just that by invoking martial language and playing the victim card, even though he himself did not fight in the war. Beirne's speech embodies Caroline Janney's description of how former Confederates, and politicians appealing to former Confederates, used Civil War memory for political purposes, "But where the Union Cause ultimately sought a reunified nation free of sectional animosity, the Lost Cause fostered a distinctive and separate Southern identity determined to resist interference by the federal government."[4]

In addition, the atmosphere of anti-Black racial terror that marked print media and literature during this period is observed by reading a small report buried on page four of the paper. The article describes, "Tom Wilson, the colored man who killed Jim Davis in Henry county Saturday night, was captured by the officers in pursuit near Mayo Forge, in Patrick county, Monday night, and brought back to Martinsville. Some threats of lynching were made, but nothing in that direction was or will be done." It is unclear what ultimately happened to Tom Wilson, but it underlines the deadly reality of everyday life for African Americans at the time. James Madison University's *Racial Terror: Lynching in Virginia* project identifies eighty-four Black people lynched in Virginia between 1877 and 1927, likely an undercount of the true number.[5]

These two articles highlight the undercurrent of partisan politics and racial violence that defined the period in which the Lee Monument was installed. However, a parallel, contradictory movement was also at play, that of sectional reconciliation. Following the tumultuous political upheavals of Reconstruction, White Northerners' support for Black civil rights began to wane. As David Blight describes, "the inexorable drive for reunion both used and trumped race."[6] Evidence of these reconciliationist ideas is evidenced in *The Daily Times* through Reverend Thomas De Witt Talmage's (1832–1902) "Forgiveness Before Sundown" sermon, given at the Brooklyn Tabernacle and reprinted on page three of the paper. Talmage, a popular evangelical preacher, discussed the spiritual importance of "not to let the sun go down on our wrath, because we will sleep better if we are at peace with everybody." While not directly invoking the Civil War, many people would have naturally made the connection between Talmage's sermon and the cataclysmic destruction that engulfed the country only twenty-two years in the past. As Janney notes, "Such frequent refrains calling on Americans to look forward and not to the past underscored the extent to which reconciliation was an arduous undertaking."[7] While difficult for both Northerners and Southerners, the 1880s saw the nation move closer to putting the war behind them. However, these efforts largely excluded African Americans and came at the expense of civil rights protections. The period of Confederate commemoration, which the erection of the Lee Monument helped kick into high gear, was defined by these contradictory ideas of sectional reconciliation on one hand, and racial and political partisanship on the other.[8]

LOCAL COLOR

While *The Daily Times* featured stories covering national and world news, the paper dedicated most of its columns to issues of local and state interest. Many of these local stories would be familiar to readers if printed today. The front page featured a story about wayward youths entitled, "The Gravel Shooter Nuisance," going on to describe, "complaints have been made to the First police station that boys with gravel shooters would break the glass in the Public School building on the corner of Marshall and Nineteenth streets." Replace gravel with paintballs or airsoft guns, and this story could be seen on the 11:00 p.m. nightly news.

The paper also featured a local feud, calling it "The Reiger-Vincent War." Invoking imagery of the Hatfields and McCoys, who were at the time murdering each other over the border in West Virginia, the article describes, "The family quarrel which has been in the Police Court one week on three warrants, one charging Mary Vincent with trespassing on the premises of Caspar Reiger, another charging John Vincent with assaulting and threatening to beat Caspar Reiger, and one charging Caspar Reiger with beating and using indecent language to Mary Vincent." The court forced all three to put up a substantial $200 bond to keep the peace, which appears to have worked.

While the reasons behind the feud may never be known, a closer look at the families' backgrounds reveals close cultural ties. Both the Reigers, also spelled Rieger, and the Vincents immigrated from Germany to join the large German community in Richmond. Court records indicate Caspar Reiger immigrated to Richmond sometime before 1876, when at the age of thirty-five he appeared before the Richmond Hustings Court to declare his intent to naturalize, becoming a full citizen in 1880.[9] While listed as a cabinetmaker in 1876, in the 1880 census, Reiger was listed as an upholsterer and lived at 205 Fifth Street, in Richmond's Madison Ward.[10] Employed in a similar line of work, the 1880 census shows shoemaker John Vincent lived less than a dozen blocks away at 402 ½ Marshall Street in Clay Ward.[11] Marriage records from 1882 disclose fifty-one year old John married twenty-one-year-old Mary Eckert, herself a German immigrant.[12] Whatever caused the rift between the Reigers and Vincents, surely the feud was the object of discussion within the tight knit German community, especially if it made it to the front page of the influential *Daily Times*.

Across the James River in Manchester, still an independent city from Richmond in 1887, *The Daily Times* reported on a case of animal cruelty; a man accused of beating his horse. However, the court dismissed the charges when it was discovered "that the horse was the master of the man." One cannot help but smile when trying to envision what exactly this means.

Last, a report from Fincastle, Virginia, mirrored recent episodes of *The Bachelor*. The paper told the story of a Ms. Jeannie Conise who "eloped with a Mr. Joseph Watkins and was married, while Miss Conise's affianced husband-to-be was patiently awaiting his prospective bride's return from a buggy ride with the man she married." Even reality TV producers could not make up better drama. The happy couple went on to have three children before Jeannie's untimely death in 1894 at the age of twenty-five.

DIFFERENT TIMES

While many articles invoke relatable modern issues, the paper regularly reminds you that it is in fact from the 1880s. One such story was the latest installment of the adventures of bicyclist Thomas Stevens (1854–1935), considered the father of bicycle travel.[13] Between 1884 and 1886, Stevens became the first person to circumnavigate the globe on a bicycle, a penny farthing to be exact. Stevens's exploits proved particularly popular in the late nineteenth century United States as enthusiasm for bicycles exploded and millions of

Figure 20. "The Seat of Intellect," *The Daily Times,* October 23, 1887.

people went "wheel crazy." By the 1890s, the League of American Wheelmen, a political organization advocating for bike friendly transportation policies, had over 70,000 members spread across every state and territory.[14] To capitalize on this interest, papers across the country reprinted Stevens's reports on his adventures.

Stevens's article in *The Daily Times* discusses his introduction to non-Western customs in the Middle East and China. Typical of a late-nineteenth-century White Westerner, Stevens uses racist, imperialistic language to describe this transition: "As one approaches the more barbarous countries of the east the natives are found expressing themselves in stranger ways, and one begins to realize that he is among alien races." He goes on to describe how he "suddenly found myself one day among a people who shook their heads when they meant 'yes,' and nodded when they meant 'no.'" Stevens's views aligned with late-nineteenth-century American conceptions of race that Paul T. McCartney describes as, "structured and legitimated along Darwinian lines . . . ranking races hierarchically while also assign[ing] to each race distinguishing characteristics."[15] These racial ideas that Stevens embodied in his reports played a leading role in America's own turn toward imperialism, which began in earnest with the 1898 Spanish-American War and lasted well into the twentieth century. While these two-wheeled adventure stories became a thing of the past with the advent of motorized transportation a few decades later, the art of travel writing continues today in the form of blogs and social media influencers.

In addition, several advertisements in *The Daily Times* reflect the popularity of patent medicines at the time. Prior to government regulation, these "snake oil" type remedies became ubiquitous in the late 1800s as they promised to cure just about any ailment a person might have.[16] By the turn of the century, capitalizing on the rise of advertising and the lack of regulation, the patent medicine industry ballooned to a $74 million business.[17] Three of these products were advertised in *The Daily Times*. The Elixir Babek claimed it was an all-natural alternative to quinine for treating malaria. Rucker's Anti-Bilious and Dyspepsia Pills, manufactured in Lynchburg, VA, promised to "remove Biliousness, Dizziness, Bad Breath, and cure Dysentery, Jaundice, Malaria, Dyspepsia, and all diseases of the Liver." John Rucker claimed his pills achieved all these wonderful results with only "powerful vegetable extracts and resenoids [sic], well known to the profession."

Unfortunately for many, these claims of all-natural materials and zero side effects did not ring true. Another advertisement in *The Daily Times* was for Botanic Blood Balm from the Blood Balm Co. of Atlanta, GA. Following early success, inventor Dr. J. P. Dromgoole was forced to sell the company to Coca-Cola owner Asa Candler after the Georgia Supreme Court ruled in favor of a customer-turned-plaintiff who, after ingesting the recommended dosage, reported red spots all over his body, sores in his mouth and throat, and hair loss.[18]

The victim of Dromgoole's Blood Balm was not alone in being harmed by these products' false promises. Civil War veterans suffering from opiate addiction helped fuel the patent medicine boom. Many companies marketed their products as addiction cures, appealing to veterans who became hooked on opium following their war-time wounding. However, many of these so-called cures contained lower doses of the same painkillers that veterans were attempting to kick, masking withdrawal symptoms instead of curing addiction. Efforts to expose the industry by reform-minded journalists and doctors eventually led to federal intervention in the form of the 1906 Pure Food and Drug Act and the formation of what would become the Food and Drug Administration.[19]

Prior to the popularity of comic strips, papers still realized the importance of entertaining their readers. Instead of comics, *The Daily Times* included a column dedicated to "Little Jokes" on the last page of the paper. Some of the jokes remain evergreen, including, "He: Did you enjoy the ser-

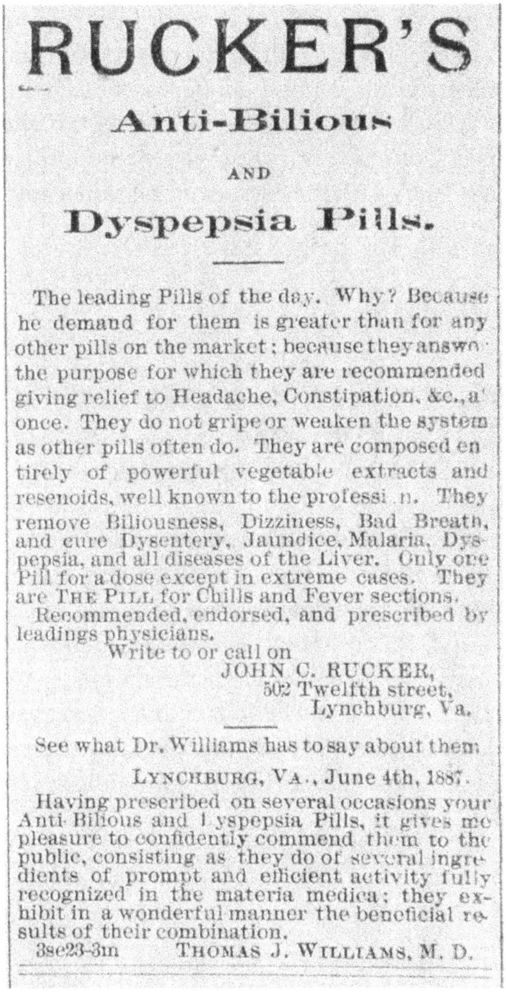

RUCKER'S

Anti-Bilious

AND

Dyspepsia Pills.

The leading Pills of the day. Why? Because he demand for them is greater than for any other pills on the market; because they answ the purpose for which they are recommended giving relief to Headache, Constipation, &c., a' once. They do not gripe or weaken the system as other pills often do. They are composed en tirely of powerful vegetable extracts and resenoids, well known to the professi n. They remove Biliousness, Dizziness, Bad Breath, and cure Dysentery, Jaundice, Malaria, Dys pepsia, and all diseases of the Liver. Only one Pill for a dose except in extreme cases. They are THE PILL for Chills and Fever sections.

Recommended, endorsed, and prescribed by leadings physicians.

Write to or call on
JOHN C. RUCKER,
502 Twelfth street,
Lynchburg, Va.

See what Dr. Williams has to say about them:

LYNCHBURG, VA., June 4th, 1887.

Having prescribed on several occasions your Anti-Bilious and Dyspepsia Pills, it gives me pleasure to confidently commend them to the public, consisting as they do of several ingredients of prompt and efficient activity fully recognized in the materia medica; they exhibit in a wonderful manner the beneficial results of their combination.

3se23-3m THOMAS J. WILLIAMS, M. D.

Figure 21. Advertisement for Rucker's Anti-Bilious and Dyspepsia Pills, *The Daily Times,* October 23, 1887.

mon? She: Of course I did. I had on a new hat and dress and the sexton seated me directly in front of that dreadful Miss Briggs." Others were topical, like one joke that belittled the growing woman's suffrage movement, "One danger of female suffrage is that the women may want the men to bet them $50 bonnets against $5 hats on the result." Richmond residents would be particularly aware of the suffrage movement following Anna Bodeker's (1826–1904) ultimately unsuccessful organizing attempts a few years prior. Bodeker founded the Virginia State Woman Suffrage Association in 1870 that sponsored many pro-suffrage speeches in Richmond over the following three years, including a two-night visit by Susan B. Anthony. However, difficulty gaining support from both lawmakers and members of the general public, combined with Bodeker's adoption of eccentric religious views, blunted the momentum she had created.[20] While it would take another thirty-three years, the suffrage movement ultimately had the last laugh with the passage of the Nineteenth Amendment in 1919.

TODAY THE PRESENT, TOMORROW THE PAST

In today's digital world, access to comprehensive local news like *The Daily Times* has dwindled. With the explosion of internet news sites and increased influence of social media platforms, local newspapers have struggled to adapt to the new form of information consumption. In addition, the prevalence of digitized historic newspapers has benefited researchers by providing remote access to records and allowing for keyword searches, but those same conveniences have reduced the need to scan individual pages for relevant information. The October 23, 1887, *Daily Times* contains plenty more interesting stories like the ones recounted above. These demonstrate the smallest news story can prove representative of larger local and national trends. Next time you read the paper or scroll through your newsfeed, think about what historians 135 years in the future will think about the stories, ads, and oddities you see today.

NOTES

1. Lester J. Cappon, *Virginia Newspapers 1821–1935: A Bibliography with Historical Introduction and Notes* (New York: D. Appleton-Century Co., for the Institute for Research in the Social Sciences, UVA, 1936), 164–94.
2. James M. Lindgren, "Joseph Bryan (1845–1908)," in *Dictionary of Virginia Biography*, Library of Virginia, last modified 2018, https://www.lva.virginia.gov/public/dvb/bio.php?b=Bryan_Joseph_1845-1908.
3. Jean L. Cooper and Brendan P. Fox, *A Challenge Was Given: The Duels of John Mason McCarty and William Page McCarty* (Palmyra, VA: Shortwood Press, 2017), 36–52.
4. Caroline Janney, *Remembering the Civil War: Reunion and the Limits of Reconciliation* (Chapel Hill: The University of North Carolina Press, 2013), 153.

5. "Research Process," *Racial Terror: Lynching in Virginia*, James Madison University, https://sites.lib.jmu.edu/valynchings/research-process/. For more on the history of Lynching in Virginia, see W. Fitzhugh Brundage, *Lynching in the New South: Georgia and Virginia, 1880–1930* (Chicago: University of Illinois Press, 1993).
6. David W. Blight, *Race and Reunion: The Civil War in American Memory* (Cambridge, MA: Harvard University Press, 2001), 2.
7. Janney, *Remembering the Civil War*, 172.
8. For more on these concepts, see Janney, *Remembering the Civil War* and Blight, *Race and Reunion*. For a synthesis of recent scholarship on reconciliation and reunion, see Nina Silber, "Reunion and Reconciliation, Reviewed and Considered," *The Journal of American History* 103, no. 1 (June 2016): 59–83.
9. Rudolph Bunzl, "Immigrants in Richmond after the Civil War: 1865–1880" (Master's thesis, University of Richmond, 1994), 139.
10. 1880 United States Census, Henrico County, Virginia, population schedule, Richmond City, enumeration district (ED) 85, page 39, dwelling 132, family 1, Caspar Rieger; database with images, *FamilySearch,* https://familysearch.org/ark:/61903/3:1:33SQ-GYBN-9L6F?cc=1417683&wc=XHWY-L29%3A1589415431%2C1589415778%2C1589394766%2C1589394992; citing National Archives and Records Administration (NARA) microfilm T9, Roll 1371.
11. 1880 United States Census, Henrico County, Virginia, pop. sch., Richmond City, ED 82, page 36, dwell. 206, fam. 338, John Vincent; database with images, *FamilySearch,* https://familysearch.org/ark:/61903/3:1:33SQ-GYBN-9GC5?cc=1417683&wc=XHWY-VZ9%3A1589415431%2C1589415778%2C1589394766%2C1589396810; citing NARA microfilm T9, Roll 1371.
12. Virginia, Marriage Records, Richmond City, 1878–1895, page 52; database with images, *FamilySearch,* https://familysearch.org/ark:/61903/3:1:3QHN-13YT-VLSS?cc=4231103; citing Library of Virginia State Archive, Virginia, Births, Marriages, and Deaths 1853–1900.
13. Gabrielle Porter and Tom Taylor, "The Impractical Scheme of a Visionary: Thomas Stevens and the Quest to Travel Round the World on a Bicycle," *World History Connected* (June 2013), https://worldhistoryconnected.press.uillinois.edu/10.2/forum_porter.html.
14. Michael Taylor, "The Bicycle Boom and the Bicycle Bloc: Cycling and Politics in the 1890s," *Indiana Magazine of History* 104, no. 3 (September 2008): 215, 217.
15. Paul T. McCartney, *Power and Progress: American National Identity, the War of 1898, and the Rise of American Imperialism* (Baton Rouge: Louisiana State University Press, 2006), 57.
16. "Balm of America: Patent Medicine Collection," Smithsonian National Museum of American History, https://americanhistory.si.edu/collections/object-groups/balm-of-america-patent-medicine-collection/history.
17. Jonathan S. Jones, "Buying and Selling Health and Manhood: Civil War Veterans and Opiate Addiction 'Cures'," in *Buying and Selling Civil War Memory in Gilded Age America*, ed. James Marten and Caroline E. Janney (Athens: The University of Georgia Press, 2021), 34.

18. Mark Pendergrast, *For God, Country, and Coca-Cola: The Definitive History of the Great American Soft Drink and the Company That Makes It* (New York: Basic Books, 1993), 52.
19. For more on the relationship between patent medicines, Civil War veterans, and opiate addiction, see Jones, "Buying and Selling Health and Manhood," 31–45.
20. Sandra Gioia Treadway, "Anna Whitehead Bodeker (ca. 1826–1904)," in *Dictionary of Virginia Biography*, Library of Virginia, 2001, https://www.lva.virginia.gov/public/dvb/bio.asp?b=Bodeker_Anna_Whitehead.

8

Calling Cards

An Introduction from the Past

Elizabeth Moore

SOCIAL CALLING CARDS

In the era before telephones and social media, calling cards provided a way for individuals to initiate visits, convey messages, and announce one's arrival at a social event. First used in fifteenth-century China, paper calling cards became popular in France in the seventeenth century and shortly thereafter in London. By the nineteenth century, they had become an essential component of social etiquette in Europe and the Americas and were an important part of the formalities of introductions, invitations, and visits.[1] Calling cards served both utilitarian purposes and as status symbols. They were a way to schedule social calls, share information, and organize events, allowing selected individuals entry to social circles and serving to keep others at a distance.

Victorian etiquette surrounding calling cards among the social elite was complex and included many rules, which, if violated, could mean social self-destruction. In typical use by wealthy individuals, a visitor would deliver a calling card to a home—sometimes in person, other times via a servant—to announce one's arrival or request a visit. If the recipient was not home or did not wish to meet, a servant would accept the calling card, or it would be left on a silver tray in the entrance hall. Even when a visit was permitted, a calling card would be left on the tray as evidence of the meeting. A tray filled with calling cards indicated one's social desirability, and cards from visitors with the most social status would be left on the top of the stack for other visitors to see. When accepted, visits were formalized and had a strict set of rules. Visiting hours were usually only in the late morning or early afternoon.

Women's cards were approximately 2.75 high to 3.5 inches wide, and messages were, by necessity, short. Women often carried their cards in protective decorative cases. Men's cards were slightly smaller, so they fit in a breast pocket. Messages could be written on the backs of calling cards or conveyed through code to express the purpose of the visit. The rituals associated with this marking of cards with messages changed over the course of the nineteenth century. At the beginning of the century, messages were encoded through the turning of a corner of the card. By 1873, Louis Dreka, card engraver and stationer in Philadelphia, stated that cards often had the words *Visite*, *Felicitation*, *Conge*, and *Condolence* printed on the back corners so that when a corner was folded the word would be visible, explaining the reason for the visit. As a member of Washington's elite and authority on social etiquette, Mrs. Madeleine Vinton Dahlgren recommended the leaving of cards in her 1873 *Social Life in Washington*.[2] A card could be critical evidence of visits in the highly structured social life of politicians and their families in the nation's capital where violation of social mores could have political implications.

At first simple rectangles printed with names, the Victorian era saw an explosion of embellishment, color, and expensive printing techniques on calling cards. Scalloped borders, fancy shapes, embossing, lithography, attached photos, and even handsewn borders were just some of the ways cards could be decorated. The function and purpose of cards continued to change over time, eventually evolving into the business card used today for professional networking.

MASONIC EMBLEM CARDS

The cards found in the cornerstone box served a different function than the more widely used social calling cards. The cards from J.H. Capers and Edward W. Price are Masonic exchange cards with emblems that indicate the cardholder's affiliation with the Freemasons or Knights Templar. Similar in form to calling cards, printers referred to these cards as emblem or exchange cards. Unlike social calling cards, emblem cards were usually exchanged in person between Freemasons. At conclaves, conventions of thousands of Freemasons or Knights Templar, emblem cards were collected and could serve as souvenirs of the event.[3]

Price's card contains a Knights Templar seal in the upper left corner, an

Figure 22. Calling card of Edward W. Price, 32°, Grand Commander, New Jersey. Price's card indicates that he was a 32nd Degree Freemason and Grand Commander of the Knights Templar, New Jersey.

Figure 23. Calling card of J.H. Capers, E.C., Richmond Commandery No. 2, Knights Templar. Richmond, VA. The Richmond Commandery No. 2 is one of thirty-six Commanderies of the Knights Templar of Virginia.

emblem of a cross in crown on top of a Maltese cross with crossed swords behind it. Encircling the cross in crown is a motto in Latin, *In Hoc Signo Vinces*, "in this you will conquer" or "in this sign we will conquer." The sign referred to is the cross of Christ. Capers' card includes the same motto, but it is above a cross in the sky that is shining light down upon a Knight Templar on horseback with his sword raised to the cross. Capers was serving on Lee's staff at the close of the Civil War and the inclusion of this card reflects his continued pride in having served with the General.

VETERAN'S CARDS

The cards from Blair Meanley and P. J. White are veteran's cards and identify their service units. Meanley and White were veterans of the Confederacy, and, like most veterans, this service was a life-defining period. Presenting a card that declared this service was a point of pride; it publicly declared the individual's political alliance during the war, it provided a means of group identification when meeting strangers, and it helped form social alliances with those of similar affiliation.

Meanley had belonged to the Walker Light Guard, which fought mostly

Figure 24. Calling card of Blair Meanley, Walker Light Guard, Co. "B", First Regt. Va. Vets. Richmond, VA.

with the Army of Northern Virginia. On August 8, 1885, Ulysses S. Grant's funeral procession in New York City was seven miles long and included veterans from both sides of the war, including the Walker Light Guard. Meanley's card contains the image of soldier surrounded by a laurel wreath, a symbol of victory, with the words *Semper Paratus*, "Always Ready."

White's card exhibits an emblem with multiple components that identify his alliance with the Confederacy, including the words "Confederate Veteran 1861–1865," an engraved image of General Robert E. Lee within a Maltese cross with symbols of the armed forces, a plaque with "CSA" (Confederate State of America), and a draped flag. The flag exhibited is the second national flag of the Confederate States of America, also known as "The Stainless Banner" or the "Jackson Flag" as it was the flag that draped the coffin of Lieutenant General Thomas "Stonewall" Jackson. Adopted in 1863, this design was supported in a series of editorials by William Tappan Thompson, editor of the *Savannah Morning News*. Placing the Confederate battle flag on a white field, Thompson argued that "The White Man's Flag" should represent the Confederacy. "As a people, we are fighting to maintain the heaven ordained supremacy of the white man over the inferior or colored race: a white flag would thus be emblematical of our cause."[4] That P. J. White chose this flag and

Figure 25. Calling card of P.J. White, Co. G, Fifth Virginia Cavalry, Payne's Brigade, Fitz Lee's Division, A.N.V. Richmond, VA. The 5th Cavalry Regiment was organized in June 1862 with the 2nd Battalion Virginia Cavalry as its core Peter Johnston White was a member of the R.E. Lee Camp No. 1 of the Confederate Veterans in Richmond.

associated symbols to be printed on his card and included in this monument sends a deliberate and distinct message of his position on emancipation and efforts toward racial equality.

The cards for both Meanley and White express pride in their service during the war by identifying their regiments. After the war, supporters of the Reconciliation Movement sought to find common ground on which they could unite. The movement portrayed the war as an honorable conflict between White men, a portrayal that allowed for honor and dignity on both sides while obscuring Black participation. The participation of the Walker Light Guards in Grant's funeral procession was a highly visible public expression of the Reconciliation Movement. Meanley's card associates him with his brigade but does not provide further commentary on the results of the war.

White's card goes beyond the representation of service, displaying a flag designed explicitly to support White supremacy. Many Southerners remained anti-union, holding onto the belief that states' rights should take precedence over decisions of the union, especially when decisions to continue chattel slavery were involved. The economic devastation wrought by the war was widespread, and only those individuals whose wealth was not primarily held in the value of enslaved people could financially recover quickly. Slavery requires that the humanity of the enslaved is called into question; that the very same people who had been viewed as less than human were now freed and starting to succeed economically and politically, was anathema to many in the South and reconciling with an enemy forcing that position was inconceivable.

AN INADVERTENT CARD

The last card presented here has handwritten information on both sides. On one side is H.L. Turner and on the other William B. Isaacs. Unlike the other cards seen here, these were not printed in advance. That they are both on the same piece of paper indicates that their inclusion may not have been planned and may have been opportunistic. Isaacs's card was not submitted by him but was submitted by W.H. Sands who also submitted a "programme Ancient Order Nobles of Mystic Shrine laying corner-stone of Lee Monument." William B. Isaacs, also a Freemason, was responsible for the collection of items for the cornerstone box. According to *The Richmond Dispatch* inventory, Isaacs provided other items for the box including "copies of charters issued by Grand

Lodge, Grand Chapter, and Grand Commandery of Virginia to its subordinates," a "Richmond Directory," and "an assortment of United States silver and copper coins." Isaacs's information is neatly written in straight lines.

Although the handwriting on both sides is similar, the information for H.L. Turner was clearly written in more of a hurry—the letters are not as neat or embellished and the lines of text are not straight and laid out as we see with Isaacs. H. L. Turner, of Norfolk, was a quartermaster for the First Battalion Virginia Artillery during the 1880s. The battalion included about 250 men from Battery 'A'-Richmond Howitzers, 'B'-Norfolk (Norfolk Light Artillery Blues), 'C'-Staunton Artillery, and 'E'-R.E. Lee Battery (Petersburg).[5] Turner was also a member of the Norfolk United Royal Arch, No. 2. The Norfolk Masonic Temple is the home for eight Masonic Lodges, the Scottish Rite, and the York Rite. The Atlantic Lodge No. 2 was chartered on December 13, 1854.[6] We do not know if Turner was present at the event, if he had a role in the cornerstone box contents, if he wished his name added to the box, or if it was added by a friend or colleague.

These five cards provide small yet telling pieces of information about the men represented. Their pride in their fraternal organizations, their military service, and their positions on the results of the war are told in the text and symbols they chose to include. The cards, like the other objects found in

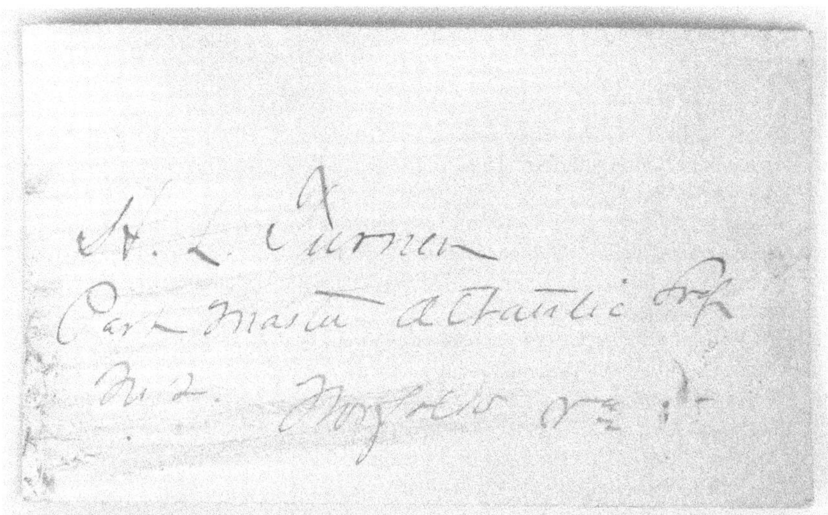

Figure 26. Calling card of H.L. Turner—Past Master Atlantic Lodge—No. 2 Norfolk, Va. First Lieutenant.

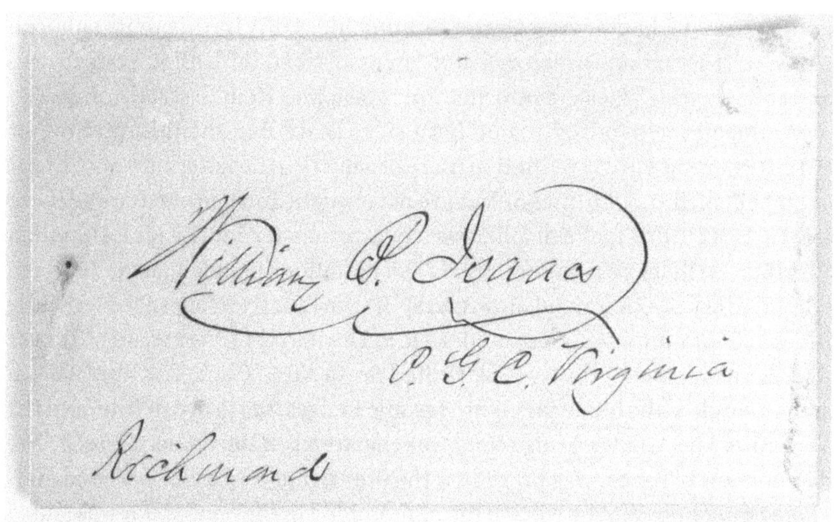

Figure 27. Calling card of William B. Isaacs, P. G. C. Virginia. Richmond.

this box, represent the opposing viewpoints of the Reconciliation Movement and the Lost Cause narrative versus post-war reconciliation, viewpoints that continue today.

NOTES

1. Edwin Banfield, *Visiting Cards and Cases* (Trowbridge, Wiltshire: Baros, 1989).
2. Madeleine Vinton Dahlgren, *Etiquette of Social Life in Washington* (Lancaster, PA: Inquirer, 1873).
3. "Masonic Emblem Cards: Victorian Tradition in a Fraternal World," *National Heritage Museum*, last modified March 3, 2015, https://nationalheritagemuseum.typepad.com/library_and_archives/2015/03/masonic-emblem-cards-victorian-tradition-in-a-fraternal-world.html.
4. George Henry Preble, *Our Flag: Origin and Progress of the Flag of the United States of America* (Albany, NY: Joel Munsell, 1872) 416–18.
5. "First Battalion Virginia Artillery," *Southern Historical Society Papers, Volume 17*, Reverend J. William Jones, ed., https://www.perseus.tufts.edu/hopper/text?doc=Perseus%3Atext%3A2001.05.0274%3Achapter%3D1.14%3Asection%3Dc.1.14.265.
6. "Norfolk Masonic Temple Atlantic Lodge No. 2, A.F. & A.M," *Norfolk Masonic Temple*, http://www.norfolkmasonictemple.com/atlantic-lodge-no.-2.html.

9

A "Picture" of Reconciliation

John Salmon

As the planning for the pedestal for the Robert E. Lee Monument in Richmond was underway in 1887, the *Richmond Dispatch* reported on October 26 that a "corner-stone" box was to be inserted in the foundation. The newspaper listed the contents of the copper box, with the names of those contributing various items and memorabilia, including "Miss Pattie Leake," who donated a "picture of Lincoln lying in his coffin."[1]

Pattie (sometimes called Patsey) Callis Leake (December 10, 1841–July 9, 1922) was the daughter of Samuel Davies and Fannie Kean Leake, who were both born in Goochland County. Pattie Leake also was born in Goochland County, and she died of "paralysis" in Wytheville, Wythe County. Her body was returned to Ashland, where she was buried in Woodland Cemetery. She never married. According to the 1880 census, when she resided in Ashland, she was a teacher.[2]

Her parents were farmers, first in Goochland County and then, by 1860, in Hanover County. The 1860 census showed that Samuel D. Leake owned a farm valued at $8,000, and that his household (in Ashland) consisted of his wife, two sons, and four daughters including Pattie, who was the oldest child. He also enslaved sixteen persons, ten males between the ages of three and fifty-eight and six females aged six to forty. On January 4, 1865, Leake advertised in the *Richmond Daily Dispatch* that "my MAN, CHARLES, who was hired to James Bolton, Richmond," had run away. Leasing enslaved persons was common; Bolton, who appeared in the 1860 census as a shoemaker, may have engaged Charles as a helper or assistant. Charles may have fled to the US Army, which was entrenched a few miles east of the city.[3]

William Josiah Leake (September 30, 1843–November 23, 1908), the elder of Pattie Leake's two brothers, was the second-oldest child in the family. He was schooled both at home and at St. George Tucker's classical school in Ashland. When the Civil War began in 1861, he left school and joined as a sergeant in the artillery company that his uncle Captain Walter D. Leake had formed. He served in it until it was disbanded in 1862, then served in two other batteries. In 1863, Leake unsuccessfully sought transfers and promotions to help support his parents and siblings, his father having become ill and unable to work. Leake served in the artillery until the end of the war.[4]

In 1867, Leake began his career as an attorney, jurist, and railroad company president. He was appointed a chancery court judge in 1890 and later served periodically as a special master in state and federal courts. Leake was general counsel for the Richmond, Fredericksburg & Potomac Railroad Company beginning in 1889 and served as president in 1905 and 1906. He died in Richmond on November 23, 1908.[5]

When Pattie Leake worked as a teacher in 1880, she resided in William Leake's Ashland household, probably in their father's dwelling. Her father and mother and several of her siblings also lived in the house. William J. Leake was listed as the head of the household then. He moved to Richmond before the end of the century, and in the 1900 census (the 1890 census was destroyed in a fire) the head of the household in Ashland, where Pattie Leake still resided, was Lavinia Leake, her and William's sister.[6]

Pattie Leake, then, was most likely teaching and living in her father's house in Ashland with her siblings when she donated the "picture of Lincoln lying in his coffin" to the cornerstone box in 1887. Her brother William J. Leake—the operative head of the family as their father declined—was a former Confederate artillerist who had become a prominent attorney and judge. Given her circumstances and the subject matter, one could reasonably suspect that she had been an ardent Confederate supporter who celebrated Lincoln's demise.[7]

In December 2021, as Team Henry Enterprises disassembled the Lee Monument a little more than 134 years after its construction, state officials, the contractors, and the general public speculated about the contents of the box and whether they would be in salvageable condition. Dale Brumfield had raised questions concerning the "picture" four years earlier, in a 2017 *Richmond Magazine* article.[8] Could it be a photograph of assassinated President Abraham Lincoln in his casket, as Brumfield conjectured, or something else?

Did someone really take such a photograph of Lincoln? The answer to that question is "Yes."

Although taking photographs of deceased persons in their coffins may seem ghoulish to modern sensibilities, the concept was widely accepted and popular during the nineteenth century, although it was the next of kin's private and personal choice to do so. In 1865, photography was only about two decades old, still a relatively new technology. Compared to portrait painting, it was far less expensive and far more accessible to average middle-class persons, at least those who lived in towns or cities with photography studios. Death was a common event. Most people died at home, and ample opportunities existed to photograph the deceased, especially babies and children who had not been photographed while alive. Such images were termed "memento mori" (literally, an admonition to "remember you must die"), or alternatively as mementos of the recently deceased. To photograph Lincoln in his coffin, then, would not have been unusual at all, although there may have been reasons for forbidding it. It was, after all, the right of the next of kin to approve or disapprove the taking of a deceased family member's photograph.

John Wilkes Booth assassinated President Lincoln on April 14, 1865, in Washington, DC. Lincoln's body was taken to the White House on April 15, autopsied, embalmed, and placed in an open coffin. Lincoln's widow, Mary Todd Lincoln, confined herself to her bedroom upstairs and never saw her deceased husband's body. His remains lay in state in the East Room on April 18, for public viewing, and then were transported to the US Capitol Rotunda, where his body lay in state again for public viewing on April 20. On April 21, Lincoln's remains were placed in the President's Car on a special train, which then transported them along a seemingly meandering route to Springfield, Illinois, for burial. Steaming slowly along 1,700 miles of railroad tracks, the train stopped in the major cities of Maryland, Pennsylvania, New York, Ohio, Indiana, and Illinois. At each stop, Lincoln's open coffin was displayed for viewing in state capitols, city halls, and other locations that could accommodate large numbers of persons. The US Army Assistant Adjutant General, Brigadier General Edward D. Townsend, commanded the escort detail during the journey to its terminus in Springfield, Illinois. Many photographs were taken of the crowds, the parades, and other ceremonies surrounding the events, but none of them showed Lincoln in his coffin, with one exception.[9]

In New York City, the coffin had been placed in city hall for public viewing on the afternoon of April 24 and the morning of April 25. The *New York Times* devoted the entire first page and more than half of the back page of its April 25 edition to the events that occurred at city hall on both days. After noon on April 24, when the procession reached the building, the coffin was carried into the rotunda and placed on a landing at the top of a double staircase. Before the public was admitted, an embalmer opened the casket and "prepared the body for exhibition." Flowers were laid inside and atop the coffin. Then, "Mr. [Jeremiah] GURNEY, Jr., to whom had been granted the exclusive right of taking pictures of the body and the scene, took possession of the hall and retained it for over half an hour, during which time he succeeded in securing material for a photograph as interesting as it will be historic."[10]

Gurney would have set up his view camera on a tripod and then would have taken more than one photograph employing "wet plates." These were glass plates that were coated with a wet silver nitrate solution in a darkroom, placed inside a lightproof holder, inserted in the camera, exposed to light coming through the lens by removing the lens cap, and then taken from the camera in the holder to the darkroom and developed in a wet solution, all in the space of about fifteen minutes. Gurney would have taken multiple photographs as quickly as possible at varying exposure lengths to get the best negative, one that was neither underexposed nor overexposed, a process of trial and error, speeded by his skill and experience in taking photographs under various light conditions.[11]

That evening, issues of the *Times* and other New York newspapers reached the desk of Edwin M. Stanton, the Secretary of War, in Washington, DC. To say that Stanton was displeased to learn that Gurney had taken photographs of Lincoln in his coffin would be a gross understatement. He was outraged. At 11:40 p.m., he fired off a telegram to Townsend in New York and demanded that the photographic plates (glass-plate negatives) and any photographic prints or other pictures, such as engravings, be seized and destroyed. He also wanted whoever was responsible for allowing the photography to be relieved of duty.[12]

Townsend was stunned by the orders, as his telegram to Stanton the next morning revealed. He explained that "the photograph was taken while I was present, [Rear] Admiral [Charles H.] Davis being the officer immediately in charge, but it would have been my part to stop the proceedings. I regret your disapproval, but it did not strike me as objectionable under the circumstances as it was done."[13]

Stanton, when he replied to Townsend, had calmed down enough to ex-

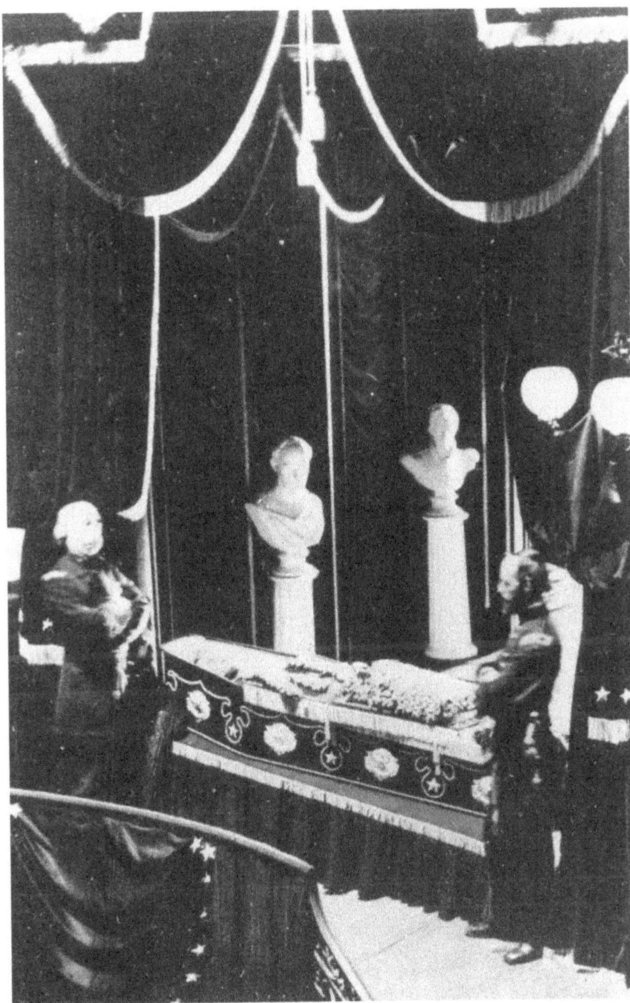

Figure 28. Gurney photograph of Abraham Lincoln lying in state. (Courtesy of the Abraham Lincoln Presidential Library & Museum)

plain the reason for his concern. "The taking of a photograph," he wrote, "was expressly forbidden by Mrs. Lincoln, and I am apprehensive that her feelings and the feelings of her family will be greatly wounded." Townsend was in Albany, New York, the next stop on the journey, when he received Stanton's answer. Townsend responded that he "was not aware of Mrs. Lincoln's wishes, or the picture would not have been taken with the knowledge of any officer of the escort. It seemed to me the picture would be gratifying, a grand view of what thousands saw and thousands could not see."[14] Townsend followed this telegram with another, also on April 26:

> [Major] General [John A.] Dix, who is here, suggests that I should explain to you how the photograph was taken. The remains had just been arranged in state in the City Hall, at the head of the stairway, where the people would ascend on one side and descend on the other. The body lay in an alcove, draped in black, and just at the edge of a rotunda formed of American flags and mourning drapery. The photographer was in a gallery twenty feet higher than the body, and at least forty distant from it. Admiral Davis stood at the head and I at the foot of the coffin. No-one else was in view. The effect of the picture would be general, taking in the whole scene, but not giving the features of the corpse.[15]

Townsend, Dix, and the funeral train departed Albany for Buffalo that afternoon. Two influential men who were there wrote to Stanton, begging him to postpone destroying the negatives until Jeremiah Gurney could speak to the Secretary of War in person. They were the Reverend Henry Ward Beecher, an ardent abolitionist leader, and Henry J. Raymond, a co-founder of the *New York Times*, chairman of the Republican National Committee in 1865 and 1866, and member of the House of Representatives from New York. Although Stanton remained convinced that the photograph should not have been taken, he agreed to postpone the negatives' destruction and ordered them turned over to Dix.[16]

Dix passed the plates by train to Major General John J. Peck, Dix's second-in-command in New York City. Probably Dix handed them off because he was to be on the funeral train to Buffalo and then would take another train back to New York City; therefore, he would be out of touch for several days. Peck telegraphed Stanton about midday on April 27, noting that a dispatch he had received from Townsend with the plates "advises of your condemnation of the taking of a photograph of the President's remains, and orders the destruction of the plates, pictures, and engravings. The plates include the pictures of General Townsend and Admiral Davis (with Lincoln's remains in city hall). They are in my hands awaiting your pleasure, as by second telegram."[17]

No further telegrams followed, or at least no others on the subject are printed in the *Official Records*. For the next eighty-seven years, the matter rested, the outcome of all the orders and telegrams unknown.

Early in the 1950s, an Iowa boy named Ronald Rietveld was becoming increasingly fascinated with American history, especially with Abraham Lincoln. After he read a newspaper article about Judge James W. Bollinger, of Davenport, who was an avid collector of Lincoln memorabilia, Rietveld corresponded with the judge about his own interest in Lincoln. He later learned that Bollinger had died and had left his collection to the University of Iowa. He wrote the university to ask if he could attend the dedication of the collection in November 1951. When he attended, one of the people he met was Harry Pratt, the state historian of Illinois, who took a liking to the fourteen-year-old boy and invited him to visit him and his wife in Springfield. In July 1952, the visit took place, and Rietveld accompanied Pratt to his office on the statehouse grounds. Pratt allowed the boy to browse carefully through the papers of John G. Nicolay and John Hay, Lincoln's secretaries, who had written a massive ten-volume biography of the president. Rietveld came across an envelope dated 1887 in which there were a letter and a folded paper. The letter was from Lewis H. Stanton, son of Edwin M. Stanton, to Nicolay, transmitting the folded paper and its contents for possible inclusion in the biography. When Rietveld unfolded the paper, "there lay a faded brown photograph" of Lincoln in his coffin in the New York City Hall. It not only depicted the scene exactly as Townsend had described it in his telegram of April 26, but it also closely resembled an engraving printed in the May 6, 1865, issue of *Harper's Weekly* that shows mourners filing up a flight of stairs past Lincoln's coffin on the landing and then down the opposite staircase. In the photograph, as Townsend had asserted, Lincoln's features were hard to discern, probably because they were overexposed on the negative.[18]

After Edwin M. Stanton died in 1869, Lewis H. Stanton inherited his father's papers. But how did the photograph get to be in Edwin Stanton's papers in the first place? Had the photographer met with Stanton and given it to him? Was the print sent to Stanton by Gurney in lieu of such a meeting? Could Townsend have had Gurney print and send it to Stanton to illustrate the points Townsend made in his telegrams? To date, no answers to these questions have been found. The most likely explanation is that before the plates were destroyed a photographic print was made and sent or presented to Stanton by Gurney or Townsend.

When conservators in Richmond opened the copper box from the Lee Monument on December 28, 2021, the "picture" proved to be neither a photograph nor an image based on a photograph, but an imaginative engraving published in the April 29, 1865, issue of *Harper's Weekly*. *Harper's*, a "magazine" as we would call it today, was printed in a format resembling that of a modern tabloid newspaper. Each issue contained articles on various sub-

Figure 29. An engraving from the April 29, 1865, issue of *Harper's Weekly* that Pattie Leake placed inside the Lee statue cornerstone box in Richmond in 1887.

jects as well as numerous large (sometimes full-page) illustrations. It was one of the most popular of several such magazines, its principal rival being *Frank Leslie's Illustrated Newspaper*. During the Civil War, these magazines shifted their focus to the conflict, the battles, the commanders, and related topics. Both magazines sent dozens of artists to the theaters of war: *Leslie's* foremost combat artist was Edwin Forbes, while *Harper's* boasted Alfred R. Waud, Winslow Homer, and Thomas Nast. Their drawings were turned into engravings and published, since the technology for printing photographs in newspapers had not yet been developed. In addition, because taking photographs required long exposure times, movement could not be captured; the combat artists could depict the action of a battle as they witnessed it, using their imagination, or based on witnesses' descriptions.

The "picture of Lincoln lying in his coffin" that Pattie Leake donated, then, was an untitled engraving by Nast, depicting a female figure in classical clothing to represent the nation in mourning, grieving beside a closed coffin labeled "Lincoln." In the upper left and right corners, Nast placed a sorrowing US soldier and sailor, respectively. Centered at the bottom, beneath the coffin, is a circular image of a congregation in a church, with the altar draped in black cloth. The completed Nast engraving represents the nation mourning for Lincoln through semi-allegorical figures. The "picture" was most definitely not a photograph and did not show the face of Lincoln as he lay in his coffin.[19]

Pattie Leake's motivation for donating the engraving remains unknown. Evidently Leake or someone else in the household subscribed to *Harper's* in 1865 and had either saved some of the issues or had cut the engraving out of the magazine. If Leake had wanted to show the face of Lincoln in his coffin, she could have clipped and donated the engraving of May 6, 1865. That image, likely based on one of Gurney's photographs, depicted the dead president and was indeed a "picture of Lincoln lying in his coffin." Instead, Leake donated the allegorical image of America mourning her loss. In addition, when conservators removed the clipping from the copper box and unfolded it, they observed that tears in the paper had been repaired by gluing other pieces of newspaper to the reverse of the image. This suggests that the illustration had been well cared for. Perhaps, rather than celebrating Lincoln's death, Pattie Leake was instead suggesting that she had joined in the mourning and had donated the engraving as a gesture of reconciliation.[20]

NOTES

1. "*Richmond Dispatch*, Oct. 26, 1887," *Genealogy Bank*, www.genealogybank.com.
2. "Pattie C. Leake, Death Certificate, Jul. 9, 1922, Virginia, U.S., Death Records, 1912–2014, LVA," *Ancestry*, https://www.ancestry.com; "Pattie Callis Leake," *Find a Grave*, "Pattie Callis Leake (1841–1922)," *Find a Grave Memorial*; "U.S. Census, Inhabitants, Virginia, Hanover County, Ashland, 1880," *Ancestry*, https://www.ancestry.com.
3. "U.S. Census, Inhabitants, Virginia, Goochland County, 1850," *Ancestry*, https://www.ancestry.com; ibid., "Hanover Co., 1860"; ibid., "Slave Inhabitants, 1860, Virginia, Hanover County," *Ancestry*, https://www.ancestry.com.; "*Richmond Daily Dispatch*, Jan. 4, 1865," *Genealogy Bank*, www.genealogybank.com; "U.S. Census, Inhabitants, Virginia, Hanover County, Ashland, 1880", *Ancestry*, https://www.ancestry.com; A physician also named James Bolton lived in Richmond in 1860, according to the census, but Leake probably would have referred to him as "Doctor" Bolton if he had been Charles's employer rather than the shoemaker.
4. "U.S. Census, Inhabitants, Virginia, Hanover County, Ashland, 1860," *Ancestry*, https://www.ancestry.com.; "St. George Tucker," *The Ashland Museum*, https://ashlandmuseum.org/explore-online/people/st-george-tucker-1828-1863/; "William Josiah Leake", *Fold3*, www.fold3.com.

5. Lyon G. Tyler, "Leake, William Josiah," in *Encyclopedia of Virginia Biography* (New York: Lewis Historical Publishing Co., 1915), 3:312, https://archive.org/details/encyclopediaofvi03tyleuoft/page/312/mode/2up; "Judge William Josiah Leake," *New York Times*, Nov. 24, 1908, https://timesmachine.nytimes.com/timesmachine/1908/11/24/104771632.pdf.
6. "U.S. Census, Inhabitants, Virginia, Hanover County, Ashland, 1880," *Ancestry*, https://www.ancestry.com; U.S. Census, 1900.
7. Dale Brumfield, "A Monument Avenue Mystery," *Richmond Magazine*, last modified December 3, 2017, https://richmondmagazine.com/news/sunday-story/a-monument-avenue-mystery/.
8. Brumfield, "A Monument Avenue Mystery."
9. Map showing funeral train route and stops, in "Funeral and burial of Abraham Lincoln," *Wikipedia*, https://en.wikipedia.org/wiki/Funeral_and_burial_of_Abraham_Lincoln.
10. *New-York Times*, last modified Apr. 25, 1865, *Times Machine*, Tuesday April 25, 1865—NYTimes.com.
11. The "dry plate," which was precoated and then exposed while dry, was not invented until 1871.
12. Robert N. Scott, ed., *The War of the Rebellion: A Compilation of the Official Records of the Union and Confederate Armies* (Washington, DC: U.S. Government Printing Office, 1880–1901), Ser. 1, Vol. 46, Part 3, p. 952.
13. Scott, *The War of the Rebellion,* 965.
14. Scott, *The War of the Rebellion,* 965.
15. Scott, *The War of the Rebellion,* 965–66.
16. Scott, *The War of the Rebellion*, 966–67.
17. Scott, *The War of the Rebellion*, 989.
18. Ronald Rietveld, "The Magnificent Find: Discovering the Lincoln Death Photograph," *Abraham Lincoln Online*, http://www.abrahamlincolnonline.org/lincoln/news/rietveld.htm. (The article includes the photograph of Lincoln in his coffin, April 24, 1865, at City Hall, New York, by Jeremiah Gurney, Jr., the original of which is in the Abraham Lincoln Presidential Library and Museum); "President Lincoln's Funeral. Citizens Viewing the Body at the City Hall, New York," *Harper's Weekly*, last modified May 6, 1865, https://archive.org/details/harpersweeklyv9bonn/page/284/mode/2up.
19. Thomas Nast, *Harper's Weekly*, last modified Apr. 29, 1865, https://archive.org/details/harpersweeklyv9bonn/page/264/mode/2up.
20. Katherine Ridgway, email to author, description of repairs to image, personal communication, Jan. 21, 2022.

10

Twelve Copper Coins from Two Little Boys

Erik Goldstein

Could there be a more appropriate thing to place in a cornerstone or time capsule than a thoughtfully chosen coin? Not in my opinion. They are almost always dated and are a cultural reflection of those who selected them for inclusion. The fact that coins were placed in the cornerstone entombed in the Massachusetts State House in 1795 by Samuel Adams and Paul Revere shows they thought so too.[1] No one should have been surprised to see American coins when the contents of the copper box found in the Lee Monument were revealed after 134 years.

A dense parcel of coins, wrapped in grungy paper and bound with crumbling twine, emerged from the coffer with its explanatory label still attached. Inked onto the back of half a business card are the words:

> 12 Copper Coins to Lee Monument from Charles E. Harwood + Walter B. Harwood
> Two little boys who love to revere the memory of R E Lee

True to the inscription, a dozen copper coins, each enveloped in its own scrap of paper, emerged from the outer wrapper. Thinking back to the America of 1887, one might expect these twelve to have been skimmed from the cream of the United States Mint's superb product line. Perhaps some specially made, proof 1887-dated cents, with surfaces as reflective as a new mirror?

Nope. In place of intrinsically or aesthetically notable examples, twelve large coppers, all well-worn, were revealed as the surprisingly modest contents of the young Harwood's cornerstone contribution. Bearing different

Figure 30. Note on business card by the Harwoods, obverse and reverse.

dates between 1798 and 1845, they are all "large cents" produced by the US Mint from 1793 to 1857 and represent all five designs struck during the time spanned by the assemblage.[2]

The same Congressional Act which sought to end the use of foreign silver coins in the United States also brought an end to the large cent.[3] In its place came newly designed smaller coins, of the same size as the current cent. First struck in copper-nickel and bearing an image of a flying eagle, they were followed by the iconic "Indian Head Penny" in 1859, produced in huge numbers for the next half century. This latter type was the "cent of the realm" in late-1880s Richmond, the world of the Harwood family.

When wrapped up for inclusion in the monument, the large cents had been superseded for thirty years and had all but disappeared from circulation. The Harwood brothers likely never had the occasion to spend such a cent in their boyish lives.

Their father, Charles W. Harwood, was a Confederate veteran of the Civil War who had served with the First Virginia Artillery and the Commissary Department.[4] Afterward, he married, started a family, and worked as a freight agent for the Southern railway, whose halved business card served as a label for the bundle of coins. If one assumes the Harwoods were a typical middle-class family in late-nineteenth-century Richmond, it is easy to understand why the offerings of their sons Charles E., age thirteen, and Walter, age eight, are unpretentious. Carefully collected, neatly packaged-up, individually labeled, and bound with a loving dedication, these worn out, old-fashioned "big pennies" represent the treasured collection of a pair of kids, though perhaps not "little boys" by either 1887 or 2022 standards.[5]

As a coin collector since early childhood, I instantly knew what these dozen coins represented from their father's label. I've been enamored with large cents since my grandfather showed me one from 1838 when I was only five or six years old. He explained the ancient coin in my hand was a huge version of the beloved "penny," and I was permanently hooked. The last large cent acquired for my personal collection came in March of 2022, proving my lust for them remains undiminished over fifty years.

Charlie Harwood, his younger brother Walt, and I are in good company. Americans—and even some Europeans—have been collecting large cents since the time they were current. Appearing in 1793, they were the first coins struck for circulation by the United States Mint and there is even a national club dedicated to their collecting, preservation, and study. One might say the large cent has its own cult following.

Today, the choicest rarities can bring well over a million dollars,[6] and many of the "mint condition" eighteenth-century large cents can be traced back to European collections.[7] Though examples were surely sold at auction in America earlier, the first "date set" of large cents was offered in 1858, when Philadelphia coin dealer Edward Cogan sold his personal collection.[8] That was the year after the last large cent popped off the coining press.

But the assemblage of these fresh-faced brothers was much humbler than those gathered by well-monied nineteenth-century numismatists. With a face value of one one-hundredth of a dollar, the ubiquitous cent could be collected for a minimal investment in 1887, just as it can be in 2022. No doubt that is why they were pursued by novice collectors, with the principal challenge lying in chasing and acquiring examples of needed dates or specific

Figure 31. Coins, individual wrappings, group wrapping, note, and twine donated to the Lee cornerstone box by the Harwoods.

varieties. The hunt is enjoyable, but success gives greater satisfaction, especially when shared with those who suffer the same affliction.

The Harwood coins bear the dates 1798, 1814, 1818, 1819, 1820, 1826, 1831, 1833, 1839, 1841, and 1845. Only one battered penny, probably struck in the late 1810s, has an illegible date. The 1814 specimen stands out, not just because it is in relatively good condition, but because it is of the rarest type in the collection. Nicknamed the "Classic Head" variety, it was only struck from 1808 until 1814, with a mere 357,830 examples made during its last year of production. By comparison with other dates in the Harwood group, one can get an idea of the 1814's scarcity; 1,841,745 cents were struck in 1798 and 4,407,550 were produced in 1820.[9] For scale, compare that to the number of cents emitted by the US Mint in 2021; about 7,908,620,000.[10] Yes, that is billions, not millions.

Were these dozen examples all the boys had, or do they represent duplicate examples? And why are there no coins made between 1846 and 1857, the large cent's final twelve years? We'll probably never know why the Harwood brothers chose to donate their collection in memory of Robert E. Lee. Or why Mr. W. B.

Isaacs, the Grand Secretary of the Grand Lodge of Virginia Masons,[11] accepted the bundle of coins for inclusion into the cornerstone of the Lee Monument.

Perhaps the answer is simple; the gift of the "little boys'" coin collection was judged a nostalgic, sincere, and heartwarming tribute. No doubt, until his death in 1955,[12] every time Walter Harwood passed the Lee Monument, he thought of the modest boyhood penny collection he and his long-dead brother had placed deep within its pedestal.[13]

NOTES

1. Mike Unser, "1795 Boston Time Capsule Contents Revealed in MFA Photos," *Coin News*, January 9, 2015.
2. R. S. Yeoman, *Official Red Book* [formally entitled *A Guide Book of United States Coins 2022*] (Whittman Publishing, LLC 2021), 96–105.
3. "A Century of Lawmaking for a New Nation: U.S. Congressional Documents and Debates, 1774–1875," *Library of Congress American Memory*, http://memory.loc.gov/cgi-bin/ampage?collId=llsl&fileName=011/llsl011.db&recNum=184.
4. "Charles W. Harwood," *fold3*, https://www.fold3.com/image/8419180?terms=civil,us,harwood,w,war,charles.
5. "Charles W. Harwood," *fold3*, https://www.fold3.com/image/8419180?terms=civil,us,harwood,w,war,charles; Pvt Charles W. Harwood (1836–1896)—Find a Grave Memorial.
6. Greg Reynolds, "Coin Rarities & Related Topics: 1793 Cent Sets $1.38 Million Auction Record for Copper Coin," *Coin Week*, January 9, 2012, https://coinweek.com/auctions-news/coin-rarities-related-topics-1793-cent-sets-1-38-million-auction-record-for-a-copper-coin/.
7. Ron Guth, "The Lord St. Oswald Coins—Where Are They Now? Part VIII," *PCGS Newsletter* 15, no. 21 (2015), https://milled.com/pcgs/the-lord-st-oswald-coins-where-are-they-now-FNz5vQ-V_LHNg3eA.
8. Edward Cogan, *Priced Catalogue of the Private Collection of the United States Cents, The Property of Edward Cogan, Sold at His Store by Private Biddings, the 1st November 1858* (Philadelphia: Edward Cogan, 1863).
9. R. S. Yeoman, *Official Red Book* [formally entitled *A Guide Book of United States Coins 2022*] (Florence, AL: Whitman Publishing, 2021), 96–105.
10. Mike Unser, "U.S. Coin Production Closed in on 14.5 Billion in 2021," *Coin News*, January 21, 2022.
11. "Masonic Relics Discovered!," *The Magpie Mason*, https://themagpiemason.blogspot.com/2021/12/masonic-relics-discovered.html.
12. "Walter B. Harwood," *Find a Grave*, https://www.findagrave.com/memorial/100059898/walter-b-harwood.
13. "Charles E. Harwood," *Find a Grave*, https://www.findagrave.com/memorial/93881196/charles-e-harwood.

11

Reconciliation and Reconstruction in Two Carved Objects

Laura Galke and Lea Lane

Two carved wooden memorial objects, created by the same hand, were carefully enclosed in an envelope and placed within the copper box ceremonially laid beneath the Lee Monument cornerstone. Contributed by a J. W. Talley, both of these tiny items were intended to be viewed in three dimensions: the front, sides, and back are highly detailed. One represents the Confederate battle flag, and the other represents the square and compasses: the emblem of the fraternity of Freemasonry. Not only were these objects symbols of their time, but the very material from which they were carved was deeply meaningful. This chapter explores new research into the artifacts and likely identity of the artist, while also considering the social context and evolving meaning of these symbols over time.

The outside of the envelope that contained these two wooden objects included a handwritten note:

> Battle flag + square + compass
> made from the tree that was
> taken from Jacksons Grave in
> Lexington, Va.
> by
> Capt. J. W. Talley

Humans have long recognized that the roots and branches of trees serve as silent observers of the history that plays out under their canopies.[1] They are

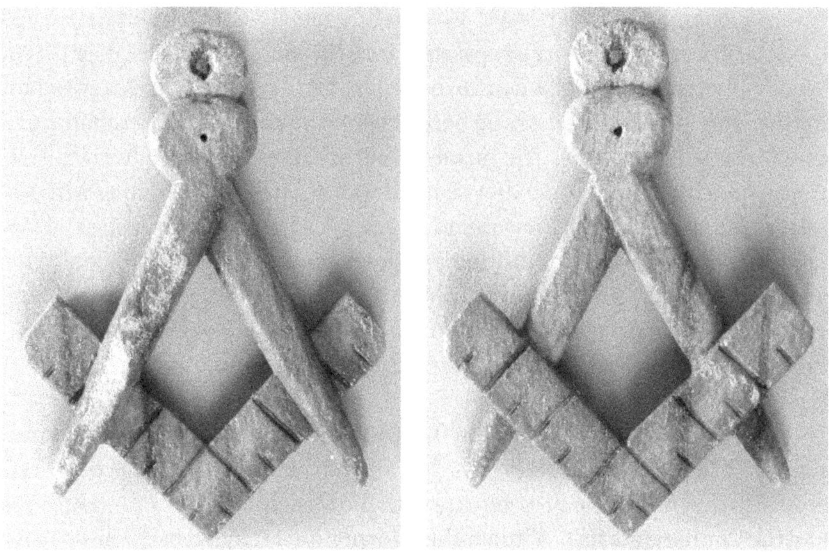

Figure 32. Carved square and compasses from the Lee Statue cornerstone box, obverse and reverse.

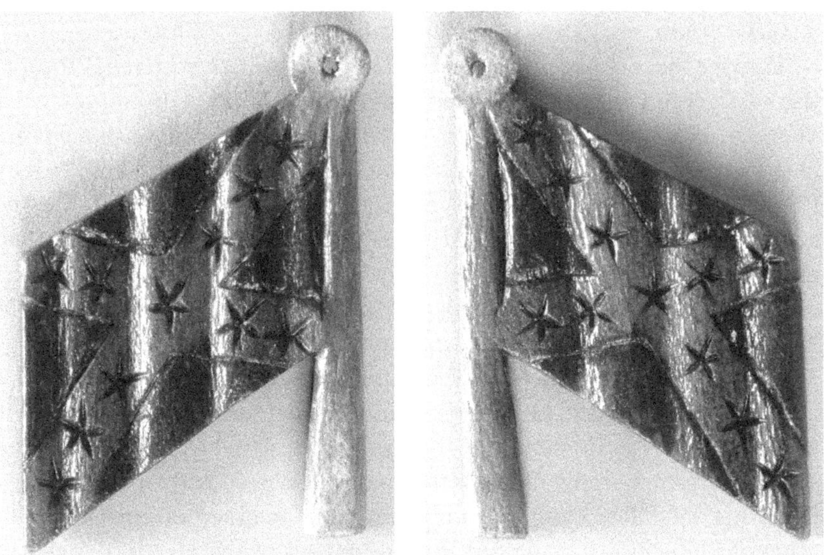

Figure 33. Carved Confederate battle flag from the Lee Monument cornerstone box, obverse and reverse.

revered as enduring witnesses. However, some Civil War soldiers turned these "witness trees" into relics even before the smoke of battles dissipated. Woody plants, especially when shredded by artillery fire, were easy fodder for the busy knives of soldiers on both sides of the conflict, who transformed them into smoking pipes, rings, and other small carvings. Indeed, the enthusiasm with which the soldiers carved was described at the time with obsessive language: mania, disease, rage, fever.[2] The soft consistency and low melting point of lead ammunition provided another medium to satisfy this addictive activity. Soldiers carved objects to kill time, to accompany tobacco consumption, to earn money, to thank others, to commemorate fallen comrades, and to have something material to return home to their family even if the soldier did not.

The objects they made were inextricably linked to the events and landscapes of their experience—even if the carving themselves had no visible reference to that origin. Such is the case with the Masonic square and compasses and the Confederate flag. Without the information included in the newspaper coverage of the dedication, they are potent symbols. With the knowledge of their connection to General Thomas Jonathan "Stonewall" Jackson's burial site, they assume a more complex identity, bound tightly with their potent material origin.

The tree that grew beside General Jackson's grave in Lexington, Virginia, was a *Paulonia imperialis*, commonly known as a Princess or Empress tree. They are native to China and burst forth with lavish foxglove-like flowers in the spring. They grow rather quickly.[3] Although only planted in 1864, by 1884 it had noticeably disturbed the burial site. The root system of this tree aggressively spreads during the early years of growth. Reports from the 1884 removal note how the "roots had gone directly to the coffin and embraced, by curious curves and bendings, the body."[4] It had embraced General Jackson in its growth—less of a witness tree, and more of an active guardian.

The sexton of the cemetery, W. C. Charlton, oversaw the removal of the tree (and the relocation of Jackson's and his daughters' graves under a new monument later in the century). He gave a cane carved from the tree and a portion of the remaining Empress tree material to Reverend John J. Lafferty. From this wood, Rev. Lafferty made or commissioned several objects sent to "men who honor the memory" of Jackson: at least two gavels, and one acorn, which are now in the collection of the American Civil War Museum.[5]

It is certainly possible that Reverend Lafferty also commissioned the carvings that were included in the cornerstone box. The report on the box

Figure 34. General Lee's last visit to Stonewall Jackson's Grave, 1872, by Louis Eckhardt. The tree is visible to the left of Jackson's grave marker. (Courtesy of Library of Congress)

only notes the source of the wood and the donor's name, one J. W. Talley, not how he obtained the material or finished items. Perhaps Captain Talley was among those identified by Reverend Lafferty as "men who honor the memory" of Jackson.

Although research pinpointed a couple of potential candidates for "Capt. J.W. Talley," the strongest option is Captain John Winn "Jack" Talley (1844–1902), who served with the Third Virginia Cavalry. Talley's whereabouts are consistent with having access to the Empress tree and potentially witnessing the Lee cornerstone box dedication ceremony. After the war, Talley became a well-known river captain and railroad conductor who later enjoyed a career as a hotel proprietor in Lexington and Buena Vista, Virginia. He was in the Lexington area in the years immediately after the removal of the tree from Jackson's gravesite and thus may have obtained a portion of the revered Empress tree wood. A newspaper account documents his visit to Richmond at the end of September 1887, less than one month prior to the Lee Monument cornerstone box dedication.[6]

In 1897, he was the commander of the Blue Ridge Camp, United Confederate Veterans, at Buena Vista, Virginia.[7] His post-war veteran activity may have also included riding with General Fitzhugh Lee at the dedication of the Confederate Soldiers and Sailors Monument in Richmond in 1894.[8] John W. Talley was a highly ranked Freemason, an appropriate background for the donor of this potent symbol of the Freemasons. In fact, the square and compasses is prominently carved on his Buena Vista, Virginia gravestone.

Why were these particular symbols important to those preparing for the statue's construction? In the decade preceding the American Civil War, Freemasonry grew popular, one of a number of fraternal societies. Men boasted their membership during peacetime by wearing the square and compasses on their lapels and watch chains. The square and compasses represent stonemason's tools and reminded members to behave in accordance with the high standards of Freemasonry.

During the Civil War, wearing Masonic pins signaled membership in this ancient fraternity, characterized by clandestine rituals and popular among soldiers of both armies. When worn as part of a uniform, embellishing rustic living quarters, or carved onto clothing accessories or pipes, these symbols entitled the owners to the privileges of this fraternal brotherhood. A system of signs, gestures, and signals notified others of their membership, overtly or covertly, as the situation warranted. This was no trifling club: displaying this symbol was an informal request by members for accommodation from fellow members—including enemy combatants—who had taken a solemn Masonic oath to provide comfort to any fellows in distress and to provide for their surviving families. Numerous examples of soldiers helping one another have survived.[9]

The Confederate battle flag, commissioned by General Pierre Beauregard and designed by William Porcher Miles, was an interesting subject for Captain Talley to carve and memorialize in the cornerstone box. The flag used the X-shaped pattern of the St. Andrew's Cross and was emblazoned with twelve stars representing each seceding state. The flag answered a desperate need for a distinctive banner around which to rally troops during the confusion of combat: at the First Battle of Manassas, soldiers on both sides were hampered by a lack of familiar emblems to coordinate their movements and rallies. The bold red color punctuated with the deep blue St. Andrew's Cross was a combination that proved to be distinctive and was first used by the Confederate army of Northern Virginia. Variations of the flag were used in other battle flags as well. In 1863, the symbol was incorporated into the Confederate national flag. Although it was popular, the flag was never adopted as the Confederacy's official symbol. The carving differs from the Confederate battle flag in that it exhibits eleven stars, not thirteen as seen in the flag design, possibly the result of the size of the carving.

At the time these items were enshrined within the Lee Monument in 1887, the "New South" embraced a revisionist history of the Civil War, in which supporters rejected that slavery was the root cause of the war. Some scholars refer to this period, from the late 1880s to the 1920s, as the "Vindication of the Confederacy" phase of reimagining the Civil War.[10] The modest obelisks that quietly adorned cemeteries in the decade after the Civil War had evolved into large statues portraying prominent Confederate military leaders in public spaces, such as courthouse grounds and state capital lawns. These public monuments bolstered the Lost Cause version of Civil War history that imagined benevolent slavery, the supremacy of Confederate military leadership, and promoted White racial supremacy.

The carved flag, and square and compasses, were placed in the cornerstone box as objects literally rooted in the figure of General Jackson, shaped into forms that projected fraternity with military and civilian groups. These items were material manifestations of brotherhood after an era of discord and preceding a future marred by segregation. Captain Talley's identity as both a Mason and Confederate soldier rooted his identity in a society that was rapidly changing: outlawing slavery and granting voting rights to all men. As the twentieth century approached, the Lost Cause ideology grew through such visible emblems and potent public monuments. These carved objects represented a material connection to imagined brotherhoods that were neither equitable nor truly fraternal.

As pieces of material culture, their meaning has changed over time, and their messages remain powerful. As communities consider the future of existing statues and the creation of new memorials, they do so with the knowledge that monuments are not passive objects, but actively inspire, discipline, and guide all who encounter them, with meanings that differ among viewers and change over time.

NOTES

1. "Witness Trees," *American Battlefield Trust*, last modified April 16, 2020, https://www.battlefields.org/learn/head-tilting-history/witness-trees; Mike Yessis, "These Five 'Witness Trees' Were Present at Key Moments in America's History," *Smithsonian Magazine*, last modified August 25, 2017, https://www.smithsonianmag.com

/travel/these-five-witness-trees-were-present-at-key-moments-in-americas-history -180963925/.

2. *Cambridge Chronicle*, May 3, 1862; L. E. Cowles, *History of the Fifth Massachusetts Battery* (Boston: L. E. Cowles, 1902); James Madison Drake, *The History of the Ninth New Jersey Veteran Volunteers* (Elizabeth, NJ: Journal Printing House, 1889); *History of the 1st Illinois Light Artillery* (Chicago: Cushing, 1899).
3. A recent study found a twenty-year-old Princess tree in Kentucky that had already reached a diameter of 20 inches, and a height of 62 feet. Christopher R. Webster, Michael A. Jenkins, and Shibu Jose, "Woody invaders and the challenges they pose to forest ecosystems in the eastern United States," *Journal of Forestry* 104 (7), (2006): 366–74.
4. Monroe, Louisiana *Daily Telegraph*, June 2, 1886.
5. Vicksburg, Mississippi *Weekly Commercial Herald,* April 23, 1886; Indianapolis *Indiana State Sentinel*, Jun 16, 1886; *The Norfolk Landmark*, December 4, 1890.
6. *Richmond Dispatch*, September 30, 1887.
7. *Confederate Military History* 3 (1899): 1197.
8. "Unveiling of the Soldiers' and Sailors' Monument," *Southern Historical Society Papers* 22 (1894): 343.
9. Michael A. Halleran. *The Better Angels of Our Nature: Freemasonry in the American Civil War* (Tuscaloosa: University of Alabama Press, 2011), 160–66.
10. Thomas J. Brown, *Civil War Monuments and the Militarization of America*. (Chapel Hill: University of North Carolina Press, 2019).

Biography of a Contribution

The Nolting Note

Maggie Creech

How many of you contributed to a time capsule as a kid? That feeling of excitement, the hope that future communities might marvel at the treasures inside? Whether or not the individuals that placed something inside the Lee Monument Cornerstone Box thought that it might one day be uncovered is a question for another chapter, but an 1887 issue of the *Richmond Dispatch* did print an inventory for interested parties. The inventory listed a "Master Nolting—$10 Confederate Note."[1] However, it did not mention the letter included with the currency, which reads:

Richmond Oct 25th/87
Mr. W. B. Isaacs

Dear Sir—

My Son a Lad of 10 years is very anxious to contribute to the Lee Monument Corner Stone and therefore enclosed you will please find a Confederate note $10—date /64 which please have deposited—and you will ever oblige

Yours Respectfully
Geo. A Nolting

Who was the father that wrote this note, and the son to whom he refers? George Augustus Nolting, Sr. (c. 1837–1900) was a Richmond native identified as a hardware merchant living at 607 North Tenth Street in the 1880 Federal Census. A two-year-old son, George Augustus Nolting, Jr. (c. 1877–1956)

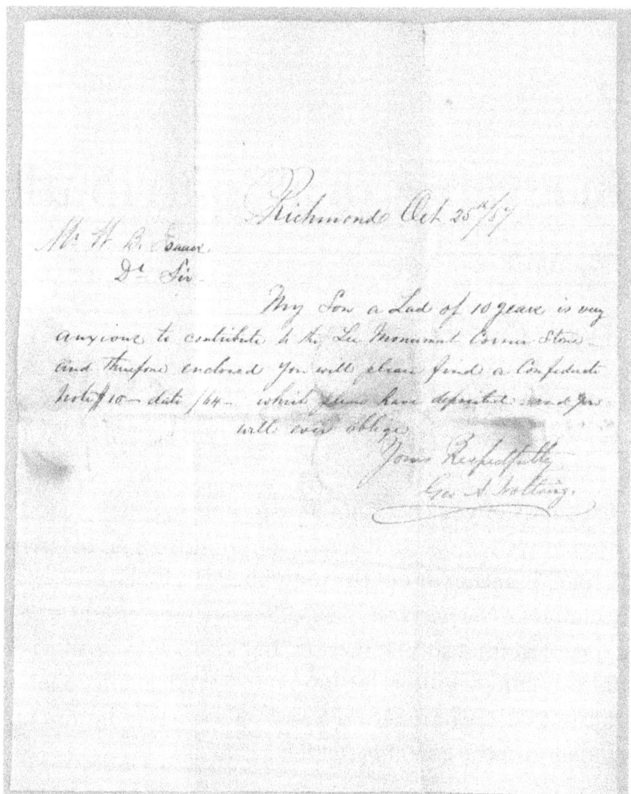

Richmond Oct 25th/67

Mr H. B. [illegible]

Dr Sir

My Son a Lad of 10 years is very anxious to contribute to the Lee Monument Corner Stone and therefore enclosed you will please find a Confederate Note $10— date /64— which please have deposited and you will ever oblige

Yours Respectfully

Geo A Nolting.

Figure 35. Letter from George Nolting from the Lee cornerstone box.

is also listed on the census, putting him at the right age to be son mentioned in this letter—but more on him later.[2]

George A. Nolting, Sr. served in the Confederate army as a sergeant in the Confederate Old First Virginian Infantry, Company H, according to a pension report filed by his widow, as well as several newspaper listings.[3] Toward the end of the war, Union soldiers captured Nolting and held him as a prisoner of war at Point Lookout, Maryland. A May 24, 1865 letter he wrote while still held at Point Lookout details his plans to take the Oath of Allegiance and return home.[4] After returning to Richmond, he appears to have traveled to New York to source materials for an employer before becoming his own boss and opening a hardware store with his brother in 1870.[5] They dissolved the partnership in 1875—maybe the old adage warning against mixing business and family came true, though we cannot say for certain—and each brother opened their

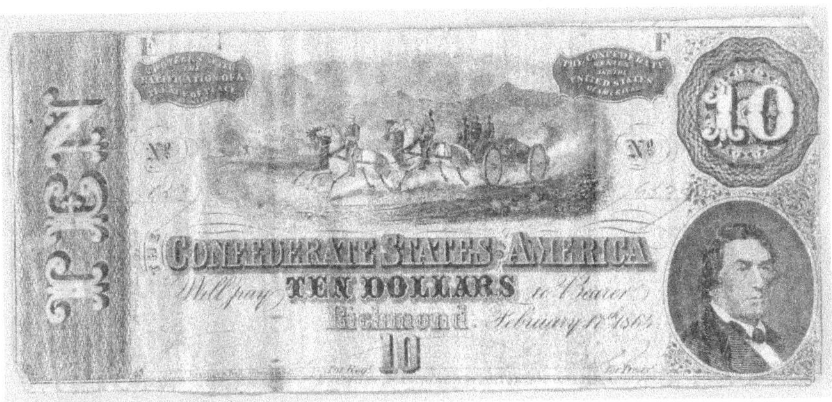

Figure 36. Confederate ten dollar note issued in 1864.

own store. Unfortunately, Nolting declared bankruptcy in 1876.[6] Toward the end of his life, he appears to have worked as a bookkeeper at the Richmond Iron Works.[7] After his death in 1900, the *Richmond Dispatch* mentioned Nolting on a list of individuals who "held high places in the public regard, and who were important figures in the social and business life of the city."[8]

Clearly this social prominence carried over to his children. George A. Nolting, Jr.'s name appears frequently in Richmond newspapers of the early twentieth century, noting his involvement in various social groups, such as the Male Choral Society of Richmond and the press committee for a convention dedicated to the Brotherhood of Saint Andrew, a men's religious organization focused on bringing more men to the Episcopal Church.[9] Nolting's personal life did not escape coverage either, with the *Richmond Virginian* announcing his 1913 marriage to Constance Bates, another Richmond native.

As with many able-bodied men in the first half of the twentieth century, Nolting registered to serve in both World Wars, though doesn't appear to have served—his age may have had something to do with it, given that he been on the upper end of the draft for World War I and over the age of the draft for World War II.[10] During, in between, and after the wars he worked in various capacities for steamship companies such as Eastern Steamship Lines and Old Dominion Steamship Company.[11] Ultimately G.A. Nolting, Jr. died at age seventy-nine on Dec. 4, 1956 from complications due to a fractured hip and was buried in Hollywood Cemetery, final resting place for many of Richmond's White elite.[12]

Figure 37. George Augustus Nolting Junior taken in 1918. (Courtesy of the Virginia Museum of History and Culture)

While this sweet note from a father advocating for his son serves as an entry point into learning more about the lives of these two men as individuals, it also reveals one of the main purposes of Confederate monuments—that the glorification of the men represented, and the ideas of the Confederate States of America, would live on in future generations. In Jefferson Davis's Farewell Address, delivered to the Senate Chamber at the US Capitol on January 21, 1861, he states a reason for secession as follows: "This is done not in hostility to others, not to injure any section of the country, not even for our own pecuniary benefit; but from the high and solemn motive of defending and protecting the rights we inherited, and which it is our sacred duty to transmit unshorn to our children."[13] Despite the surrender of the Confederate States of America, this quote emblazoned the 1907 Jefferson Davis Monument erected several blocks down Monument Avenue from the Robert E. Lee Monument.

"*Transmit unshorn to our children*"—What better way to communicate these ideals than a citywide celebration of the installation of the Lee Monument, lending it legitimacy and tacit approval from political and social leaders? What better way to create a sense of Southern pride, and clear continuation of Confederate ideology, than to include donations from children? George A. Nolting, Jr. was not the only child to donate to the cornerstone box. The inventory also includes Charles E. and Walter B. Harwood—"two little boys who love to revere the memory of Lee"—and their contribution of twelve copper coins (chapter 10).[14] Here I ask readers to consider the perspective of a young boy, staring at the monumental Lee statue, surrounded by friends and family, feeling the pride of contributing to such a celebratory and important day for the City of Richmond.

Sociopolitical groups like the United Daughters of the Confederacy in late nineteenth and early twentieth century Jim Crow Virginia recognized the power of children to carry narratives through to a new generation. The United Daughters of the Confederacy (UDC) formed in 1894 with a stated mission of "the objects of this Association are educational, memorial, literary, social and benevolent; to collect and preserve the material for a truthful history of the war between the Confederate States and the United States of America; to honor the memory of those who served and those who fell in the service of the Confederate States."[15]

This manifested in the funding of Confederate monuments, such as the Jefferson Davis Monument on Monument Avenue, as well as a dedication to (mis)educating students about the history of the Civil War and the institution of slavery. They did this through informal education in groups like their Children of the Confederacy organization, which welcomed youth under eighteen who could trace their ancestry to someone who served in the Confederacy. The Children of the Confederacy learned patriotic songs and ceremonies, and would often be incorporated at monument unveilings or veteran events.[16] In addition, the Children of the Confederacy focused on memorization of Lost Cause tenets focused on portraying enslaved workers as faithful and devoted, the North as aggressive and unjust, and the cause of the Civil War as the defense of states' rights. Manly's Battery Chapter, out of Raleigh, North Carolina, published a pamphlet entitled *Lincoln as the South Should Know Him*. This publication asserts, "he gave the North dominion over the South. He carried out Northern ideals of centralism, imperialism. The Southern ideal, States rights, home rule . . . met destruction at his hands." It calls Southerners (the reader must note that Black individuals are not considered to be Southerners, despite generations living and laboring in the area) "the purest-blooded branch of the sane and virile Anglo-Saxon race." Finally, the pamphlet charges Lincoln with unleashing "four million savages . . . in our very midst, against our defenseless women and children."[17]

While this rhetoric was employed at Children of the Confederacy meetings, it was not confined to them. The UDC's reach also extended to formal classroom education. In 1908, the UDC created an office of historian-general who was charged, in part, with reviewing textbooks for distribution throughout the South. In 1919, historian-general Mildred Lewis Rutherford created a document called "A Measuring Rod to Test Text Books, and Reference Books in Schools, Colleges and Libraries." Guidelines included, "Reject a book that says the South fought to hold her slaves" and "Reject a book that speaks of the slaveholder of the South as cruel and unjust to his slaves."[18] Again, it is easy to understand how a child surrounded by this content, taught by adults who he or she is meant to love and respect, could grow up with a foundational misinterpretation of Southern slaveholding culture, the Civil War, and Reconstruction.

The efforts of the UDC are not surprising—as Victoria Ott states, "Southern daughters who came of age in the Confederacy held tight to the gender ideals and racial ordering of the slaveholding culture."[19] Ideas instilled at a young age can be difficult to shake free, and often beget a cycle wherein one generation grows older and works to replicate their belief system in the next. Caroline Janney sums this up with the statement, "Through their textbook campaigns, scholarship funds, and library funds, the UDC encouraged the next generation of White Southerners to demonstrate pride in their White Southern heritage in an effort to quell the political, social, and cultural changes unleashed by the war, emancipation, Reconstruction, and the industrializing society around them."[20]

When we reflect back on the story of a young George Augustus Nolting, Jr., it is easy to understand how a seemingly innocuous donation to a cornerstone box can mean so much more—how it can be indicative of a culture of Lost Cause nostalgia and generational misunderstandings. Though discussions of Confederate monuments have been ongoing since installation, renewed discussions around Richmond's monuments since 2017 have brought to light these misunderstandings and misinterpretations. And, as we think forward to current and future generations of young Virginians, it is clear to see that we must do a better job in building a more equitable, more truthful tomorrow.

NOTES

1. "*Richmond Dispatch*, October 26, 1887," *Chronicling America*, last modified October 26, 1887, https://chroniclingamerica.loc.gov/lccn/sn85038614/1887-10-26/ed-1/seq-1/.
2. "1880 United State Census, Henrico, Virginia, United States 'George A. Nolting,'" *Family Search*, FamilySearch.org.
3. "2120 Hanover Ave," *Richmond Narratives*, last modified November 22, 2019, https://richmondnarratives.com/2120-hanover-2/.

4. George A. Nolting to unidentified addressee, May 24, 1865, Virginia Historical Society Research Library.
5. George A. Nolting to John W. Bradbury, 1866, Virginia Historical Society Research Library; "The Daily Dispatch", *Chronicling America*, last modified September 2, 1870, https://chroniclingamerica.loc.gov/lccn/sn84024738/1870-09-02/ed-1/seq-4/.
6. "The Daily Dispatch," *Chronicling America*, last modified June 27, 1876, https://chroniclingamerica.loc.gov/lccn/sn84024738/1876-06-27/ed-1/seq-1/.
7. "2120 Hanover Ave," 4.
8. "Richmond Dispatch," *Chronicling America*, last modified January 1, 1901, https://chroniclingamerica.loc.gov/lccn/sn85038614/1901-01-01/ed-1/seq-8/.
9. "The Richmond Virginian," *Chronicling America*, last modified December 16, 1917, https://chroniclingamerica.loc.gov/lccn/sn90052005/1917-12-16/ed-1/seq-18/; *Richmond Dispatch*, October 11, 1900, https://chroniclingamerica.loc.gov/lccn/sn85038614/1900-10-11/ed-1/seq-1/.
10. "'United States World War I Draft Registration Cards, 1917–1918,' 'George Augustus Nolting, Jr.,'" *Family Search*, FamilySearch.org; "'United States World War II Draft Registration Cards, 1942,' 'George Augustus Nolting, Jr.,'" *Family Search*, FamilySearch.org.
11. 1920 United State Census, 1920, Richmond, Henrico, Virginia, United States, "George A. Nolting, Jr.," *Family Search*, FamilySearch.org.
12. "Virginia Department of Health; Richmond, Virginia; Virginia Deaths, 1912–2014". *Family Search*, FamilySearch.org.
13. Jefferson Davis, "Jefferson Davis Farewell Address," transcript of a speech delivered at the Senate Chamber, U.S. Capitol, January 21, 1861, *Rice University* last modified January 21, 1861, https://jeffersondavis.rice.edu/archives/documents/jefferson-davis-farewell-address.
14. *Richmond Dispatch*, October 26, 1887.
15. United Daughters of the Confederacy, "Constitution of the United Daughters of the Confederacy," *Encyclopedia Virginia*, last modified 1895, https://encyclopediavirginia.org/entries/confederacy-constitution-of-the-united-daughters-of-the-1895/.
16. Caroline Janney, "United Daughters of the Confederacy," *Encyclopedia Virginia*, last modified March 3, 2023, https://encyclopediavirginia.org/entries/united-daughters-of-the-confederacy/.
17. O. W. Blacknall, *Lincoln as the South Should Know Him,* (Raleigh, NC: Manly's Battery Chapter, Children of the Confederacy, 1915), 12, 18, 22.
18. Mildred L Rutherford, *A Measuring Rod to Test Text Books, And Reference Books In Schools, Colleges and Libraries* (Athens, GA: United Confederate Veterans, 1919), 5.
19. Victoria E. Ott, "Love in Battle," in *Children and Youth During the Civil War Era*, ed. James Marten (New York: New York University Press, 2012), 125.
20. United Daughters of the Confederacy, "Constitution of the United Daughters of the Confederacy."

13

Virginia is for Huguenot Lovers

Laura Lavernia

On a cold, bleak day in December of 2021, a crew charged with removing the Lee Monument pedestal finally found what they thought to be the long-sought-after cornerstone box. A large granite stone containing a small metal box was removed and rushed over to the conservation lab at the Virginia Department of Historic Resources. After painstakingly opening the box, DHR conservators Kate Ridgway and Chelsea Blake ultimately revealed the contents of the box. None of the items inside matched newspaper listings of the contents of the cornerstone box that was placed and dedicated on October 27, 1887. Soon it was surmised that this was not "the" cornerstone box from 1887 but *another* box.

The box's contents, wet from condensation, included: an 1875 almanac; a plumbing supply catalog; a silver 1887 British Victorian penny; an envelope with a photo of master stonemason James Netherwood (1834–1899), made by Virginia Artists Studio; an 1888 brochure by Collinson Pierrepont Edwards Burgwyn (1852–1915) titled *Civil Engineer of the Natural Advantages and Water Power Facilities of the City of Manchester and the County of Chesterfield with Accompanying Maps.* Unlike the cornerstone box that held items related to the Civil War, the Lost Cause, Freemasons, and life in Virginia, the contents of the lead box documented the builders of this monument—and this particular box served as a vanity project for Netherwood and Burgwyn. All of the contents made sense, except for one final historic inclusion: a copy of the 1889 book *The Huguenot Lovers: A Tale of the Old Dominion* by Collinson Pierrepont Edwards Burgwyn, A.B., C.E., M. Am., Soc. C.E.

I immediately decided I absolutely, positively, *had* to read this novel. Mr.

Figure 38. The 1889 book, *The Huguenot Lovers: A Tale of the Old Dominion,* by Collinson Pierrepont Edwards Burgwyn, was removed from the Lee Monument time capsule on December 22, 2021.

Burgwyn was the consulting engineer for the monument; but was it possible that a civil engineer could also pen a "bodice-ripper" romance novel? *This is good stuff*, I thought, so I sat down with a large matcha latte in hand and read an original scan of the book available for free on Google Books[1]—and so began my introduction to the tidy literary oeuvre of C. P. E. Burgwyn.

The story is an amorous tale of courtship between a young woman of the Bostonian elite and a former Confederate General. The couple not only suffer the slings and arrows of love itself but also manage to wound each other with words. They wield their merciless tongues and sharp wits as weapons in the latest struggle of North vs. South—their courtship. Our heroine—Ms. Edyth Prescott—is brought to Richmond by her father so she may learn about his native city. This Southern sojourn ends up being more than she bargained for. But no spoilers here. That said, it should be noted, that the ending of *The Huguenot Lovers* is both sudden and ambiguous—and open to interpretation.

The first paragraph of the Preface explains how and why the book came to be: "In the Autumn of 1888, the Author was engaged in assisting at the transferring of the Monitor fleet from City Point to an anchorage near Richmond, Va. After the heavy vessels were under way, there was an interval of several hours each day, in which he had no duties to perform, and it was during that brief respite from the demands of a busy professional career that most of the pages were written."

The novel is very much of its time. There are good aspects, but Burgwyn also uses racist characterizations of people as did many White authors of the period. However, it is still an interesting portrait of Richmond after the Civil War. The Colonel takes our young heroine on carriage rides and introduces her to Libby Prison, the James River, and other sites around the former Capital of the Confederacy. I don't know if I would choose Libby Prison as one of my destinations for an evening rendezvous, as it was a location where much human misery ensued during the Civil War—but Burgwyn clearly wanted to make a point about the South and dispel "rumors" here. It is oft said that all art is autobiographical. The book was not just the dalliance of a bored Southern engineer between projects. C. P. E. Burgwyn was a Southerner, yes, but also a Harvard graduate whose mother (Anna Greenough Burgwyn) belonged to a distinguished New England family and whose father (Henry King Burgwyn) was of New England and Southern heritage.[2] The novel captures the internal turmoil and difficulties many, including C. P. E. Burgwyn, must have felt during the war. He lost a brother (Colonel Henry K. Burgwyn) at Gettysburg, and another was wounded and captured at Cold Harbor. The book and much of his other work—both professional and para-professional—are decidedly pro-South.

C. P. E. Burgwyn was born on April 5, 1852, in Northampton County, North Carolina. Immediately following the Civil War his family moved to Boston where Burgwyn attended school, and lived, until 1877. He became a civil engineer for the US Coastal Survey, designing harbor improvements for the federal government. He won the commission for the expansion of Richmond's Hollywood Cemetery—a design compatible with the original 1848 plan by John Notman. He also supervised the installation of Richmond's first tele-

Figure 39. Portrait of C. P. E. Burgwyn, 1873. (Courtesy Harvard University Archives)

phone lines. In 1886, Burgwyn worked for the City Engineer, Wilfred Emory Cutshaw, and assisted with supervision of the construction of Richmond's city hall. The building, recently renovated, stands on Broad street and was designed by architect Elijah E. Myers in the High Victorian Gothic style. Burgwyn also worked on several mammoth public works projects along the James River.

The novel takes its title from its final setting: the Huguenot Springs Hotel. Located in Powhatan County, Huguenot Springs is a twelve-acre rural property once popular as a summer resort where Richmonders took in the waters at nearby sulfur springs. The Huguenot Springs Mining Company constructed the original hotel between 1847 and 1850. Curiously, John Notman designed the hotel's landscape—a fact Burgwyn would have known. The landscape was an ample bowling green with a semicircular driveway directly in front of the three-story wood frame hotel with wraparound porches. Cottages located along the carriage lane provided additional accommodations. A very popular location for antebellum socials, balls, and dances, the hotel also served as a Confederate hospital during the Civil War. In the post-war era, the hotel was once again a site of social activity, visited by many. Robert E. Lee and other notable Confederates served on the hotel's board. The three-story hotel burned down in 1890, and today what remains are the brick outline of its foundation and one extant free-standing cottage.[3]

What compels me to write about this is not to discuss political sympathies, nor to debate the book's literary merit. As an architectural historian and preservationist, I do feel that *Huguenot Lovers* serves as a primary source providing us insight into the thoughts, opinions, and look of Richmond during a period when the city was attempting to rebuild and remarket itself as a rising beacon of the industrialized "New South." Promoters embraced ideas from the vanguard in landscape architecture, which would crystallize shortly thereafter in the City Beautiful Movement. The best example of Burgwyn's work is Monument Avenue. A National Historic Landmark (NHL), Monument Avenue is regarded as one of the best examples of the City Beautiful Movement. As stated in the NHL nomination, "when a grand avenue as a setting for the Lee Monument was proposed, it appealed to many different desires and goals. A grand avenue could provide a showcase of residences for the wealthy merchants and professionals of Richmond's changing community, lay out a modern civic centerpiece for the Richmond of the New South, and combine forces with the evolving movement to express pride in the 'Lost Cause.'"[4] Indeed, Burgwyn sings the song of Richmond in this passage, perhaps an attempt to not only expose the *Huguenot Lovers*, but also to breathe life into a city hollowed out by the ravages of a fratricidal Civil War. The engineer leaves us with a vignette:

"In all her ideas of Richmond she had imagined it a low-lying city, surrounded by flat lands and waste woods. Her surprise was great when she found it what it is. This was the city of which she had heard so much and knew so little. This long, broad street, down which the train was passing, was apparently unending, and what a beautiful park, what fine residences, and how bright the sun was reflected from the large windows. Presently the train shot into a tunnel, from which it emerged and soon came upon the long bridge across the James. What a sight to see the water breaking over the rocks and glittering like streaks of light, and how high the train was up in the air; what colossal foundries were underneath, and what a picturesque castle on top of the hill overlooking the river!"

NOTES

Editors' note: All other chapters in this book are based on artifacts from the copper cornerstone box that was placed in the Lee Monument cornerstone in October 1887.

This chapter addresses a book found in the lead container in the Lee Monument placed on or after March 1, 1889.

1. Collinson Pierrepont Edwards Burgwyn, *The Huguenot Lovers: A Tale of the Old Dominion* (Richmond, VA: Published by author) https://www.google.com/books/edition/The_Huguenot_Lovers/x8Q0AAAAMAAJ?hl=en.
2. "Biography of Collinson Pierrepont Edwards Burgwyn," *Dictionary of Virginia Biography, Library of Virginia*, https://www.lva.virginia.gov/public/dvb/bio.php?b=Burgwyn_C_P_E.
3. Virginia Department of Historic Resources (DHR) Architectural Survey Form "Huguenot Springs" (DHR ID #072-0092)
4. "Virginia Department of Historic Resources (DHR). Monument Avenue National Historic Landmark Nomination Form, 1997," *Virginia Department of Historic Resources*, https://www.dhr.virginia.gov/wp-content/uploads/2018/04/127-0174_Monument_Avenue_HD_1997_Nomination_NHL-4.pdf. For discussions of Richmond's progressive era, see Michael Chesson, *Richmond After the War, 1865–1890* (Richmond: Virginia State Library, 1981) and Kathy Edwards, Esme Howard, Toni Prawl. *Monument Avenue, History and Architecture*. (Washington, DC: HABS, National Park Service, 1992), chapter 1.

Militariana

14

Buttoning on a Navy in Haste

Brendan Burke and Patrick Boyle

The contents of time capsules are meant to convey concepts, sentiments, and even characters from one age into another. As small markers to big ideas, places, or people, we often find symbolic emblems or logos on, or even comprising, items within time capsules. A small brass button contained within the cornerstone box of the Lee Monument bore witness to a life at sea and a hidden part of the war often overlooked. Examining the button, we find an intricate design and some hints as to the life of the artifact through the war years and modification that gave it new life after the war. Embossed on the front is a fouled anchor overlaid onto crossed cannons. The design was for officers in the Confederate navy. Both anchor and cannon elements are found throughout military buttons of the past several centuries but this busy design packs together the concept of military might afloat. Below the anchor are the three letters "C S N" for the Confederate States Navy. A cable borders the design which is overlaid onto a background of fine horizontal lines. Lightly gilded, the button is small and was meant for frock cuffs or waistcoats.

While the basic design of uniforms and naval standards remained relatively unchanged from the Union to the Confederate navies, the button design demonstrated a distinct break. In 1861, regulation buttons for officers in the US Navy consisted of the federal eagle uplifted grasping a wooden stock anchor on a lined background surrounded by thirteen stars and a cable border. The eagle and anchor combination were a venerated tradition since 1775 and the loss of the eagle, the federal bird, was a conspicuous elimination. Tradition-bound sailors in the newly established Confederate navy balked at

Figure 40. Front of Bremond's naval button depicting a fouled anchor overlaying crossed cannons.

the switch from navy blue to steel gray and one wonders how the button design found acceptance.

The little button in the cornerstone box not only bore the emblem of the Confederate States Navy, but also a tale of its role in the war. Its job to adorn a cuff, or close a vest, was long over but the symbology and connection to the conflict gave the button new value in post-war years as remembrances of the war turned into a political fight against reconstruction. To explore the button's functional and allegorical roles, let us step back to the beginning of the Civil War to set the stage for a new navy and sailors in steel gray.

RICHMOND AND THE CONFEDERATE STATES NAVY

The Provisional Congress of the Confederate States of America established a navy on February 21, 1861, only eighteen days after the prototypic government's formation. Stephen Mallory was appointed as Secretary of the Navy. Formerly Chairman of the Senate Committee on Naval Affairs for the United States, Mallory arrived in Richmond in June of 1861 and began assembling his navy for war. Virginia also recognized a need for naval defenses and organized the Virginia State Navy, which ended up as a squadron within the Confederate States Navy. This role, harkening back to the Revolutionary War where colonies maintained regional navies, also challenged the concept of the federal republic.

Building a navy is no small task for any government. As many discovered, cash or credit reserves required to build, man, and maintain a fleet can be astounding. No matter how expensive, Confederate ports required protection and sea-lanes for outbound cotton and inbound war supplies which were crucial to keep the economy running. The United States Navy, under the direction of the War Department, enacted a total blockade on the Confederacy early in the conflict. Warships stationed around Southern states bottled up ports and choked trade. The Confederate navy's upstart status and limited tonnage prevented any serious threat to the US Navy. Rather, the Confederate fleet was intended to prevent important ports from capitulating to naval bombardment, interrupt the shipping of the United States, break the blockade, and demonstrate to global powers the legitimate sea power of the Confederate States.

Blue water Confederate naval aspirations were grand in scheme and on paper but a more functional role for the navy was to keep US Navy gunboats from shelling the capital of the Confederacy in Richmond. At the beginning of the war, Confederate naval defenses of the lower Chesapeake and James River centered on Norfolk.[1] The hope was to create a strong outer defense, but these hopes were dashed with the fall of Norfolk and the capture of Gosport Navy Yard in May of 1862. With the yard in flames and much of the valuable captured tonnage sitting on the bottom of the bay, what remained of the Confederate Naval forces withdrew up the James River and closer to the capital.

The residue of the Confederate navy instead formed into the James River Squadron. An ersatz flotilla of tugboats and repurposed civilian vessels armed with deck guns that sulked up and down the river to show the flag. Aboard the CSS *Patrick Henry*, flagship to the squadron, a naval academy formed to teach young officers the art of war on the water. The Yankee-built sidewheeler had served the Old Dominion Steam Ship Line as the *Yorktown* and struggled to shed her ironic name. At Rocketts, a low-lying shoreline below the city, sawmills buzzed, and hammers banged away to build real warships. Since the loss of CSS *Virginia* in 1862, the race to add ironclads to the fleet was furious. Foundries in Richmond rolled out the armor plating and lathes spun metal into revolving engine parts for hulking casemate ironclads such as CSS *Richmond*, *Fredericksburg*, and *Virginia II*. By this time, Richmond's role in the Confederacy could not have been more complete with its full complement of government and military apparatus.

BUTTONED DOWN AND BOTTLED UP

During the first half of the nineteenth century, decorative military buttons were typically cast from brass or pewter. Casting in molds allowed decorated buttons to be manufactured, but was slow, even in batch production. An amalgam of pure gold was brushed onto buttons to gild the front face, but was also a slow, hand-done process. Flat faced buttons of the eighteenth century gave way to round faced buttons, but the true innovation was die-struck buttons. Brass sheeting pressed over the die produced finer detail with higher production speeds. Button machines introduced during the midcentury sped up production and lowered costs allowing even the lowly army private a frock bedecked with shiny brass.

With the creation of the Confederate States Navy, the War Department took the opportunity to advertise their breakaway status with the color of the uniform and the change in button design. Jack tar sailors, bedecked in steel gray and officers glittering with crossed cannon and fouled anchors, were more of a dream than reality as the new government struggled to find suitable tonnage and construct warships. Due to the lengthy time to contract and build a vessel, most of the purpose-built Confederate floating force entered service late in the war. Early Confederate sailors relied heavily on captured US Naval equipment, including uniforms. Some were even reluctant to diverge from the traditional navy blue, invoking superstition of the sea that changing color would bring bad luck to their ship. Officers, required to supply their own uniforms, were more frequently clad in regulation gray and would have purchased a set of buttons from a private contractor.

As the war progressed, blockading efforts of the US Navy reduced Southern port traffic by as much as 95 percent and, with dedicated coastal bombardment, Confederate-controlled ports dwindled with each passing year. More than two dozen steam-powered ironclads patrolled Southern rivers and harbors to keep Union gunboats at bay. Thick iron plating over their casemates covered "tween" spaces reserved for ammunition, fuel, smoldering boilers, and often-underpowered steam engines. Confederate naval officers in the ironclad service more frequently dealt with bad engineering problems aboard their commands as well as desertion from a seemingly futile endeavor than other ships in the Confederate navy. Confederate sailors' alternatives to ironclad hell were life in the cruiser or gunboat service.

Nearly one hundred gunboats and a handful of cruisers carried the designation "Confederate State Ship." Gunboats were exclusively captured vessels of various designs, including mail packets and tugboats. The term merely indicated commissioned armed service for the Confederate government. Life aboard a gunboat meant frequent boredom in port as Confederate gunboats were ill equipped to steam out an inlet to face broadsides from the US Navy. Confederate sailors seeking adventure on the high seas found it more often in the cruiser service. Cruisers were designed to be fast enough to outrun the US Navy and overtake merchantmen with a pair of heavy guns or single pivot gun.

Darting out from a Southern port, cruisers hunted the seas for merchant traffic inbound and outbound from states not in rebellion. Northern cargoes, by the thousands of tons, were burned at sea, sunk, or captured as prizes of war. Interrupting trade would break the economic backbone of Uncle Sam, so the Confederate government thought, but the United States simply outproduced and out-shipped the Confederate navy's ability to have a lasting effect. Even exorbitant insurance rates for cargo and tonnage due to commerce raiding merely singed the whiskers of Yankee merchants.

One of the first ships to fly the Confederate naval jack was CSS *Florida*. While a subsequent cruiser carried the same name, the original *Florida* was a converted sidewheel packet built for the Mobile Mail Line in 1856. On April 22, 1861, *Florida* was commandeered for Confederate naval service. Taken to Lake Pontchartrain, Louisiana for refit and modification, an upper deck was removed, armor plating was added to protect machinery, and *Florida* was equipped with three guns. Lt. H. Dennis Bremond (1832–1870) was appointed as Acting Master on September 24, 1861.[2] A *New York Times* article from February 9, 1863, indicates Bremond was a commissioned officer in the US Navy prior to the war and like many of his fellow junior officers, the Civil War fast-tracked his command career.[3]

Acting Master Bremond fell into the doldrums of a blockaded warship. Daily duties involved drilling what crew was available and performing ever-present maintenance on the gunboat. After nearly six months blockaded in Mobile, CSS *Florida* fired her first shot in the war. Near Biloxi on October 19, 1861, *Florida* encountered USS *Massachusetts* and neatly placed a nine-inch projectile through its wheelhouse. The injured *Massachusetts*, with its eye poked out, broke off from the engagement.

On December 4,1861, *Florida* put USS *Montgomery* to its heels while guarding the Confederate troop ship *Pamlico*. For the ignominy of *Montgomery's* retreat, Capt. Darrah Shaw was relieved of command. In February of 1862, Bremond was transferred from CSS *Florida* briefly to the Richmond, Virginia, station. At the same time, he resigned his commission yet continued to serve with the Confederate navy. It is likely that Bremond's resignation from official service opened him up to the possibility for command of a blue water vessel, a blockade runner or privateer. However, for the time being, the War Department returned him to brown water ignominy aboard CSS *Louisiana*. Designed as a casemate ironclad to guard the lower Mississippi River, *Louisiana* was ill fated from the beginning. Problems with construction and design made the hulking ship a floating liability. *Louisiana* was prematurely commissioned, and her gun crew struggled to drill among workmen installing equipment and armament. Like many early casemate ironclads, the ship's engines could barely make way against the river current. Novel steering screws, used to force water over the rudders to induce turning, were never installed and the vessel could simply not navigate without help from tugs. Crippled, *Louisiana* was tied to the bank.[4]

When US Flag Officer David Farragut led assaults on fortifications of the lower Mississippi, *Louisiana* found itself stuck in the middle of the fray. After firing a dozen feeble shots, the ship was burned by her officers to prevent capture. In the fray, Acting Master Dennis Bremond was given permission by Capt. Mitchell, along with a number of other officers, to abandon ship and avoid capture. The perceptible loss of command ability within the Confederacy outshone any illusions of valor by going down with the ship.[5]

From the smoldering remains of CSS *Louisiana*, the Confederate naval command ordered Bremond back to Richmond aboard CSS *Patrick Henry* for temporary duty. Almost immediately, he was reassigned to CSS *Chattahoochee* in Saffold, Georgia. Lt. Catesby Jones, superintendent of the conversion of the famed ironclad CSS *Virginia*, oversaw *Chattahoochee's* construction on behalf of the Confederate navy. Bremond arrived at a shipyard partially idled for lack of construction materials and a crew consisting entirely of commissioned officers. During *Chattahoochee's* construction a number of serious setbacks occurred that rendered the vessel nearly obsolete. Confederate abandonment of Apalachicola meant the ship could no longer reach the Gulf of Mexico to carry out its role of interrupting the US merchant fleet. Moreover, even if *Chattahoochee* had been able to blast her way through Apalachicola's Union defenses, a giant chain stretched across the river collected logs and debris to form an impenetrable barrier to outbound shipping. With *Chattahoochee* still in the yard, Dennis Bremond was transferred to the Charleston station in late 1862.

Bremond's departure from CSS *Chattahoochee* was well-timed, an April boiler explosion killed nineteen crewmen. The Confederate outlook in

Charleston during the fall of 1862 was marginally sunnier than Bremond's previous posts. The city's natural harbor was the second largest port in the South and heavily defended. Ironclads under construction in the city were heralded as the saviors to break an increasingly restrictive blockade. However well defended maritime assault, the US Navy did their best to keep shipping bottled up. Charleston was a blockade runner's haven with its packed warehouses and rich merchants desperate to get cargo out. A new blockade runner fitting out in early 1862 was the former CSS *Huntress*. Sold out of the Confederate navy in October of 1862, *Huntress* was renamed *Tropic* and Dennis Bremond was named captain. The low-slung sidewheeler was loaded with cotton and turpentine. Hardly a more combustible and dangerous cargo could be chosen for a ship meant to steam flat out through a blockade of shot and shell. On January 18, 1863, while standing out to sea, *Tropic* caught fire. Whether accidental or an act of sabotage, the crew and passengers escaped the conflagration by lifeboat and were picked up by USS *Quaker City*. This time, Capt. Bremond's luck ran out. For the remainder of the war, Capt. Dennis Bremond remained a prisoner in Fort Delaware. On April 25, 1865, he was paroled and rejoined civilian life.

The little cuff button found tucked into the Lee Monument cornerstone came from the uniform of Capt. H. D. Bremond. Whether or not the cuff button witnessed all that Bremond experienced through the war, it is a touchstone to the naval aspirations of the Confederacy. Focus on the Civil War is often myopic and limited to tactical victories and losses by both armies. Less considered is the war at sea, moreover the strategic victory set into motion by the blockade contemporarily called the Anaconda Plan. As its squeeze drew tighter around Richmond's neck, efforts by Confederate blockade runners, cruisers, and privateers amounted to little more than a bother. The Confederate naval efforts may indeed have been the penultimate Lost Cause.

FROM EUROPE TO CONFEDERACY AND FROM CUFF TO LAPEL

The maker's mark on the back of the button was damaged by alteration and corrosion but appears to have a name at the top ending in ". . . ith" and the manufacturer's location, Piccadilly, on the bottom. Charles Smith & Sons was a military accoutrement manufacturer during the mid-nineteenth century in Piccadilly, London, who stamped, or had stamped on commission, gilt buttons. Surviving Confederate naval officers' buttons include common back

Figure 41. Reverse side of Bremond's naval button. Note the back mark of the manufacturer that reads "C. Smith Piccadilly."

marks such as Isaacs & Campbell (London), Firmin & Sons (London), and Courtney & Tennent (Charleston, SC). This specimen is likely a rare example of Smith's work and, like many Confederate buttons, was imported through the blockade.[6]

We know that H. D. Bremond willingly resigned his commission as an officer in the Confederate navy in early 1862. At the time, the Confederate navy was awash with officers.[7] Experienced lieutenants flooded the ranks at the war's outset only moments after resigning their commission in the US Navy. Bremond, among them, began to realize the diminishing opportunities for command even with his post as acting master aboard CSS *Florida*. Perhaps, combined with the hasty retreat from the pitifully incompetent CSS *Louisiana*, Bremond's final straw was drawn. No more ungainly floating batteries for him, but life aboard a cruiser or blockade runner. One of the most notorious blockade runners during the war, John Maffitt, also escaped the Confederate navy for an opportunity to strike a blow for the South and make a pile of cash.[8] With the idle life of a river-bound naval officer behind him, no longer was the steel blue and brass buttoned frock necessary. When Bremond moved into the civilian blockade running world, did he have a cuff button converted into a pin as a reminder of his service to the cause?

Maybe the little button was never part of Bremond's uniform at all. When the Lee Monument cornerstone box was placed, Charles A. DeVilliers (1826–1879) included the C.S.N. button lapel pin in honor of his brother-in-law. The selection was likely chosen by DeVilliers' wife Sylvanie Bremond DeVilliers, H. D. Bremond's sister. Col. Charles De Villiers had ironically led a more swashbuckling life than Capt. Bremond.

Born in Guadeloupe, DeVilliers' French army service transferred to a colonelship with the Eleventh Ohio Volunteers. Captured on July 17, 1861, at the Battle of Scary Creek, DeVilliers was sent to Castle Godwin in Richmond, a prison for Union officers. Carefully observing the sign-countersign measures to allow passage of prison guards he disguised himself as one and managed to talk his way out of the prison. So began a long sojourn eastward which included carrying a pine board upon which DeVilliers crossed rivers and creeks, including crossing the James River near Jamestown.

For two weeks, DeVilliers worked for a German blacksmith with Union sympathies. However, the colonel's zeal for command and excitement led him to adopt an old character used prior to the war, that of a disaffected French subject. Wearing green goggles and rags, his German acquaintance led DeVilliers to Confederate General Huger's command post. DeVilliers feigned blindness, disability, and pled to be ferried under flag of truce to Fortress Monroe so he could continue to a US port and return to France. Union Gen. Wool, commanding exchange operations at Fortress Monroe, initially refused the exchange but after DeVilliers let slip to a US soldier taking part in the exchange that he was an escaped Union officer, Gen. Wool sent a special plea and boat to Gen. Huger to rescue the "poor old Frenchman." According to testimony from the exchange, once DeVilliers boarded the exchange boat and was safe in Union hands, he whipped off the goggles and rags, stood upright and proclaimed to his former Confederate handlers that they were witnessing the escape of a colonel from the Eleventh Ohio Volunteers.[9]

DeVilliers was rarely out of trouble during the Civil War. After his escape from Virginia, DeVilliers was charged with theft of goods from a Washington, DC, merchant amounting to twenty-five dollars and sentenced to eighteen months in prison. President Lincoln issued a pardon for the wayward colonel along with an admonition to depart the city and not return for at least five years.[10]

Departing Washington and returning to the Eleventh Ohio, Col. DeVilliers was once again in hot water for "appropriating the property of private citizens for his own use." At the time, he commanded US forces at Point Pleasant and was charged with seizing property of Union sympathizers for his personal use. His denial of the charges was basis for refusal to surrender to Federal Marshals charged with his arrest. Intervening, Gen. Rosencrans summoned DeVilliers but no surviving correspondence remains on how the matter was settled.[11]

After the war DeVilliers married Sylvanie Bremond and the two established a music school and musical emporium in Norfolk. The Bremond Institute, a boarding and day school located at 25 Fenchurch Street, first held classes in 1869 and offered classical education as well as musical training.[12] Charles DeVilliers was listed as its principal and Sylvanie an instructor. During 1876, the Bremond Institute arranged several musical events to raise money for the construction of the Lee Monument.[13] In 1878, Charles and Sylvanie DeVilliers moved to Richmond and opened a "Select English and French School for Girls" at 312 North Twelfth Street.[14] Charles DeVilliers was buried in Hollywood Cemetery on May 10, 1881, six years prior to the placement of the cornerstone. However, in the October 26, 1887, listing of items contributed to the cornerstone box, DeVilliers is included as having donated three programs from the fundraising concerts and the small Confederate naval button. It was Sylvanie who likely donated the items on her late husband's behalf and likely included the button as a tribute to her deceased brother, Capt. Dennis Bremond.

Little did the button know that it would once again see the light of day only to reveal the storied careers of Dennis Bremond and Charles DeVilliers. Did Sylvanie have the button converted into a pin to wear in her brother's honor? Why did a man who once led a Union regiment against the Confederate army hold fundraisers for a monument to their leader's honor? Virginia's post-war milieu was a complex series of interconnected political and social circles. From Reconstruction's end to the frenzied movement of the Readjusters, the new balance ended up much the same as it looked prior to the war. Not surprisingly, construction of monuments to Confederate heroes acted as a capstone to efforts that wiped away progressivism. Beneath a stoic Lee on his horse, and embedded within the copper box, were deep rooted sentiments of the monument's proponents. Some of the items with direct connections to the war, such as the Confederate naval cuff button, were relics from a lost holy land that was the American Civil War. Regardless of their meaning when placed, each item contains a story, or series of stories, which reflect on a conflicted past that was the bloodiest single chapter in American history. Each story is an allegory representing something lost, a sacrifice for unachieved goals, and arguably, a touchstone for seeking a more perfect union.

NOTES

1. John M. Coski, *Capital Navy: The Men, Ships and Operations of the James River Squadron* (El Dorado Hills, CA: Savas, 1996), 1–2.

2. *Register of Officers of the Confederate States Navy 1861–1865* (Washington, DC: Government Printing Office, 1931).
3. "From the Southern Coast: Arrival of the United States Gunboats Circassian and Water Witch," *New York Times*, February 9, 1863, 8. https://www.nytimes.com/1863/02/09/archives/from-the-southern-coast-arrival-of-the-united-states-gunboats.html.
4. Saxon T. Bisbee, *Engines of Rebellion: Confederate Ironclads and Steam Engineering in the American Civil War* (Tuscaloosa: University of Alabama Press, 2018).
5. *Official Records of the Union and Confederate Navies in the War of the Rebellion*, series I, vol. 18 (Washington, DC: Government Printing Office, 1904).
6. Daniel A. Binder, *Civil War Collectors Guide to Albert's Button Book: A Handbook of Updates, Corrections, and New Discoveries* (Orange, VA: Publishers Press, 1993).
7. Ivan Musicant, *Divided Waters: The Naval History of the Civil War* (New York: Castle Books, 2000).
8. Charles D. Ross, *Breaking the Blockade: The Bahamas During the Civil War* (Jackson: University Press of Mississippi, 2021).
9. "How Col. De Villiers Escaped from the Rebels," *New York Times*, last modified December 8, 1861, https://www.nytimes.com/1861/12/08/archives/how-col-de-villiers-escaped-from-the-rebels.html.
10. "Pardon of Col. Charles DeVilliers," *Raab Collection*, https://www.raabcollection.com/presidential-autographs/abraham-lincoln-pardon-dc.
11. " 'Serious Charges—A Federal Colonel Under Arrest' Richmond Semi-Weekly Enquirer, Vol. 13, No. 131, 18 February 1862," *Virginia Chronicle*, https://virginiachronicle.com/?a=d&d=RSWE18620218.1.2&srpos=8&e=---en-20—1—txt-txIN-%22charles+de+villiers%22---.
12. "Bremond Institute Advertisement. Norfolk Landmark, Vol. 4, No. 123. 31 August 1875," *Virginia Chronicle*, https://virginiachronicle.com/?a=d&d=TNL18750831.1.2&srpos=15&e=---en-20—1—txt-txIN-%22bremond+institute%22---.
13. " 'Children's Tribute to the Confederate Soldiers' Monument'. Norfolk Landmark, Vol. 6, No. 72. 23 June 1876," *Virginia Chronicle*, https://virginiachronicle.com/?a=d&d=TNL18760623.1.1&srpos=1&e=---en-20—1—txt-txIN-%22bremond+institute%22---.
14. "Girls School Advertisement. Daily Dispatch, Vol. 53, No. 38. February 13, 1878," *Virginia Chronicle*, https://virginiachronicle.com/?a=d&d=DD18780213.1.1&srpos=45&e=---en-20—41—txt-txIN-%22bremond+institute%22---.

15

Carlton McCarthy's *Detailed Minutiae of Soldier Life*

Christopher A. Graham

Carlton McCarthy (1847–1936) picked fights. As mayor of Richmond in 1908, while in the city's Police Court on routine business, he spotted a reporter for the *News-Leader*, a paper that McCarthy had determined was out to get him. McCarthy hailed verbal abuse upon the surprised victim in front of the judge, which resulted in a twenty dollar fine for the mayor and a spate of embarrassing national news reports. He was not sorry. In 1915, the former mayor punched another *News-Leader* reporter at city hall.[1]

The combative Richmonder did not shrink from fights over Confederate memory. In the same year as the first assault on a newsman, McCarthy again made the national news when a newspaper reported him to have said that he had loyalty to only two flags—that of Virginia and that of the Confederate States. The alleged slight of the US flag (and thereby the United States itself) moved Union Civil War veterans to encourage Northern state legislatures to condemn the mayor of the former capital of the Confederacy. His remark even outraged conservative Southerners, who long before had accepted a renewed allegiance to the United States as part of the post-war reconciliation project. The top newspaper in South Carolina, *The State*, carried a letter that called him a "freak" and declared "people of this kind ought to be ossified and stacked away in the Confederate museum." Again, McCarthy was not sorry. He claimed the reporter who had taken down the remark, "made evident his illiteracy by his efforts to translate his notes into English" and noted that he had a US flag entwined with a Confederate flag in his mayoral office.[2]

In 1893, McCarthy had tussled with Thomas Nelson Page (1853–1922), the then-renowned novelist who had solidified the White Southern historical imagination of an idyllic, pre–Civil War plantation society of gallant aristocrats living in harmony with their happy and loyal "servants." McCarthy thought one story that Page penned had insulted ordinary White people, and he used temperate language to suggest that Page had committed slander, saying, "the rudest hand can with ease disfigure that which is grandest."[3]

What bothered McCarthy so much about Page's assertions was that the latter had cast aspersions on the men who would make up the rank-and-file of the Confederate army, and McCarthy styled himself the champion of the common soldier and his memory. McCarthy channeled his combativeness, his loyalty to the Confederate cause, and his opinions on the proper way of commemoration into his 1882 book, *Detailed Minutiae of Soldier Life in the Army of Northern Virginia*, that he placed in the Lee Monument cornerstone box. *Detailed Minutiae* made a foundational and enduring contribution to the way that twentieth-century Americans imagined the Civil War and the soldiers who fought it.

The son of an Irish immigrant who grew up in a slaveholding household in Richmond, Carlton McCarthy was passionate about military service during the war but too young to join the army in 1861. He fell in with a number of local defense companies before formally enlisting in the army in October 1864, just after turning seventeen. McCarthy joined the Richmond Howitzers (Second Company), an artillery command. It was notable for being the military home of central Virginia's wealthiest and most influential citizens. The Howitzers had been commanded by McCarthy's older brother who was killed in action at Cold Harbor. By the time the young soldier entered camp, the Howitzers were hunkered down with the Army of Northern Virginia in the Siege of Petersburg. Five months later the Siege broke, and McCarthy experienced his first and last open campaign and combat of the war on the retreat toward Appomattox.

McCarthy did not intend *Detailed Minutiae* to be a memoir of his own service, though he drew on his time in the army to inform several chapters. Instead, he meant it to be a broad claim for the place of common Confederate soldiers within Lost Cause memory. In its contradicting bundle of truthful insights, historical inaccuracies, romance, and racism, *Detailed Minutiae* insisted that the men who populated the ranks of the armies deserved an equal amount of respect and admiration as the General officers whom Richmond had rushed to honor with statues.

In the primary chapters, McCarthy relied on general observations about military service while the last few chapters clearly narrated his own experi-

Figure 42. *Minutiae of Soldier Life* as found in the Lee cornerstone box.

ences on the Appomattox campaign. His interest lay in describing the mundane details of soldier life: dividing up miniscule and rotten rations between too many men, the animated reveries around campfires that helped foment a sense of family in the ranks, the joy of lighting a pipe after a cup of coffee, the giddiness of boy-soldiers in possession of "camp slaves" to polish boots, and the pain of seeing comrades killed in battle. Examples are many, but one will suffice:

Troops on the march were generally so cheerful and gay that an outsider, looking on them as they marched, would hardly imagine how they suffered. In summer time, the dust, combined with the heat, caused great suffering. The nostrils of the men, filled with dust, became dry and feverish, and even the throat did not escape. The "grit" was felt between the teeth, and the eyes were rendered almost useless. There was dust in eyes, mouth, ears, and hair. The shoes were full of sand, and the dust, penetrating the clothes, and getting in at the neck, wrists, and ankles, mixed with perspiration, produced an irritant almost as active as cantharides. The heat was at times terrific, but the men became greatly accustomed to it, and endured it with wonderful ease.

McCarthy's point was not to simply elicit pity, to weave tales of glory, or to reminisce about the old days. Instead, McCarthy meant to claim that the soldiers' very real struggles against a materially superior foe, deprivations, and death were made endurable and admirable because of the enormously high spirits of the soldiers that were rooted in their unmatched sense of duty and self-sacrifice. It was a character trait that he insisted US soldiers simply lacked.

What made McCarthy's description stand out, however, is that he portrayed the Confederate soldier as possessing so elevated and abstract a sense of duty that the particulars of what the war was about (aside from opposing a tyranny that McCarthy did not define) simply didn't matter. He disassociated Confederate soldiers from the Confederate cause to preserve slavery and defined it solely as one of youthful romance, battlefield courage, and the comradeship of the campfire.

White Southerners carried McCarthy's sensibility into the twentieth century. Despite contrary evidence, it was possible for them to imagine the Civil War as nothing more than the clash of two honorable armies of White men. Anything that touched on politics or race was considered an unwarranted and unwanted intrusion on that romance. Even today, advocates for the Confederate flag claim that it represents not the Confederate States' political and racial implication, but instead, that it meant nothing more than the unsullied character of brave but forlorn soldiers. Indeed, McCarthy made that exact point in the last chapter of his book.

Many of McCarthy's observations are decidedly truthful. He notes battlefield deaths, starvation, and material deprivation in ways that suggest the real trauma that he and his comrades must have endured. Yet many of his other claims about the universal virtue and ingenuity of Confederate soldiers have not stood up to historical scrutiny. Some Confederates had to be forced into the army while others took whatever means to desert it.

Figure 43. William L. Sheppard (top left) and Carlton McCarthy (top center) at a reunion of the Richmond Howitzers, ca. 1870. (Courtesy of the American Civil War Museum)

Many died in a gruesome and anonymous fashion to which no sense of glory could be attached. They operated on behalf of a War Department that made policy decisions that adversely affected soldiers. Finally, Confederate soldiers, from the beginning to the end of the war, were conscientious that the causes and stakes revolved around slavery, and continued awareness of evolving racial politics informed their commitment to the Confederate States until the end.[4]

Carlton McCarthy adored Robert E. Lee and, despite the former's protestations about the imbalance of praise between leaders and men, it was no contradiction to him to place his book in the pedestal of the Lee Monument. After all, veterans of the Army of Northern Virginia, from general to private, regarded their hard service together to have forged an organic cadre united in the post-war South.

Besides his book, Carlton McCarthy shaped Richmond's memorial landscape in other ways. He and other veterans from the Richmond Howitzers—including William Ludwell Sheppard, who illustrated McCarthy's book and sculpted several statues in Richmond—were influential movers in the ongoing Confederate veteran reunion calendar, particularly in the Association of the Army of Northern Virginia, represented by the medal McCarthy placed in the box. They joined together to raise up the Richmond Howitzer statue in Richmond's Fan neighborhood. McCarthy also took a leadership role in the fundraising for the Confederate Soldiers' and Sailors' Monument on Libby Hill.[5]

Unlearning McCarthy's take on common soldiers has been the work of generations. However, understanding the ways that he revealed differences within the Lost Cause movement and how he shaped Civil War memory with his book of facts, purposeful omissions, and breezy romance will always be useful.

NOTES

1. "Mayor Before Police Court," *The Times-Dispatch* (Richmond, VA), January 26, 1906.
2. "Ice Kings Have Big Convention," *Richmond Times-Dispatch*, March 22, 1906, "Not One in a Thousand Men," *The Cincinnati Enquirer*, March 23, 1906, *The State* (Columbia, SC), March 28, 1906, and "M'Carthy Enters Denial," *The Baltimore Sun*, March 26, 1906.
3. Carlton McCarthy, "People of Virginia: As They Are Portrayed by Thomas Nelson Page," *The Times* (Richmond, VA), April 9, 1893.
4. This scholarship includes, among numerous other works, John M. Sacher, *Confederate Conscription and the Struggle for Southern Soldiers* (Baton Rouge: Louisiana State University Press, 2021); Mark A. Weitz, *More Damning Than Slaughter: Desertion in the Confederate Army* (Lincoln: University of Nebraska Press, 2008); Drew Gilpin Faust, *This Republic of Suffering: Death and the American Civil War* (New York: Vintage, 2009); and Chandra Manning, *What This Cruel War Was Over: Soldiers, Slavery, and the Civil War* (New York: Vintage, 2008).
5. Pamphlet, "Souvenir Unveiling Soldiers and Sailors Monument. Richmond, Virginia, May 30, 1894," (n.p.: 1894), "Three of the Workers," *Richmond Times-Dispatch*, May 30, 1894.

16

Analyzing the Past

Analysis of an Army of Northern Virginia Badge

Hannah Sanner

Nestled among the collection of books, papers, and mementos in the Lee Monument cornerstone box was a small medal suspended on a ribbon. This object is one of only three textile-based artifacts found within the box. On first glance, the medal appears to be an enamel Confederate flag attached to a red and white striped ribbon that is missing the pin. The placard is the Army of Northern Virginia battle flag inscribed with "A.N.V" at the bottom.[1] Other iterations of this medal are marked with the respective soldier's division or engraved on the back, but this award, donated by Richmond Mayor Carlton McCarthy, is unpersonalized.

Composite artifacts present a conundrum to conservators. Different materials require different preservation methods; a composite object requires conservators to prioritize one part of an artifact over another. In the case of the medal, the Department of Historic Resources (DHR) conservation staff decided the object should not be placed in silica gel like the rest of the metal objects. Silica gel adsorbs water to prevent metal corrosion. However, this loss of moisture can also render textiles, paper, and other organic materials brittle and more fragile. Given the medal is one of few textile artifacts found within the cornerstone box, the DHR staff prioritized the safety of the ribbon and did not place the object in a dry environment.

Identifying the ribbon's fiber proves challenging, even though the artifact predates synthetic textiles. The ribbon could be woven from cotton, flax, or silk. Given the object is a military award, a silk ribbon would be a likely choice. However, the ribbon exhibited a ridged cord weave that would be an unusual pattern for silk. Satin weaves are more commonly used to highlight

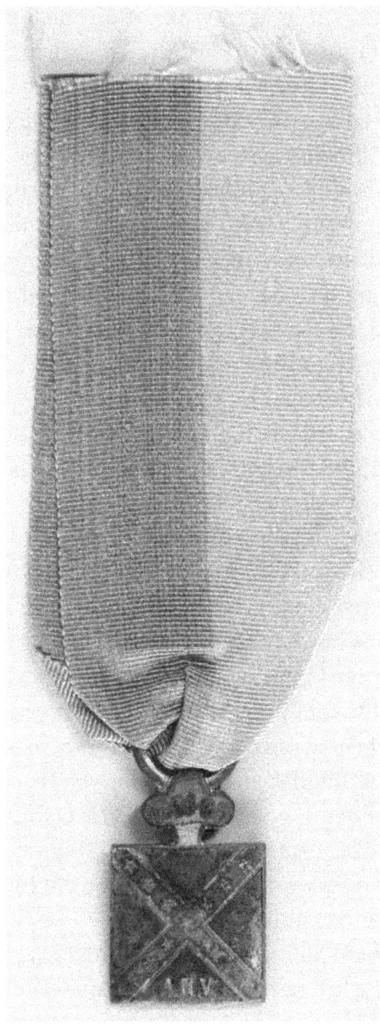

Figure 44. Carlton McCarthy's Army of Northern Virginia Badge from cornerstone box, dated "1861–1865."

the fiber's luster, while cord weave is ridged for strength. Examination of the ribbon's fraying edge also yields no answers. The threads possess a sheen, which may indicate silk, but this property does not eliminate any possible materials for this textile.

Under a microscope, flax appears visually similar to bamboo with segmented units defined by rings. Cotton looks like flattened and twisted tubes. Comparatively, silk appears flexible and smooth. These microscopic structures affect the properties. The mercerization process used on cotton and flax was invented in 1844. This is a process that improves the luster, strength, and dye uptake of both cotton and flax by regularizing their microscopic structures.[2] While silk can usually be recognized for its shiny smoothness, once cotton and flax are mercerized, they are difficult to discern from silk by eye.

Polarized light microscopy would allow greater insight into the textile composition through the magnification of the fibers' microscopic structures. Under polarized light, mercerized fibers can be distinguished from one another on the basis of "extinction."[3] Extinction occurs when portions of a sample do not refract polarized light, rendering some of the sample invisible under magnification. Silk refracts polarized light in an "undulating pattern" when rotated under a microscope.[4] Even if cotton has been hydrated to resemble silk, the fiber will uniformly reflect light no matter how the sample is manipulated. Bast fibers like flax will appear brightest around the rings, regardless if mercerization has minimized these physical characteristics.

The ribbon is discolored: the red has faded and the white has yellowed. Additionally, there are tide lines at the border between the colors, indicating the red dye is not sufficiently colorfast. Tide lines occur when pigments dissolve in water and cause wave-like discolorations on the object. Potential natural dyes include cochineal and madder, which can be successfully applied to both protein (silk and wool) and celluloid (cotton and linen) based fibers. Cochineal is a pigment derived from an insect of the same name, which is native to Central and South America. The European madder pigment is derived from the roots of the *Rubia tinctorum* plant. Madder was generally valued less than cochineal as the herbaceous dye was more susceptible to sun bleaching and produced inconsistent hues. Though both dyes were equally prevalent in the mid-nineteenth century given the expense of cochineal.

However, the ribbon may have been concurrent with the invention of synthetic dyes. The dates on the medal note the full duration of the Confederacy from 1861–1865, meaning the medal could have been issued anytime from 1865–1887. Notable figures like Julia Christian (née Jackson), daughter of General "Stonewall" Jackson, were issued honorary A.N.V medals after the conclusion of the war. Given that the medals were not distributed in connection to a particular event or date, their date range could include the rise of synthetic dyes after 1856.

A possible synthetic red dye, alizarin red, was synthesized from madder in 1869. Its invention toppled the cultivation of natural madder dye throughout Europe.[5] In 1881 the French district of Midi produced over half of the world's

Figure 45. Unidentified Civil War veteran wearing A. N. V. badge, dated 1903. (Courtesy of Library of Congress)

madder. By 1886, the township sold no dyestuffs due to competition with alizarin red.[6] The red dyed ribbon could be anything from natural madder, natural cochineal, or synthetic alizarin.

Mass spectrometry tests could more definitively identify the ribbon's dye. Mass spectrometry relies on the measurement of an ion's mass to charge ratio, which correlates to specific chemical groups and structures. For example, alizarin dye should exhibit a mass of 241.0501 daltons when the energy of the compound's unique bonds and atoms are all totaled.[7] This analytical tool functions on protein and celluloid fibers alike. Mass spectrometry can identify both modern and historic dye samples equally successfully.[8]

The metal placard of the award was able to be tested in the DHR conservation lab. The lab utilizes a pXRF (portable X-ray fluorescence) machine for identifying non-organic elements, such as the metal used to make the placard and composition of the enamel pigments. The machine uses X-rays to excite the electrons of the object being scanned. As the electrons give off their extra energy, they revert to their original state. The machine is able to identify the unique distances between energy levels, which correlate to specific elements as the electrons move from their excited energy state to their normal energy state.

Scanning the placard revealed the medal is brass, as the pXRF indicated the presence of both copper and zinc. The red and blue enamels within the

Army of Northern Virginia battle flag were determined to be a lead-based pigment and a copper-based pigment, respectively. Copper's corrosion products that are used for pigments can be red, blue, or green in hue. Artists and pigment manufacturers took advantage of this to make blue pigments. These metals could be informative regarding the availability of materials if examined alongside other artifacts produced before, during, and after the Civil War.

Unlike the placard, the ribbon composition could not be definitively identified. DHR lacks the necessary equipment for mass spectrometry dye tests, but the technique could be pursued elsewhere. Comparatively, polar light microscopy (PLM) is an unlikely candidate for future analysis. PLM requires a sample to be cut from the object to prepare a microscope slide. Even snipping a piece of unraveling thread from the ribbon compromises the integrity of the original artifact. The DHR is not the permanent owner of the cornerstone box and its artifacts, so any destructive testing will not be conducted at this time. Questions regarding post-War industry and materials are best answered through other more common artifacts. This medal is unique given its association with the cornerstone box and Mayor Carlton McCarthy.

NOTES

1. John M. Coski, *Confederate Battle Flag: America's Most Embattled Emblem* (Cambridge, MA: Harvard University Press, 2005), 3–4.
2. J. T. Marsh, *An Introduction to Textile Finishing* (London: Chapman and Hall 1948), 111–33.
3. Denyse Montegut, "Textile Study Group Chapter V. Analysis and Testing Methods for Textiles—Section C. Fiber Identification," (American Institute of Conservation Wikipedia, February 6, 2016).
4. Montegut, "Textile Study Group Chapter V. Analysis and Testing Methods for Textiles—Section C. Fiber Identification."
5. François Delamare and Bernard Guineau, *Colors: The Story of Dyes and Pigments* (New York: H. N. Abrams, 2000), 101–2.
6. Delamare and Guineau, *Colors: The Story of Dyes and Pigments.*
7. Cathy Selvius DeRoo and Ruth Ann Armitage, "Direct Identification of Dyes in Textiles by Direct Analysis in Real Time-Time of Flight Mass Spectrometry," *Analytical Chemistry* 83, no. 18 (2011): 6924–28, https://doi.org/10.1021/ac201747s.
8. Selvius DeRoo and Armitage, "Direct Identification of Dyes in Textiles by Direct Analysis in Real Time-Time of Flight Mass Spectrometry."

17

The Richmond Sharpshooters

Company H, Twenty-Third Virginia Infantry Confederate Veterans Muster Roll

Robert L. Jolley

THE DONOR

George T. Mattern, a private in Company H of the Twenty-Third Virginia Regiment, gave a muster roll to be placed in the Lee Monument cornerstone box. His service records indicate he enlisted in May 1861, was captured in 1864, and released from confinement at Fort Delaware after taking an oath to not take up arms against the United States government in May of 1865.[1] Little is known about Mattern other than he enlisted at age twenty and was a blacksmith in civilian life.[2] He does not appear to have been involved with Confederate Veteran organizations but it is known that he served as a police officer during the unveiling of the Lee Monument.[3] Only George Mattern knows the reasons why he deposited his unit muster roll in the cornerstone box, but perhaps he thought it fitting since his unit was part of General Robert E. Lee's Army of Northern Virginia.

THE TWENTY-THIRD VIRGINIA INFANTRY REGIMENT

The Twenty-Third Virginia Infantry Regiment was organized early in the war and consisted of ten companies. One company was from the City of Richmond (Company H), and the other nine companies were from Louisa, Amelia, Goochland, Prince Edward, Charlotte and Halifax counties. Mattern and other members of Company H enlisted for a year in the spring of 1861.

The regiment was actively engaged in several campaigns until they surrendered at Appomattox Court House at the close of the war in April 1865. The Twenty-Third fought in several engagements and sustained casualties in battles fought in the Eastern Theater including Corrick's Ford, Kernstown, McDowell, Cedar Mountain, Antietam, Gettysburg, Spotsylvania Courthouse, Chancellorsville, and Petersburg.[4]

THE POST–CIVIL WAR MUSTER ROLL

Civil War era company muster rolls are informative documents that contain information on the names of the men, their rank, when and where they enlisted, when they were last paid, where they are currently located, and the name of the commanding officer. Each roll contains a remarks section that is used to indicate if the soldier has been killed in battle (and if so, in what battle), wounded, absent without leave (AWOL), in prison, sick, deserted, or furloughed.

The Richmond Sharpshooters (Company H), Twenty-Third Virginia Infantry Regiment muster roll is an uncommon document-a post-war roll of the unit veterans from war records. This muster roll contains information about the soldiers themselves along with their service history and may have been printed for a special occasion, possibly the laying of the cornerstone for the Lee Monument.

THE MEN OF COMPANY H

The post–Civil War muster roll lists the original eighty-one members of the unit when they mustered into service on May 16, 1861. What is known about these men?

Most soldiers were nineteen or twenty years old when they enlisted and their ages ranged from eighteen to thirty-five. The average age of a soldier was twenty-one years. Two soldiers who stated their age as eighteen at enlistment were discharged after they were found to be seventeen. Another soldier was discharged as being too old because the Confederate Conscription Act of 1862 only allowed men up to the age of thirty-five to serve.

The men in the Richmond Sharpshooters had diverse occupations. Of the original eighty-one members of the unit, thirty-two different occupations are represented. The greatest number were carpenters followed by painters,

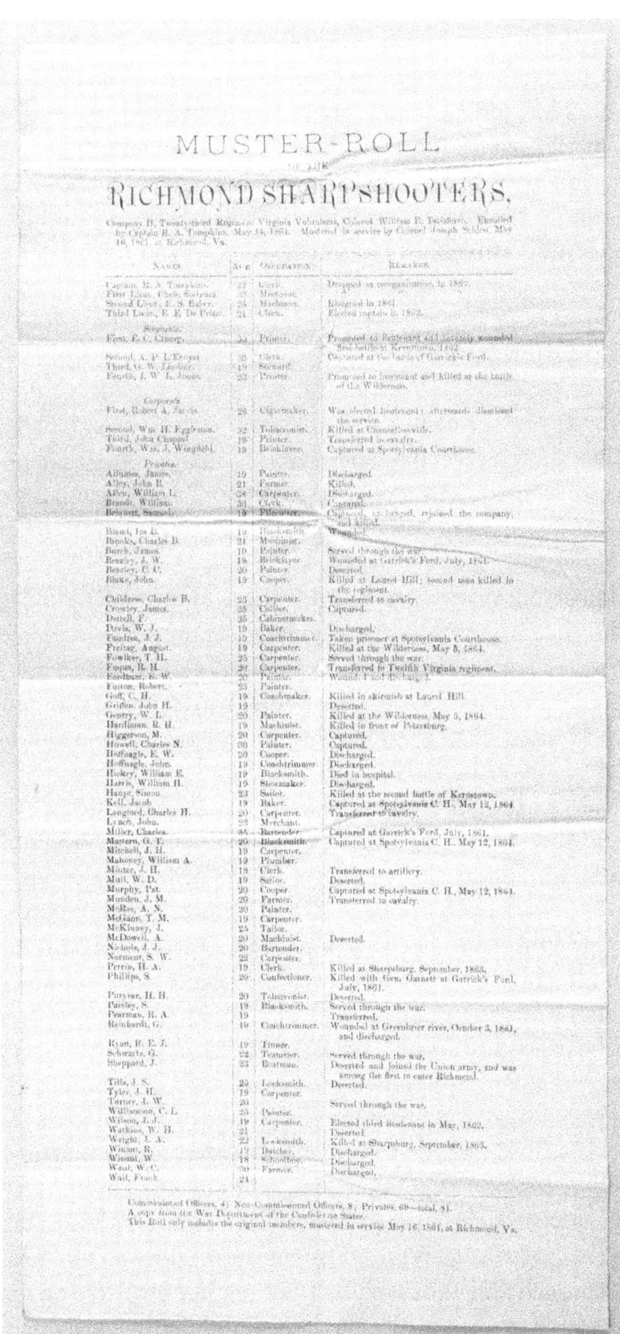

MUSTER-ROLL

OF THE

RICHMOND SHARPSHOOTERS,

Company B, Twenty-third Regiment Virginia Volunteers, Colonel William B. Taliaferro. Enrolled by Captain R. A. Tompkins, May 14, 1861. Mustered in service by Colonel Joseph [illegible], May 16, 1861, at Richmond, Va.

Names.	Age.	Occupation.	Remarks.
Captain, R. A. Tompkins.	27	Clerk.	Dropped at reorganization, in 1862.
First Lieut., Chris. [illegible]	27	[illegible]	
Second Lieut., E. S. Baber.	25	Machinist.	Resigned in 1861.
Third Lieut., E. E. De Prizer.	21	Clerk.	Elected captain in 1862.
Sergeants.			
First, E. C. Crump.	30	Printer.	Promoted to lieutenant and severely wounded first battle at Kernstown, 1862.
Second, A. P. L'Enyer.	26	Clerk.	Captured at the battle of Garrick's Ford.
Third, G. W. Lindsay.	19	Steward.	
Fourth, J. W. L. Jones.	23	Printer.	Promoted to lieutenant and killed at the battle of the Wilderness.
Corporals.			
First, Robert A. Jarvis.	28	Cigarmaker.	Was elected lieutenant; afterwards dismissed the service.
Second, Wm. H. Eggleston.	32	Tobacconist.	Killed at Chancellorsville.
Third, John Chappel	19	Printer.	Transferred to cavalry.
Fourth, Wm. J. Wingfield	19	Bricklayer.	Captured at Spotsylvania Courthouse.
Privates.			
Allumes, James.	19	Painter.	Discharged.
Alley, John R.	21	Farmer.	Killed.
Allen, William L.	38	Carpenter.	Discharged.
Brandt, William.	33	Clerk.	Captured.
Brissett, Samuel.	19	Filecutter.	Captured, exchanged, rejoined the company, and killed.
Blunt, Ira B.	19	Blacksmith.	Wounded.
Brooks, Charles B.	21	Machinist.	
Burch, James.	19	Painter.	Served through the war.
Beazley, J. W.	18	Bricklayer.	Wounded at Garrick's Ford, July, 1861.
Beazley, C. C.	20	Painter.	Deserted.
Blake, John.	19	Cooper.	Killed at Laurel Hill; second man killed in the regiment.
Childress, Charles B.	23	Carpenter.	Transferred to cavalry.
Crowley, James.	25	Collier.	Captured.
Dettell, F.	35	Cabinetmaker.	
Davis, W. J.	19	Baker.	Discharged.
Faudree, J. J.	19	Coachtrimmer.	Taken prisoner at Spotsylvania Courthouse.
Freitag, August.	19	Carpenter.	Killed at the Wilderness, May 5, 1864.
Fowlkes, T. H.	25	Carpenter.	Served through the war.
Fuqua, R. H.	29	Carpenter.	Transferred to Twelfth Virginia regiment.
Fordham, E. W.	20	Painter.	Wounded and discharged.
Fulton, Robert.	25	Painter.	
Goff, C. H.	19	Coachmaker.	Killed in skirmish at Laurel Hill.
Griffen, John H.	19		Deserted.
Gentry, W. L.	20	Painter.	Killed at the Wilderness, May 5, 1864.
Hardiman, R. H.	19	Machinist.	Killed in front of Petersburg.
Higgerson, M.	20	Carpenter.	Captured.
Howell, Charles N.	30	Painter.	Captured.
Hoffnagle, E. W.	20	Cooper.	Discharged.
Hoffnagle, John.	19	Coachtrimmer.	Discharged.
Hickey, William E.	19	Blacksmith.	Died in hospital.
Harris, William H.	19	Shoemaker.	Discharged.
Haupe, Simon	23	Sailor.	Killed at the second battle of Kernstown.
Kell, Jacob	19	Baker.	Captured at Spotsylvania C. H., May 12, 1864.
Langford, Charles H.	20	Carpenter.	Transferred to cavalry.
Lynch, John.	23	Merchant.	
Miller, Charles.	35	Bartender.	Captured at Garrick's Ford, July, 1861.
Mattern, G. T.	20	Blacksmith.	Captured at Spotsylvania C. H., May 12, 1864.
Mitchell, J. H.	19	Carpenter.	
Mahoney, William A.	19	Plumber.	
Minter, J. H.	19	Clerk.	Transferred to artillery.
Mull, W. D.	19	Sailor.	Deserted.
Murphy, Pat.	20	Cooper.	Captured at Spotsylvania C. H., May 12, 1864.
Munden, J. M.	20	Farmer.	Transferred to cavalry.
McRae, A. N.	20	Painter.	
McGann, T. M.	19	Carpenter.	
McKinney, J.	25	Tailor.	
McDowell, A.	20	Machinist.	Deserted.
Nichols, J. J.	20	Bartender.	
Norment, S. W.	23	Carpenter.	
Perrin, H. A.	19	Clerk.	Killed at Sharpsburg, September, 1863.
Phillips, S.	20	Confectioner.	Killed with Gen. Garnett at Garrick's Ford, July, 1861.
Puryear, H. H.	20	Tobacconist.	Deserted.
Parsley, S.	19	Blacksmith.	Served through the war.
Pearman, R. A.	19		Transferred.
Reinhardt, G.	16	Coachtrimmer.	Wounded at Greenbrier river, October 3, 1861, and discharged.
Ryan, R. E. J.	19	Tinner.	
Schwartz, G.	22	Teamster.	Served through the war.
Sheppard, J.	23	Boatman.	Deserted and joined the Union army, and was among the first to enter Richmond.
Tilts, J. S.	25	Locksmith.	Deserted.
Tyler, J. H.	19	Carpenter.	
Turner, J. W.	20		Served through the war.
Williamson, C. L.	25	Painter.	
Wilson, J. J.	19	Carpenter.	Elected third lieutenant in May, 1862.
Watkins, W. H.	21		Deserted.
Wright, J. A.	22	Locksmith.	Killed at Sharpsburg, September, 1863.
Winans, R.	19	Butcher.	Discharged.
Winans, W.	18	Schoolboy.	Discharged.
Wall, W. C.	20	Farmer.	Discharged.
Wall, Frank	24		

Commissioned Officers, 4; Non-Commissioned Officers, 8; Privates, 69—total, 81.
A copy from the War Department of the Confederate States.
This Roll only includes the original members, mustered in service May 16, 1861, at Richmond, Va.

Figure 46. Muster-Roll of the Richmond Sharpshooters.

clerks, machinists, printers, blacksmiths, coopers, farmers, coach trimmers, tobacconists, sailors, bartenders, bakers, and locksmiths. Other occupations represented by soldiers include mechanic, steward, cigar maker, file cutter, collier, cabinet maker, baker, coach maker, shoemaker, merchant, plumber, tailor, confectioner, tinner, teamster, boatman, butcher, and schoolboy. Unlike Company H, other companies in the Twenty-Third Virginia Infantry were from rural areas comprising mostly farmers.

THEIR WARTIME EXPERIENCE

The men of Company H saw the elephant. The term "seeing the elephant" or "seeing the monkey show" were idioms used by Civil War soldiers to describe the experience of combat.[5] These colorful expressions originated from attending circus events featuring never before seen exotic animals when they were boys or adolescents.

Some survived almost four years of war and privation. Many were wounded in action. Some were killed in action. Others deserted. Many fell ill, suffered disabilities, and received medical discharges. Several were taken as prisoners of war (POW) and held in Union POW camps. While a prisoner of war, one member of Company H was used as a human shield and later became known as one of the "Immortal 600."[6]

As is always the case with Civil War sources, the written accounts differ. The post–Civil War muster roll and modern-day research conducted over one hundred years later by a historian do not always agree.[7] Although the post–Civil War muster roll states at the bottom that the information was obtained from war records, flawed memories compounded by personal bias, post-traumatic stress, and the phenomenon known as the "fog of war" may have been at play when the roll was compiled.

The Richmond Sharpshooters muster roll lists thirteen original members of the company that were killed in action however, research by Rankin indicates that only eight were killed in action or died of wounds received.[8] Four of those listed as KIA (killed in action) on the veterans' muster roll are listed as captured, and one is listed as a deserter in the roster compiled by Rankin. One other member of the unit died of disease in a hospital in Staunton, Virginia.

Over twenty-five, or approximately one-third, of the original members of Company H were discharged for various reasons. Six soldiers are listed on the veterans muster roll as having survived wounds received on the battlefield.

Some of these soldiers were discharged with medical disabilities. Other soldiers were discharged due to sickness.[9] Robert Jarvis, listed as having been dismissed from service on the veterans muster roll after being elected as an officer, was relieved of command on the charge of drunkenness.[10]

Other soldiers were discharged early in the war after they had been captured and paroled, an action consistent with the terms of their parole, but a few reenlisted. Later in the war, when Grant's policy of attrition was applied, Confederate prisoners were no longer exchanged but confined in Union prisoner-of-war camps. Nine were confined at Fort Delaware, a fort on the Delaware River originally designed to protect American harbors. Fort Delaware prisoners were not released until May or June of 1865 after they had signed an oath indicating they would no longer take up arms against the US government.[11]

The veterans' muster roll lists eight men as deserters and that number increases when the research conducted by Rankin is considered.[12] The issue of desertion is clouded as some of those listed as deserters on the veteran's muster roll are listed as captured in other records. One soldier listed on the veterans' muster roll earned the distinction of not only being a deserter but also joining the Union army and having been one of "the first to enter Richmond."

THE END OF COMPANY H AND THE TWENTY-THIRD VIRGINIA INFANTRY REGIMENT

Toward the end of the war, both the company and regiment were decimated. The Company H muster roll for November-December 1864 had only six privates listed.[13] When the Twenty-Third Virginia Infantry Regiment evacuated Petersburg on April 2, they retreated westward. Only fifty-five men of the Twenty-Third Regiment made it to Appomattox Courthouse to surrender with Lee's Army of Northern Virginia.

None of the original members of Company H of the Twenty-Third Virginia Infantry Regiment were present when what remained of the Twenty-Third regiment surrendered at Appomattox Courthouse in April 1865. Both the veterans muster roll and Rankin's history of the regiment are in agreement that none were paroled at Appomattox. All eighty-one original members of the company had been killed in action, discharged for various reasons, deserted, transferred to other companies or were still actively held as prisoners of war. The remaining members of Company H captured at Spotsylvania Courthouse in 1864 and held in confinement at Fort Delaware were released in May-June of 1865. They all signed a solemn Parole of Honor to no longer "take part in hostilities against the Government of the United States."

Several original members of Company H lived long after the Civil War, including the private that deposited this muster roll in the cornerstone box in 1887. Their captain, Emmett DePriest, lived until 1903 and is buried in Hollywood Cemetery. Today, the tradition of the Twenty-Third Virginia Infantry Regiment is remembered by a reenactor group by the same name that maintains a website with information about their history.[14]

NOTES

1. "George T. Mattern," *fold3*, https://www.fold3.com/.
2. Thomas M. Rankin, *23rd Virginia Infantry* (Lynchburg, VA: H. E. Howard, 1985), 119.
3. *Southern Historical Society Papers* 17 (1889): 257.
4. Rankin, *23rd Virginia Infantry.*
5. Tracy L. Barnett, "Seeing the Elephant," *The Civil War Monitor* 11 (2021): 4.
6. Mauriel Joslyn, *The Biographical Roster of the Immortal 600* (Shippensburg, PA: White Mane, 1995), 86.
7. Rankin, *23rd Virginia Infantry.*
8. Rankin, *23rd Virginia Infantry*, 100–138.
9. Rankin, *23rd Virginia Infantry.*
10. Rankin, *23rd Virginia Infantry*, 116.
11. Rankin, *23rd Virginia Infantry*, 93.
12. Rankin, *23rd Virginia Infantry*, 100–138.
13. "History of the 23rd VA," *23rd Regiment of Virginia Volunteer Infantry Companies A-K*, https://23rdvirginiainfantry.org/hist23.htm.
14. "Welcome to the 23rd VA," *23rd Regiment of Virginia Volunteer Infantry Companies A-K*, https://23rdvirginiainfantry.org/welcome.htm.

18

Muster at High Tide

The June 30th Muster Roll of the Petersburg Old Grays, Co. B, Twelfth Virginia Infantry

Brendan Burke

The American Civil War has often been described as a "rich man's war—poor man's fight," a perspective borne out by the disproportionate suffering of the lower and middle-classes compared to an educated, wealthy elite. Wealth frequently allowed men the ability to buy their way out of service by hiring a substitute or being exempted from service in the South by owning more than twenty slaves. Most regiments, both North and South, were filled with poorer farmers or industrial laborers. As the war drew on, and the armies grew hungrier for soldiers, more and more farms and factories were emptied of their labor to feed the bloodbaths that were Antietam, Cold Harbor, Chickamauga, and many more battles. Many were conscripts, immigrants who stepped off the boat and into a foreign war, or volunteers who simply had no other choice but to fight. The Twelfth Virginia Regiment of Virginia Infantry was a bit different.

The newly formed Confederate government formed several armies in 1861 including the well-known Army of Northern Virginia. Each army consisted of two to four corps, which were made up of two to four divisions. A division likewise consisted of two to four brigades, each of which included four regiments. A regiment ideally contained one thousand men and was broken into ten companies. While each of these units within an army was important, the real soul of an army was the company. The Twelfth Virginia consisted largely of men from Petersburg and the surrounding countryside. It was more common for a regiment to include companies from far flung areas of the state as the army was assembled from varying components of local militia companies and so the Twelfth Virginia was uniquely local. More common were amalgamations of various locales such as the Twenty-Third Virginia Infantry, which included men from Goochland, Louisa, Charlotte, Richmond, Prince Edward, and Halifax counties. However, within each company was a community. The men within a company had often grown up together, and during the Civil War, suffered and died together.

Every few months a company was mustered for inspection, condition, strength, and composition. A form called a muster roll was filled out and signed by the company's commanding officer, a captain or lieutenant, and certified by an inspecting officer. These periodic inspections were critical for army brass to track field strength. Without muster rolls, General Lee and his command would have been blind as to the strength of their forces. Historians and scholars of the conflict rely on muster rolls to accurately represent the ebb and flow of forces, including predations on armies by sickness and the conspicuous absences around the planting and harvesting of crops.

Contained within the copper box placed below the Lee Monument was a muster roll of the Twelfth Virginia, Company B, known as the "Petersburg Grays." Companies often carried a nickname that referenced their locality such as the "Riverton Invincibles" (Tenth VA Inf. Co. I), "Grayson Dare Devils" (Fourth VA Inf., Co. F), or the "Richmond Light Infantry Blues" (First VA Inf., Co. E). The Petersburg Grays were an old militia company first mustered in 1828. They fought in the Mexican War during the 1840s and in 1859, the Petersburg Grays were dispatched to Charlestown, Virginia (now West Virginia) to oversee the hanging of John Brown. Colonel David Addison Weisiger (1818–1899), who signed this muster roll, served as the Officer of the Day to preside over the hanging. According to eyewitness David Hunter Strother, the troops stood "mute and motionless" for half an hour while Brown's body silently dangled from the noose. It was their job to witness for the nation "the awful majesty of the law."[1]

In May of 1861, the Petersburg Grays became Co. B of the Twelfth Virginia Regiment of Volunteer Infantry for the Confederacy. During the organization, the Petersburg Grays swelled in numbers and a new company (Co. C) was split off to become the Petersburg New Grays Co. B now became known as the Petersburg Old Grays. Formed in Norfolk, the regiment consisted of six companies from Petersburg with the remaining four coming from across Southside Virginia. They were collectively known as the Petersburg Battalion. The Twelfth Virginia was combined with the Sixth, Sixteenth, Forty-First, and ultimately the Sixty-First Virginia regiments under the direction of General William Mahone (1826–1895) to form Mahone's Brigade.

Figure 47. Brigadier General David Addison Weisiger of the First Virginia Infantry battalion, 1861, by J. R. Rockwell. (Courtesy of the Library of Congress)

The first year of General Mahone's command was quiet and their main action was the capture of Gosport Navy Yard, a critical success for the formation of any Confederate naval force. That all changed at 5:30 p.m. on July 1, 1862, at the Battle of Malvern Hill. Mahone's Brigade was swept up into a charge across open ground. Federal sharpshooters intentionally withdrew to clear the field for a withering artillery barrage. The Twelfth Virginia was caught in the open and pounded with canister shot. Each cannon was turned into a large shotgun and the result "was not war—it was murder," according to the General D. H. Hill, who was ordered to lead the charge.

Less than two months later the Twelfth Virginia fought as part of Anderson's Division at Second Bull Run/Manassas. Despite their participation in the successful counterattack on the second day of the battle, sixty-nine men were killed or wounded in the action. With little time to recover, the regiment marched north as part of the Maryland Campaign in September of 1862. At the Battle of Crampton's Gap on September 14, the Twelfth Virginia lost sixty men. By this time, combat, sickness, and fatigue had taken a ghastly toll on the Petersburg Old Grays and when the unit was thrown into battle at the Battle of Antietam/Sharpsburg the regiment fielded only twenty-three men. They were thrown into the worst part of the conflict, wherein the

Sunken Road became known as Bloody Lane. In three hours of fighting, over 5,500 men were killed or wounded with no strategic victory for either side. The Maryland Campaign took a huge toll on the Army of Northern Virginia. Dr. Powhatan Bledsoe, assistant surgeon with the Thirty-Second Virginia, remarked that "men could have been tracked for miles by blood from their feet."[2] Hunger was rampant, and men became desperate for food and water. Less than three months after Antietam, the remains of the Twelfth Virginia held the Confederate line at the Battle of Fredericksburg. Thus, they ended 1862 with a major Confederate victory but at a terrible cost.

Spring brought additional loss to the Twelfth Virginia. At Chancellorsville, the regiment lost thirty-six by death or wounding with an additional fifty-one prisoners taken. By then, desertion stalked the ranks and muster rolls from late in the season show that nearly two-thirds of the regiment was absent without leave. Most historians would explain such a desertion rate in the spring as a temporary loss suffered by the army as soldiers returned to their farms to plant crops, but the Twelfth Virginia was uncharacteristically urban.

When the muster roll found in the Lee cornerstone box was taken on June 30, 1863, the men present were unaware that the tide of the war was only days from turning. It was a Tuesday and General Meade, the newest commander of the Army of the Potomac, stalked western Maryland to "find and fight" General Lee. The Petersburg Old Grays remained at Fayetteville, Pennsylvania about eighteen miles west of a quiet town named Gettysburg. It was "the most delightful camp which I remember during the war" according to Westwood Todd (1831–1886), a private in the Twelfth Virginia.[3]

Mahone's Brigade, then part of Anderson's Division, broke camp early on July 1, 1863, and marched eastward to join the Army of Northern Virginia. While the battle of Gettysburg would mark the high tide of the Confederacy, as defined by the repulse of Pickett's charge, Mahone's Brigade stood by in reserve and watched. General Mahone's decision to remain in reserve was confusing as more battle-weary regiments were thrown into brutal combat. However, reorganization of the Confederate officer corps had led to communication breakdowns that may have contributed to one of Lee's most hard-hitting commanders keeping his brigade on the bench.

In 1864, the Twelfth Virginia opposed General Grant's overland campaign at the Battle of the Wilderness. The battle, fought through a large, densely thicketed region, resulted in more than one case of friendly fire. When Mahone's Brigade entered a chaotic scene where lines and sides were crossed, he halted the troops. Unaware of the order to halt, Col. Weisiger led the Twelfth

Virginia in its rapid advance through the underbrush. Realizing he was well in advance of the brigade line, Col. Weisiger turned the Twelfth around and reversed direction. General Longstreet, attempting to reconnoiter the melee, became accidentally trapped between the lines as the Twelfth Virginia ran into the Forty-First Virginia. Sporadic, nervous fire from both sides increased to full volleys. When the smoke cleared, Gen. Longstreet was badly wounded and several soldiers from the Twelfth Virginia lay dead.

As 1864 drew on, the war settled on Petersburg, home to many of the Twelfth Virginia, and nearly all of the Petersburg Old Grays. Gen. Grant focused the might and power of the US Army on the city and began the final siege of the war. From June 18, 1864, until April of 1865, the regiment was largely entrenched at Petersburg. The Battle of the Crater, an attempt by the US Army to blow a hole in the Confederate defenses, was Mahone's Brigade's last notable action in major combat. When 320 kegs of gunpowder blew up beneath the Confederate line in the early hours of July 30, 1864, more than two hundred soldiers were immediately killed. A giant hole, ripped open from the earth, smoked and steamed. For about an hour, the confusion slowly abated. Leveraging the confused lines on both sides, Gen. Mahone led a counterattack. What resulted was one of the most futile and gory battles of the war. Its result was tactically meaningless, and more than 800 soldiers died. US "colored" troops who took part in the US advance were targeted by Confederates and even Mahone had trouble stopping the bloody reprisal.

When Petersburg fell in the spring of 1865, Mahone and the Twelfth Virginia moved westward on what would become Lee's Retreat, or the Appomattox Campaign. Mahone's men guarded the crossing of the Appomattox at Goode's Bridge before joining what was left of the Army of Northern Virginia on its march toward Lynchburg. After numerous skirmishes between the two armies and a major engagement at Sailor's Creek where Lee lost one-fifth of his army, the Petersburg Regiment surrendered a total of sixteen officers and 180 men at Appomattox.

Mahone's Brigade is unique in that it remained intact throughout the war. The Twelfth Virginia, the Petersburg Regiment, was remarkable since it was one of the most urban units in the Confederacy. It was also one of the most well educated. More men in the Twelfth had some form of formal education than in most other units. Today, we may easily fail to see Petersburg for the thriving urban center it once was. The "Cockade City," as it was known, was once the Southern literary and theatre capital. The Twelfth Virginia was its own regiment and so we return to the concept of a "rich man's war and a poor man's fight." The regiment took its share of body blows during the war, was never favored for being a bunch of rich "city boys," and even included farm lads from Meherrin and Brunswick. Like many units, the ranks swelled and, more often, dwindled, but the unit persisted.[4]

So why did muster roll end up in the Lee Monument? Furthermore, why *this* muster roll? What is the importance? There are likely three parts to this answer. First, a muster roll is a snapshot of a unit's composition and health. Comparing regimental muster rolls over time, we can see how its composition changed according to addition, loss, and absenteeism. In this muster roll, while much of the descriptive text is barely legible, we can see that many men were listed as "absent sick." A few were "absent without leave" (AWOL), and several were detailed to hospital or other duties. Was some of this favoritism for the rich boys to keep them out of combat? Maybe, but most regiments were drawn from to support the needs of the army. It is more likely that the higher degree of literacy or mathematical aptitude led the Twelfth Virginia to poaching by army brass for clerical and professional tasks. This muster roll provides a snapshot of the regiment by name and rank, it is a representative sample of the complex military organism. This form of recognition became a way to put names of the rank and file in a silent place to share the intended grandeur of the booted and spurred bronze hero, Lee.

The second part of the answer is purely conjectural but bears a moment of contemplation. When Captain T. A. Brander (1839–1900), former artillery commander under W. J. Pegram (1841–1865), placed the muster roll in the box, he did so not only as a proponent for the monument's construction but as a fellow veteran marking the names of many of his fellow soldiers. Prior to the war, Brander served with many of the Petersburg men who watched John Brown hang. The moment may have been the bond that lasted through, and after, the war. June 30, the date of the muster roll is symbolic. It was the last muster of the Petersburg Regiment prior to Gettysburg at their encampment at Fayetteville, Pennsylvania. Taken only moments before Lee's crushing defeat, it represents a time that Faulkner painted so well with words:

> It's all now you see. Yesterday won't be over until tomorrow and tomorrow began ten thousand years ago. For every Southern boy fourteen years old, not once but whenever he wants it, there is the instant when it still not yet two o'clock on that July afternoon in 1863, the brigades are in position behind the rail fence, the guns are laid and ready in the woods and the furled flags are already loosened to break out and Pickett himself with his long oiled ringlets and his hat in one hand probably

and his sword in the other looking up the hill waiting for Longstreet to give the word and it's all in the balance, it hasn't happened yet, it hasn't even begun yet, it not only hadn't begun yet . . . but there is still time for it not to begin against that position and those circumstances which made more men than Garnett and Kemper and Armistead and Wilcox look grave yet it's going to begin, we all know that, we have come too far with too much at stake and that moment doesn't even need a fourteen-year-old boy to think This time.[5]

The third part to the answer is what some members of the Twelfth Virginia and Mahone's Brigade did after the war. The uncharacteristically educated regiment played a big part in the Readjuster movement, led by Mahone and supported by a number of veterans from the Twelfth Virginia. This complex political party crossed many traditional boundaries, including race, and sought to refinance the state debt to establish a system of public education. They 'readjusted' war debt owed to Northern creditors and leveraged it to support such things as the Virginia Polytechnic Institute, more commonly known as Virginia Tech. Under the party, poll taxes and public whippings were eliminated. The Readjuster movement was over nearly as soon as it began, being seen by wealthy, power-brokering Whites as a threat. Capt. Brander's feelings toward, or involvement with, the Readjusters is unknown, and by the time the copper box was placed beneath the Lee Monument cornerstone in 1887 the movement had lost momentum four years prior. Nonetheless, veterans of the Twelfth Virginia were notably involved with the Readjusters and perhaps, just perhaps, Brander meant for their ameliorative attempts to be silently memorialized.

The faded paper, ink, and pencil of this muster roll is a snapshot of individuals, a unit, and a complex history. It glimpses John Brown's hanging, the "high tide" of the Army of Northern Virginia at Gettysburg, and the struggle to rebuild a war-ravaged Virginia. Tucked inside the stone of the monument in a silent moment, it speaks once more as a contemporary commentator in a sea of new voices.

NOTES

1. Boyd B. Stutler, "An Eyewitness Describes the Hanging of John Brown," *American Heritage* 6, no. 12, https://www.americanheritage.com/eyewitness-describes-hanging-john-brown.

2. "Application of Mary E. Beal to United Daughters of the Confederacy, Virginia Division, Scottsville Chapter, Henry Gantt Camp C.V.75; 23 September 1908," Collections of Scottsville Museum, Scottsville, VA.
3. Todd A. Westwood, *Reminiscences of the Civil War, #722* (Southern Historical Collection, The Wilson Library, University of North Carolina at Chapel Hill, 1936).
4. John Horn, *The Petersburg Regiment in the Civil War: A History of the 12th Virginia Infantry from John Brown's Hanging to Appomattox, 1859–1865* (El Dorado Hills, CA: Savas Beatie, 2019).
5. William Faulkner, *Intruder in the Dust* (New York: Random House, 1948).

19

Annual Reunion Pegram Battalion Association

Christopher A. Graham

The Virginia veterans of Pegram's Battalion marched into the House of Delegates chamber of the Virginia State Capitol and sat to witness what was to them a sacred ceremony. It was 1886, twenty-one years after the battlefield death of their namesake commander, Colonel William R.J. Pegram (1841–1865), in the last week of the war. After a prayer, W. Gordon McCabe, the battalion's wartime executive officer, arose and presented the battalion's battle flag to the Pegram's Battalion Association for safekeeping. McCabe recounted the battalion's history and launched into an oratory about Pegram. Almost as an afterthought, the association also took possession of Pegram's saber. The ceremony closed with a benediction, and the attendees crossed Broad Street and settled into dinner, drinks, and ceremonial toasts at Sagner Hall.[1]

The association subsequently published the proceedings of the event, and one unknown member donated this copy to the Lee Monument cornerstone box. (All quotes herein are from this document.)

The 1880s and 1890s had seen the flourishing of veterans' organizations and activities in Richmond. Groups like Pegram's Battalion Association, the Richmond Howitzers, the Association of the Army of Northern Virginia, and the Veteran Cavalry of the Army of Northern Virginia were social and cultural gathering spaces for veterans at the peak of their economic and political power. These groups met in annual meetings to reminisce with comrades and remember the old days. Every gathering from an association picnic to the funeral of prominent members earned a notice in Richmond's White newspapers.

Veterans met for more than just nostalgia. These associations worked

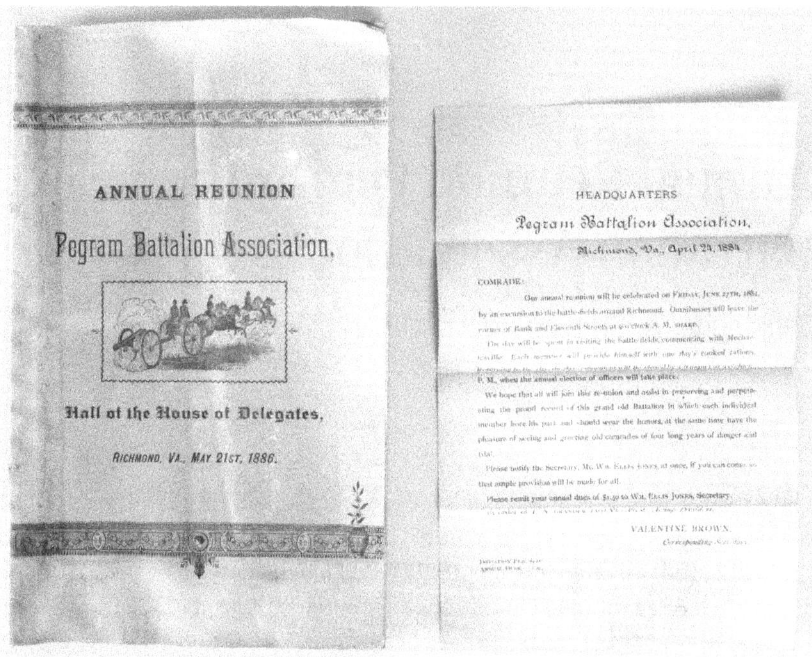

Figure 48. *Annual Reunion Pegram Battalion Association* program from Lee cornerstone box.

hard to fundraise and lobby for the erection of monuments to their men and their commanders. After the 1886 meeting, Pegram's Battalion Association took a leading role in the creation of the A. P. Hill burial site and monument formerly at the intersection of Laburnum and Hermitage in Richmond. They also raised funds for the care of elderly and infirm veterans at the R.E. Lee Camp No. 1's Soldier's Home, where they honored themselves with a memorial window to the battalion in the Soldier's Home chapel.

Richmond's web of Confederate veteran associations also worked hand-in-hand with United States veterans in the Soldier's Home project. The Grand Army of the Republic, spearheaded by Richmond's Phil Kearney Post, No. 10, donated a great deal of money in the early 1880s to the Confederate veteran home. This cooperation made sense to the men involved. After all, four years of killing one another had given way to an anxious peace as former Confederates resisted efforts to enforce racial equality during Reconstruction. Symbols of sectional cooperation like the partnership between Richmond veterans and the Phil Kearney Post were not ubiquitous in the 1880s.

Figure 49. Colonel William R. J. Pegram. (Courtesy of the American Civil War Museum)

The veterans therefore sought any opportunity to celebrate fraternal moments that promised peace and satisfied the emotional and political needs of both sides.[2]

The Pegram's Battalion veterans in 1886 did not emphasize those specific needs in the speeches contained in this pamphlet, but they are still apparent.

The pamphlet began with McCabe's tribute to Pegram, noting that "he needs no panegyric in the presence of the men who knew him" and then proceeded to deliver such a public speech to the men who had known him. He traced Pegram's military career. The twenty-year-old Richmond native left his studies at the University of Virginia to join the Confederate army and quickly rose through the ranks to command, first, the Purcell Artillery battery and then the battalion of cannoneers attached to General A. P. Hill's infantry division. McCabe described an unassuming and near-sighted youth with tightly pursed lips who enforced strict discipline and became a battle captain seeking the most desperate assignments and delivering frightful damage to the enemy. Pegram's adherence to discipline and his love of combat made him a magnetic commander whose men revered him.

McCabe's adjectives made his points. Resolute, youthful, generous, brilliant, Christian, exact, cheerful, boyish, and noble: they sustained a character study of Pegram and of the Confederate soldier in general as almost perfect and forever pure. Pegram's former comrades, no doubt, regarded

Figure 50. Photograph of Pegram's Battalion memorial window from the Confederate Memorial Chapel found in the Lee cornerstone box, next to a picture of the same window in 2020. (Courtesy of the Virginia Department of Historic Resources; Virginia Museum of Fine Arts)

him in such lofty estimation, but it was also an abstraction applied to any Confederate veteran about whom veterans talked. These veterans regarded themselves and their lost comrades as having survived the most grueling test because of their character, courage, and virtue. They insisted so strenuously that it defies credulity. Confederate veterans were "the embodiment of what is noblest in human nature," one 1886 association speaker claimed, "and the incarnation of all that is God-like in man!"

They demanded that this incarnation made them able to govern in the present, receive adulation of future generations, and be regarded as the *best* Americans in the reunified United States.

More American than actual United States soldiers who had preserved the Union? One Pegram's Battalion speaker had an answer for that: "The Confederate infantry was distinctively an American infantry and its victories distinctively the triumph of Americans over armies composed, perhaps in greater part, of recruits drawn from the half civilized nations of the world."

It was this same assumption—their own native ethnic and racial superiority—that drove their cultural politics in their present. If their former foes and their former slaves would just accept the fact of their wartime courage and of their superiority in the present, they reasoned, then they would be happy to "rejoice . . . in the integrity of the Union" and even to be "glad that the slaves had been set free." Reunion was a fact settled by Appomattox, but reconciliation would only happen on their terms.[3] The rhetoric worked. It became a trope of the Lost Cause and of Civil War memory that Confederates represented something wholesome while the US Army had been composed of the flotsam of the modern world.

The association found these sentiments so compelling that they had the speeches printed and distributed widely. It survived not only in the cornerstone box but also in numerous libraries and archives today, a testament to the veterans' regard for their fallen comrades and to what they wanted from the present and the future.

NOTES

1. Pegram Battalion Association, *Annual Reunion of Pegram Battalion Association: In the Hall of House of Delegates, Richmond, Va., May 21st 1886* (Richmond, VA: W. E. Jones, 1886).
2. Elizabeth L. O'Leary, *Across Time: The History of the Grounds of the Virginia Museum of Fine Arts* (Richmond: Virginia Museum of Fine Arts, 2019).
3. M. Keith Harris, *Across the Bloody Chasm: The Culture of Commemoration Among Civil War Veterans* (Baton Rouge: Louisiana State University Press, 2014).

20

A Lasting Impression

Inspecting the Seal of the Office of the Adjutant and Inspector General's Office, CSA

Brendan Burke

In this chapter, we explore the Office of the Adjutant and Inspector General, its role in the Confederacy, a wax impression of the office's seal, and the man who saved the wax impression for posterity. The small wax seal was made by pouring molten sealing wax onto a piece of cardstock and then impressing the seal itself into the viscous wax. The seal, a negative impression of the actual wax seal, contains crossed cannon topped by what appears to be seven stars. A ring surrounds the motif and is wrapped with the text "ADJT. & INSP. GEN.OFFICE.CSA." A dotted border forms the outer bounds of the seal. The wax sealing material is somewhat pink in color and may have originally been a different hue and altered by the conditions in the copper box. Contrary to popular culture, not all sealing waxes were red. In fact, red was often used in personal or business correspondence during the nineteenth century to signify bad or urgent news.

TO MAKE OFFICIAL—CREATING A GOVERNMENT, ARMY, AND CREDIBILITY

If the pen is mightier than the sword, then perhaps the seal is mightier than the pen. Many documents, even when signed, are not complete without an official seal. The concept of sealing is ancient and still venerated. From notaries to clerks of the court, much of our business is simply not official until sealed. When an entity becomes official, it needs a seal. When the Confederate States of America sought to gain legitimacy as a political organization in

Figure 51. This is a wax impression from the seal of the Adjutant and Inspector General's Office of the Confederate States Army. Collected by Capt. John Mayer, who worked within the office, this seal would have been affixed to important documents to indicate they were originals issued from the central office.

1861, it created offices and organizations to do the business of a government in rebellion. The same was true of its military, a near carbon copy of the US military but dressed in Cadet Gray. Outside of symbology and uniform color, there were few distinctions. One such difference was the amalgamation of the roles of the adjutant general and inspector of the Confederate State Army. Unlike the US Army system that supported two separate offices with two very different purposes, the Confederate version combined the roles.

ORGANIZING FOR VICTORY

The word "adjutant" is one rarely used outside of a military context. An adjutant is an administrative assistant, a commissioned officer, who serves and assists a higher officer. An adjutant general is thereby the highest-ranking administrative officer in an army. While the role may not direct troop movements or pull the lanyard on a cannon, the role of the adjutant general is critical to organizing an armed force. General orders flow from the adjutant general's office. These are the overarching orders that function as an administrative code for officers to consult. General orders cover a wide variety of topics and may include military law. Adjutants are constantly collecting data on troops, battles, and conditions. The combined information is fed to the command structure to allow them to keep track of the disposition of their fighting forces and help make decisions concerning troop movements.

INSPECTING TO SUCCEED

On October 29, 1777, the first inspector general was appointed to help mold the Continental Army into a fighting machine. Inspectors general are charged with oversight of training, reviewing troops, establishing discipline, and ensuring justice within the command structure. The first inspector general of note was Baron Frederick William Augustus von Steuben (1730–1794). By 1778, Lt. Gen. von Steuben, who spoke no English, created an Office of the Inspector General and began to mold the Continental Army into an effective force. From that point on, the US Army maintained, and maintains, an Office of the Inspector General whose duties are to ensure the fighting trim of our soldiers.

A CONFEDERATE COMBINATION

The roles of adjutant general and inspector general are typically two separate commands. However, due to the necessity to mobilize rapidly in 1861, combined with a preference by President Davis for appointing personal relationship over talent, Samuel Cooper (1798–1876) was appointed to a combined office. Cooper and Davis were not only well known to each other, both had served as Secretary of War during the 1850s. Cooper, a New York native, had also served in the army's Adjutant General office since the late 1830s. His service in the Second Seminole War (1841–1842) and the Mexican American War (1846–1848) prepared Cooper well for the monumental administrative role of establishing a Confederate army.

Samuel Cooper was the first full general officer in the Confederacy and while the names of Lee, Johnston, and Beauregard are more well known, Gen. Cooper was technically senior to them all and served throughout the war as the senior-most Confederate military officer. While Lee and his fel-

Figure 52. This image of Adjutant and Inspector General Samuel Cooper was included in an 1895 chromolithograph. The broadside includes a central image of the Lee Monument, a portrait of Lee, and is surrounded by famous Confederate military commanders and politicians. Note that Gen. Cooper is not shown in uniform, a common depiction of Adjutant Generals as they have periodically eschewed martial dress. (Courtesy of Library of Congress)

low field commanders assembled armies from local militias, Gen. Cooper was busily erecting an administrative and organization architecture for the army. His headquarters was in the War Department building, formerly the Richmond Mechanic's Institute, and just southwest of the Capitol Grounds where the modern Eighth & Main building now sits. General orders outlined everything from the mustering of troops, to compiling manuals of arms, to uniform standards. The *Uniform and Dress of the Army of the Confederate States*, published in 1861, was a valiant attempt at standardizing the Confederate fighting uniform. Not surprisingly, it followed basic tenets of the US Army such as the colors for piping or facings for artillery, cavalry, infantry, and medical departments. The color of gray for the Confederate uniform was assigned by the manual to be "cadet gray." While the adjutant and inspector general may prescribe a cut and color of uniform, the manufacturing capacity of the South, even supported by imports ferreted in through the blockade, was insufficient to create uniformity in material.

When not engaged in updating manuals or drafting general orders, the adjutant and inspector general's office was swamped in field reports. As the chief administrator of the armies, Gen. Cooper's office was a central node for information. Field reports included a basic synopsis of a skirmish or battle, a list of wounded/killed/missing, and any weapons seized. Field intelligence reports also came into Cooper's office. To be in the Adjutant and Inspector General's office meant having your finger on the pulse of the war.

Behind the pomp and circumstance of dashing sabers, sparkling bullion, and cockaded slouch hats was always the adjutant and inspector general. It was in that office that the true cost of war was measured in cold, calculating figures. It was in that office that some semblance of order was to be maintained by regulating the role of partisan rangers out in the hinterlands. And it was through the inspections of garrisons, posts, and facilities that the office attempted to hold together an army partially ruled by thirteen governors. Meanwhile, silently sitting on Gen. Cooper's desk was a seal. A little more than an inch wide, it would have been repeatedly pressed into sealing wax to dispatch letters from Gen. Cooper to the field and pass the word to the Confederate government on the status of their war.

RECOGNIZING THE MOMENT

So how did an impression of this seal come to be in the copper box? Capt. John F. Mayer (1840–1919) served in a clerical role in the Adjutant and Inspector General's office in Richmond during the Civil War.[1] Mayer also collected signatures and documents from his office that were determined to be redundant. At some point, Capt. Mayer took it upon himself to make a seal on card stock using the brass seal of the office, a special privilege. According to collections records of the American Civil War Museum, Mayer may have accompanied the records of the Adjutant and Inspector General's office when they were evacuated from Richmond to Charlotte, North Carolina in April of 1865. He saved a flag that had been the headquarters ensign for Robert E. Lee from being turned over to the US Army. So, we may assume that not only did Capt. Mayer have a close association with the office records, but also a penchant for saving iconographic items associated with the Confederacy. The seal and a registered $100,000 bond were donated by Capt. Mayer to William Isaacs (1818–1895), a leader of the Lee Monument movement who oversaw collecting items for the cornerstone box.

As to Gen. Cooper, his role in the Civil War may best be summed up as the chief curator of the records of the Confederate armies. At the end of the war, fire ravaged building after building as Richmond set itself ablaze. However, it was the careful assemblage and curation of the records of the Adjutant and Inspector General's office that allowed the Civil War to be documented. Years later, as the 127 volume *War of the Rebellion: A Compilation of the Official*

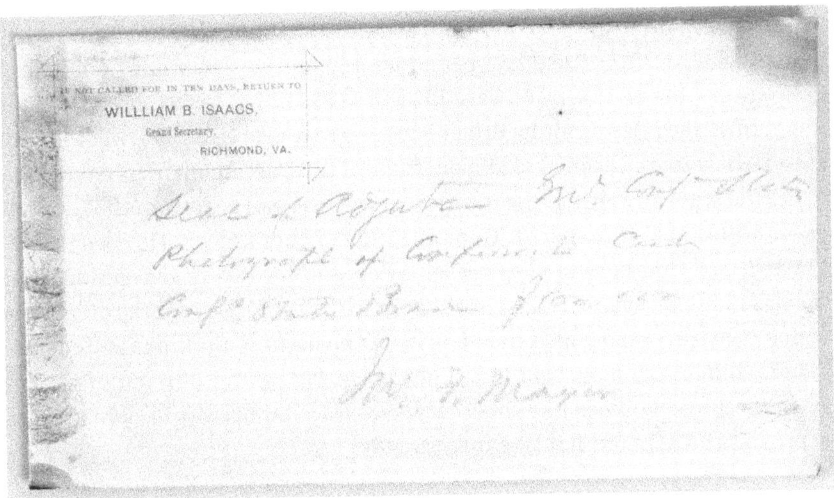

Figure 53. William Isaacs placed this envelope in the copper box set beneath the Lee Monument cornerstone.

Records of the Union and Confederate Armies was assembled (referred to as the "Official Record"), much of the documentation was saved by Gen. Cooper.

EXPLORING THE SYMBOL

The seal itself may still exist but has not been viewed by the author. It is likely that it was made from a copper-alloy blank. An engraver would have carved the design in reverse into the face of the seal. Seals of this size were often heavy and meant to have the mass to absorb heat and cool the wax, especially where multiple seals were required such as in a busy government office. A warm seal prevented the wax from cooling and hardening. What is interesting here is that the clarity of the wax impression is poor. Many wax seals, if kept clean, offer a perfect impression of their surface. Perhaps the wax itself was of poor quality, maybe even diluted with lesser materials to stretch it out during the war. If this impression was made during the Civil War that may account for the poor quality of the sealing wax.

A historic seal of New Kent County was authenticated by DHR in 2021. That seal, a solid brass disk, was engraved by William Wagner, of York, Pennsylvania, sometime during the mid-nineteenth century. Wagner was a popular engraver and made several hundred seals for counties, courts, and companies. The New Kent seal had been taken from the New Kent Courthouse grounds in June of 1862 by Edward Brown, a US soldier. In October of 2021, it was returned to New Kent by Brown's great-great-grandson. During the process, DHR was approached to inspect the seal for assessment of its condition.

At the time of writing, the location of the original seal from the Confederate Adjutant and Inspector General's office is not known. However, Capt. Mayer saved this small, wax representation of it for future generations that we may now appreciate it. It is a testament to the hidden role of the office, one which has nearly concealed the identity of the highest-ranking Confederate general officer from our common knowledge. No matter how out of view, it was functionary offices like this that have, since before the Roman armies, arranged and kept our fighting forces ready.

NOTE

1. Robert J. Raynor, *Raynor's Compendium of Autographs & Biographies of the High Commanders of the Confederate States of America* (Raynor's Publishing, 2007).

21

Investing in the Confederacy

The Role of Bonds in Funding the Confederacy

Robert L. Jolley

CONFEDERATE NEED TO RAISE REVENUE

When the Confederacy seceded from the Union, they were confronted with the task of establishing a new government. They needed to act quickly to enact laws and establish offices to manage the affairs of state. Of immediate concern was the need to raise revenue through borrowing, taxation, and printing currency.

The Confederate government turned to issuing bonds and printing currency to generate the revenue needed to run government affairs and fund the war effort. According to one researcher, Confederate bonds accounted for 32 percent of Confederate States of America (CSA) revenues compared to 60 percent from printing currency.[1] Imposing taxes was not politically feasible in a newly established country advocating states' rights, and collecting tariffs from imported goods was impeded by the Union blockade. As a result, taxation accounted for only 8 percent of the revenue the Confederacy was able to raise.

THE BOND

A bond authorized by the Confederate legislature was one of the items deposited in the cornerstone box. The bond depicts the image of a man and woman in the center and a woman standing with a shield (an allegorical depiction of Liberty) in the lower left-hand corner. The bond has a value of $100,000, yielded 8 percent interest, and was issued on March 17, 1864. The bond had an 1871 redemption date, six years after the CSA ceased to exist. This type of bond is considered rare as it is estimated that only 445 were issued and only five in the amount of $100,000.[2] The large denomination of this bond is unusual as the value of most bonds ranged from $100 to $1,000.

The first bonds authorized by Confederate legislation were intended to raise $15,000,000 to meet the immediate needs of the new government. Additional bond acts from 1861 through 1864 authorized greater sums to support the war effort.[3]

The bond was deposited in the cornerstone box by John F. Mayer who also deposited the adjutant general's seal. Who was Mayer and why did he leave this item in the box? His service records indicate he was a clerk at the War Department in Richmond during the war.[4] He contributed archival material relating to the Civil War on several occasions to the Southern Historical Society and was noted as being "an industrious collector of Confederate material."[5] He was not only present at the unveiling of the Lee Monument but was also actively involved, pulling ropes when the monument was transported from the railroad station to Monument Avenue.

Who invested $100,000, an amount equivalent to $1,776,000 in today's money in 1864 when the South was in dire straits and had lost decisive battles at Gettysburg and Vicksburg?[6] The bondholder is not legible, as the ink is smeared due to water damage, but the last two legible letters "Co" indicate it was held by a company, not a person. Since the company was able and willing to purchase a $100,000 bond, they must have had a vested interest in the Confederacy. Additional examination of the bond in the future using advanced imaging techniques may reveal the identity of the bondholder.

As with most CSA bonds and currency, this bond was printed by a lithographer in a Southern state, J. T. Paterson & Co. of Columbia, South Carolina. Paterson, a Scottish dentist living in Georgia when the Civil War started, was one of twelve known printers of Confederate bonds. He entered the security engraving business to avoid the Confederate Conscription Act of 1862 because occupations that served the public interest were exempt from conscription.[7]

Other printers of Confederate bonds include an unknown firm in England and the American Bank Note Company of New York. Ironically, the first order for the printing of Confederate bonds was placed with the New Orleans branch of the American Bank Note Company but was actually printed at the American Bank Note Company in New York before war commenced with the bombing of Fort Sumter.[8] After war broke out, US marshals seized the plates

Figure 54. Obverse and reverse of the bond found in the Lee cornerstone box.

used to print the bonds from the New York branch of the American Bank Note Company.

The person who signed the bond, Robert Tyler (1816–1877), Register of the Confederate States Treasury, was the son of US President John Tyler. Before war broke out, Robert Tyler was the head of the Democratic Party in Pennsylvania and after the war, he became the head of the Democratic Party in Alabama.[9]

OTHER TYPES OF CONFEDERATE BONDS

The first attempt to categorize Confederate bonds was made in the twentieth century with the goal to provide a guide for collectors.[10] A more detailed study, involving the examination of tens of thousands of bonds, resulted not only in the publication of a definitive catalog but also the completion of a PhD dissertation from the University of London's School of Economics. Ball's research also led to the discovery and study of a large hoard of forgotten CSA bonds that had been stored in England for over a century.

Confederate bonds depict a variety of images. Most have lithographs of CSA figures (elected officials and cabinet officers) but also include historical American figures (George Washington and Andrew Jackson), monuments, ships, trains, bales of cotton, soldiers, allegorical figures (Liberty, Columbia, and Ceres) and other subject matter. The most common figures depicted on Confederate bonds were the first two Confederate States Secretary of the Treasury, C.G. Memminger (Feb 21, 1861–July 18, 1864) and George A. Trenholm (July 18, 1864–April 27, 1865).

The Confederate practice of depicting portraits of contemporary political figures on their bonds and currency differs from the US tradition of never depicting living figures on currency, a practice still held to this day. US coinage in the nineteenth century relied on Liberty style images and it was not until 1909, when an image of Lincoln was placed on the penny to commemorate the hundredth anniversary of his birth that an exception was made to place a deceased figure on US coinage.

Over 360 varieties of CSA bonds are recognized based on differences in vignettes, their value, or other attributes such as the paper they were printed on. Interest rates on CSA bonds varied from 4 to 8 percent and the maturation date varied from 1864–1893 depending upon the amount of interest authorized by the Confederate legislature.

The CSA issued mostly domestic bonds but also collaborated with European countries to market bonds. One of the foreign bonds was backed by cotton, which traded mainly in England, and the other was a high risk (junk bond) traded in Amsterdam. The cotton bonds were redeemable in cotton during the war, but the holder of the bond had to navigate through the Union blockade to receive bales of cotton at designated Southern ports. There was a political motivation behind the foreign bonds, especially the cotton bonds, for they provided an incentive for European intervention to support the South.

During the brief four-year history of the Confederacy, monetary reforms were implemented to encourage the conversion of currency into bonds. These reforms also had the effect of increasing the price of goods.[11] The inflation rate in the Confederacy rose to over 9,000 percent at the end of the war as compared to only 80 percent for the Union.[12]

Despite numerous legislative acts to control the fiscal economy, rampant inflation caused social unrest. In March and April of 1863, the price of basic commodities led to bread riots in Southern cities, including an organized riot in the City of Richmond.

POST WAR SPECULATION AND TWENTIETH-CENTURY HOARD DISCOVERY

CSA bonds were actively traded on the London and Amsterdam stock markets and their value steadily declined as the war progressed due to CSA military setbacks. The bonds continued to be traded after the Civil War based on speculation that the United States government may partially redeem their value. However, the Fourteenth Amendment to the US Constitution, passed on July 9, 1868, prevented this from happening: "neither the United States nor any state shall assume or pay any debt or obligation incurred in aid of insurrection or rebellion against the United States, or any claim for the loss or emancipation of any slave; but all such debts, obligations and claims shall be held illegal and void."

Despite the passing of the Fourteenth Amendment, speculation continued in European markets with offers to buy the bonds for 10 percent of their face value during the period 1879–1884. At that time, there was a Confederate depositary in Europe that was still receiving assets after the war and a Confederate Bond Holders Committee was established in England to redeem the bonds. Bonds flowed into Great Britain from Southern states during this period.[13]

Once it was finally determined that the bonds had no monetary value, many if not most were discarded. However, more than 100,000 unclaimed and unredeemable CSA bonds, held in a vault by the Coutts Bank of England for over a century, were rediscovered and sold to an American numismatic company in the 1980s.[14] Today they sell and trade on the open market as Civil War memorabilia.

NOTES

1. Marc D. Weidenmier, "Money and Finance in the Confederate States of America," *Explorations in Economic History* 30, no. 1 (1993): 352–76.
2. Douglas B. Ball, *Comprehensive Catalog and History of Confederate Bonds* (Port Clinton, OH: BNR Press, 1998), 42.
3. Ball, *Comprehensive Catalog and History of Confederate Bonds*, 246–47.
4. "John F. Mayer," *fold3*, https://www.fold3.com/.
5. Rev. J. William Jones, DD, *Southern Historical Society Papers* 3 (1877): 95.
6. *CPI Inflation Calculator*, Accessed March 6, 2022, https://www.bls.gov/data/inflation_calculator.htm.
7. Ball, *Comprehensive Catalog and History of Confederate Bonds*, 18.
8. Ball, *Comprehensive Catalog and History of Confederate Bonds*, 18.
9. Ball, *Comprehensive Catalog and History of Confederate Bonds*, 21.
10. Grover C. Criswell, *Confederate and Southern States Bonds*, 2nd ed. (Criswell Publications, 1980).
11. Richard C. K. Burdekin and Marc D. Weidenmier, "Suppressing Asset Price Inflation: The Confederate Experience, 1861–1865," *Economic Inquiry* 41, no. 3 (2003): 420.
12. Douglas B. Ball, *Financial Failure and Confederate Defeat*. (Urbana: University of Illinois Press, 1991).
13. Ball, *Comprehensive Catalog and History of Confederate Bonds*, 10.
14. Ball, *Comprehensive Catalog and History of Confederate Bonds*, 10.

Epilogue

Julian Maxwell Hayter

Yet remembrance is always a form of forgetting, and the dominant narrative . . .–distilled from history and memory, twisted by ideology and political contestation, and embedded in heritage tours, museums, public rituals, textbooks, and various artifacts of mass culture—distorts and suppresses as much as it reveals—Jacquelyn Dowd Hall, 2005.[1]

Richmond, Virginia, is most often remembered as the former capital of the Confederacy. Richmond was essential to American liberty. Patrick Henry gave his celebrated "Liberty or Death" speech at Richmond's St. John's Church in 1775. Some of America's loudest cries for liberty came not from Massachusetts or Pennsylvania, but from Maryland and Virginia.[2] Yet, bondage too became a defining characteristic of Richmond's identity. During the mid-nineteenth century, the capital of the Commonwealth was the second-largest slave trading center in the South, second only to New Orleans. By the dawn of the Civil War, slave trading and slave-based tobacco production had made a good number of Richmonders extraordinarily wealthy. Richmond's factories specialized in tobacco production, manufacturing iron, and milling flour. The River City was one of the few industrialized cities in the American South prior to the Civil War. Many of these industries often used enslaved labor. The ideas and institutions that made slavery possible survived the Civil War. To this day, the city has struggled to unfetter itself from the history of American slavery and the Confederate cause that arose to defend it.

Richmond was the epicenter of Confederate identity long after the American Civil War. No place better embodied the city's centrality to the Confederacy, and remembrance of it, than Monument Avenue. Until recently, Monument Avenue and the statues that dotted its landscape seemed like permanent fixtures. The statues of Jefferson Davis, Stonewall Jackson, Robert E. Lee, Matthew Maury, and J. E. B. Stuart stood relatively uncontested for decades.[3] During the Jim Crow era, Monument Avenue effectively separated White neighborhoods on Richmond's West End from the almost exclusively Black enclaves east of Broad Street. In fact, the Lee statue, erected in 1890, was the only statue on Monument Avenue built in the nineteenth century. Richmond built its last Confederate statue, a memorial to Confederate naval Commander Matthew Maury, sixty-four years after the Civil War, in 1929. Celebrated by some, detested by many, these statues were more than war memorials. They were testaments to the order of racial apartheid that arose throughout the American South after the Civil War.

In the summer of 2020, protestors initiated the process of demonumentalizing the avenue. At the height of the COVID pandemic, on June 10, 2020, a diverse group of activists and protestors ripped the statue of Jefferson Davis from its pedestal. The day before, the same protestors had torn down a statue of Christopher Columbus and threw it into the Fountain Lake of Byrd Park. In time, protestors began to use the scale and grandeur of Richmond's Confederate monuments as mediums for protest art. They first graffitied protest messages onto the statues. Artists Alex Criqui and Dustin Klein, as a part of the Black Lives Matter movement, then began to project images of Black heroes onto the Lee Monument. The *New York Times* called the projections onto the Lee Monument the most powerful piece of protest art in American history since the Second World War.[4] Politicians answered the call. Richmond's mayor, Levar Stoney, and Virginia's governor, Ralph Northam, finally activated the machinery of government to remove the monuments. Lee, the largest monument on the avenue, was the last to go. In September of 2021, contractors from Team Henry Enterprises, began to bring the Lee Monument down. They eventually pulled the copper cornerstone box (and an unexpected box placed by the builders) from the pedestal shortly after.

The Lee Monument epitomizes how many White Richmonders (and Southerners) felt about not just Lee, but the cause he fought to defend. The contents of the copper box (and the boxes embedded in the pedestals of Monument Avenue's other statues) were equally intentional in their veneration and vindication of the Confederate cause. In fact, the artifacts, which had been enshrined in the statue's pedestal since 1887, give rise to deeper questions about the making, recording, and interpreting of history. In this way, memorabilia matter—it tells the story of the post–Civil War South and the people who weaponized history to help make sense of a world that the Civil War turned on its head.

In some ways, the previous pages are only technically about the contents found in the boxes under the Lee Monument. This effort is, more broadly, an examination of the distinctions between history and heritage: material culture and memory. To be sure, the authors treat the contents of the copper box as important historical artifacts—on their own terms, as memento mori of a people who fought for, and lived in the shadow of, a defeated and defunct nation. The pages above move beyond merely observing and chronicling these items. In fact, if heritage is based on features of the past that people choose to keep (namely because these features are inherited and cherished), the authors are attempting to reconstruct and understand the past by contemplating the evidence and considering their context. These are fundamentally historical endeavors. In thinking about why historical actors placed certain objects in the box, we begin to understand what historical actors did, and *did not*, value. Readers begin to understand what these Richmonders wanted us to remember, and perhaps forget, about their world.

In telling this story, the pages above contemplate the relationship between memory and material culture. The effort first delineates the historical context that gave rise to Monument Avenue. The next section considers the cultural values that gave rise to the contents of the copper box, while the last section uses military memorabilia to consider how historical actors made sense of the war and the postbellum South. Beneath the three sections lie very fundamental questions about not only the cornerstone box, but the people affiliated with its enshrinement. Namely, what were these people trying to convey about their world? What do the objects tell us about what they valued? What does the omission of certain objects tell us about these actors' preferences? How do we, despite the many intolerably anachronistic ways these people thought, begin to view these talismanic materials on their own terms? And, ultimately, do these artifacts tell us *the story* of what happened or *a story* that people wanted us to believe?

In answering these questions, a larger theme begins to emerge from this work—while primary documents and artifacts may belong to the past, *history* is what experts make of the surviving materials. And, it is impossible to understand the contents of these boxes—or the Confederate statuary on Monument Avenue—without considering the context that shaped them: namely, the history of the American Civil War, the demise of American slavery, and the segregated order that arose after slavery's end. Much has been made over the motivations of the people who erected the statues on Monument Avenue—the copper cornerstone box is an important glimpse into the ways postbellum Richmonders saw their world, their war, and their memory. Here is what these accounts seem to illustrate:

The first chapter sets the tone. It is, readers come to understand, impossible to remove the memorialization of the Confederacy and the lionization of the war effort from the anomie that came to characterize life in Richmond after Confederate soldiers razed the city during their retreat on April 3, 1865. Richmond was built upon the ashes of the Confederacy's defeat, and Monument Avenue arose in the crucible of what we might call late-nineteenth-century suburban expansion. In their anxious pursuit to remember the past and build a neighborhood in its memory, the second and third chapters demonstrate precisely how the architects of the Lost Cause (see below) very purposefully celebrated certain history yet seemed to intentionally omit certain actors. In fact, White women, who played a central role in memorializing the Confederate Cause, were very curiously left out of the copper box. So too, for obvious reasons, were African Americans. These sins of omission tell yet another story—we not only see both that women and Black people were essential to Confederate remembrance, African Americans (who helped erect the Lee Monument), especially, were the first people to recognize that Confederate memory had gravely mythological implications.

Over the next several sections, the chapters dedicated to material culture and memorabilia demonstrate not just how people made sense of the war in real time, but how those that placed the items in the box wanted posterity to remember Southerners and Confederate veterans. The contents of these boxes, from elites' calling cards to copper coins, carved objects, and military memorabilia emphasize a specific type of history—a history of elitism, loyalty, duty, and purpose. Even the contents of the other (lead) box unearthed in the Lee pedestal, namely the 1889 book, *The Huguenot Lovers*, is a literary window into how Southern socialites, many who lost out on the possibility of slaveholding, thought about life after the war. A world where chivalry, romance, and reverence for the antebellum past began to masquerade as real history. Here we begin to see two distinct trends taking place in the boxes—people are attempting to preserve artifacts of importance (real history) while romanticizing the antebellum South and the Confederate cause (nostalgia).

We are then left to contemplate Monument Avenue and these artifacts (and those responsible for them) considering what we now know about the history of late-nineteenth-century Richmond. On the one hand, former Confederates, their veterans' associations, and mutual aid societies claimed that Confederate iconography and statuary were war memorials—they were material manifestations of bereavement and commemoration.[5] On the other hand, Black Southerners found it difficult to divorce the rise of Confederate statues from the rise of the segregated system. Southerners designed segregation to strip recently emancipated freed people of their constitutional rights (especially the Reconstruction amendments). In time, Jim Crow laws reduced Black Southerners to second-class citizens, marginalized their labor, controlled the movement of Black bodies and, for the purposes of this effort, allowed Whites to reorganize public spaces. In this way, Confederate monuments, even if we consider them war memorials, are inextricably linked to the politics of Jim Crow segregation.

And the politics of Jim Crow segregation paved the way for Confederate iconography. Following the American Civil War, Southerners met the challenges of Black emancipation with restriction. By the dawn of the twentieth century, America watched as Southerners nullified Black citizenship.[6] While racial segregation in the South did not happen uniformly or instantaneously, by the early 1880s, Jim Crow became synonymous with a set of customs and laws that not only separated Black and White peoples but stripped Black Southerners of economic and political power.[7] None of the memorials erected on Monument Avenue were built with a popular mandate. Although most Confederate statues were funded and erected privately, their placement (and maintenance) in public spaces was made possible only by White overrepresentation on Southern legislative bodies.[8]

Apart from the Lee Monument, which Richmond unveiled twenty years after his surrender at Appomattox, all the Avenue's Confederate statues were built in the twentieth century, at the very moment when Virginia's undemocratic proclivities were at the high-water mark. In fact, the Constitutional Convention of 1901–1902 used poll taxes and literacy tests to remove undesirables from the electoral process. These direct disenfranchisement measures effectively removed 80 percent of African Americans from the voting ranks. It also removed 50 percent of Whites from the rolls. Virginia had the lowest voter turnout rate in the United States and one of the lowest rates of any free democracy in the world for most of the early twentieth century.[9] It is difficult to separate Monument Avenue and the placement of Confederate statues in public space from the segregationist politics of exclusion.

Richmond has never been un-segregated. And Monument Avenue was "but one of many examples of the fiendishly covetous ways that Southern politicians and profiteers used urban development" and the Lost Cause to keep neighborhoods racially homogeneous.[10] In fact, Virginia's then-governor, Fitzhugh Lee (who also happened to be the nephew of Robert E. Lee) openly rejected attempts to place Lee's statue at the Commonwealth's capital. He also very openly referred to Monument Avenue as a "plain business proposition."[11] In many ways, Monument Avenue was the late-nineteenth-century precursor to the discriminatory residential laws and housing patterns that defined most (if not all) of the twentieth century: racial zoning, redlining, restrictive covenants, urban renewal, and slum clearance. In fact, Richmond was second only to Baltimore, Maryland, in codifying racially restrictive zoning laws in the early twentieth century.[12] The effects of residential segregation survived the segregated system—Richmond was more residentially segregated by race and class in 1980 than it was in the 1960s.[13]

If the Lost Cause eventually emerged more prominently in Virginia, it did not begin there. The Lost Cause of the Confederacy not only resolved to justify slavery and the Civil War; its proponents rewrote history to affirm segregation. It emerged while the war was still taking place, eventually sought to justify the South's role in initiating the conflict and attempted to rationalize the carnage. Often put forward by former Confederate elites, Confederate military leadership, and women affiliated with both (namely The United Daughters of the Confederacy), the Lost Cause promoted several major mythologies about slavery, the Civil War, and former slaves.[14] Confederate apologists argued:

- Slavery was a benign institution and slaveowners were benign paternalists.
- The Civil War was about states' rights rather than slavery.
- The Confederacy was a heroic effort to maintain the Southern way of life.
- The Confederacy was destined to lose because the North had more resources and men.
- Black people were unprepared for freedom.[15]

The remnants of the Lost Cause have outlived Confederate statuary. During the 1950s, state officials began the process of overseeing the writing of civics and history books throughout the state. In 1950, Virginia's General Assembly created the Virginia History and Government Textbook Commission to directly supervise their content. Governor John S. Battle appointed a seven-member board made up of politicians, historians, and teachers. This board, which disbanded after agreeing upon material for the textbooks, eventually mandated that millions of public school students in the Commonwealth read books such as, *Virginia: History, Government, and Geography, Virginia's History*, and *Cavalier Commonwealth: History and Government in Virginia*.[16] These books' depictions of slavery, the Civil War, and Confederate leadership were direct reflections of Lost Cause assertions and informed later scholarly books written by children educated during this era—namely, *Richmond: The Story of a City* by Virginius Dabney.[17] Many of these ideas are still with us—history textbooks with Lost Cause talking points were often not phased out of American classrooms until the late twentieth century. In Virginia, you can still find many of these points tucked away in public school textbooks.[18] In 2011, the Pew Research Center reported that nearly half of Americans still believe that states' rights primarily caused the Civil War—only 38 percent of Americans believed that slavery was the primary cause of the Civil War.[19]

I say all of this to underscore a point that cannot be overstated: things done purposefully can only be undone on purpose. Jim Crow segregation and Confederate memorialization were intentional endeavors designed to enforce racial apartheid. Any attempt to reconcile this history must be equally intentional. In fact, Monument Avenue is not the only artifact of the Jim Crow system that remains in Richmond. To this day, Richmond is a hypersegregated city with disproportionately high rates of concentrated Black poverty. The public funds spent on Monument Avenue came at the expense of developing Richmond's Black communities. Very few people know this—the City of Richmond failed to install modern sewage systems in the African American sections of Church Hill until 1953! Richmond had one of the highest Black mortality rates in the United States during the mid-twentieth century.[20] These are the lasting artifacts of Jim Crow and they have been difficult to reconcile.

It is impossible to contemplate the future of Monument Avenue without first looking backward. The relics of the Jim Crow system still exist in Richmond. And ignorance of this history has made it difficult to devise real solutions to current problems: namely the failures of Richmond Public Schools (RPS) and entrenched poverty. To this day, the areas where students and families live often dictates educational and health outcomes. In 2020, RPS had the lowest on-time graduation rate and highest dropout rate in the Commonwealth of Virginia. The graduation rate in 2020 stood at 71.6 percent. Only 33 percent of Latinx students graduated on time and 80 percent of African

American students.[21] These graduation rates, we know now, are a reflection not just of contemporary racial and socioeconomic problems, but of history. Or rather, Richmond's reluctance to deal with it. Student performance in RPS cannot be divorced from the sordid historical legacy of racial segregation and the ideas that arose to defend this order. To this day, very few African Americans or people of color live on Monument Avenue. Residential segregation and the ideas that rationalized it have had real material consequences. Consequences that are as real as the artifacts unearthed in the cornerstone box.

Since 2021, very little has happened on Monument Avenue or with what remains of the statues. The City of Richmond currently has no plan to imagine the future of Monument Avenue. People have demanded very little after removal and politicians have obliged the silence. Lee Circle is now filled with mulch, plants, and trees. Its current state, in the words of one Monument Avenue resident, Caroline Bowers, "diminishes the historical significance of the place."[22] The Black History Museum & Culture Center of Virginia is currently in possession of most of the statues that once lined Monument Avenue. They have not declared what they plan to do with the statuary. There is, however, one notable exception to this lethargy—the Valentine Museum and its recumbent display of the Jefferson Davis statue. In the middle of the museum's first floor, "Davis lies covered in graffiti and damaged from his fall—with a large gash in his upper right arm and a severely smushed face. Tufts of toilet paper clump to the pink paint around his neck, where a noose placed by protestors formerly hung."[23] The Davis statue is also surrounded by historical context—curators have encircled the statue with language that more accurately describes slavery, the Civil War, and Jim Crow segregation.

Apart from the Jefferson Davis exhibit at Richmond's Valentine Museum, removal has, for many, facilitated what experts feared forgetting. Removing statuary and examining the contents of cornerstone boxes was merely the beginning of a more complex phase—a phase that requires coming to terms with hard, tortured history. In fact, negotiating this history will require a diverse range of input. Monument Avenue now needs what it failed to have at its creation—diversity (e.g., landscape architects, urban planners, local people, political representatives, artists, educators, scholars, children, and others).

Reconciliation requires recognition. Cities are never blank slates—they are the result of brilliant human innovation and human limitations. We know now that historical actors brought their biases to bear on the development of cities like Richmond, and without knowledge of the history, we will struggle to designs cities of the future. Can civic and community actors design spaces that reflect true democratic input? Can we use Monument Avenue as an education tool—a vehicle, if you will, for truth and reconciliation? In an age characterized by heightened incivility, reimaging public space to facilitate public discourse could be used as a revolutionary tool—a tool toward a better understanding of Richmond's past and how that past paved the road to now.

NOTES

1. Jacquelyn Dowd Hall, "The Long Civil Rights Movement and the Political Uses of the Past," *The Journal of American History* 91, no. 4 (2005): 1233.
2. Julian Maxwell Hayter, *The Dream Is Lost: Voting Rights and the Politics of Race in Richmond, Virginia*, (Lexington: University of Kentucky Press, 2017), 2–3.
3. For more on Monument Avenue, see https://onmonumentave.com.
4. Thessaly La Force, Zoë Lescaze, Nancy Haas, and M. H. Miller, "The 25 Most Influential Works of Protest Art Since World War Two," *The New York Times Style Magazine*, October 15, 2020.
5. Heather Cox Richardson, *No Common Ground: Confederate Monuments and the Ongoing Fight for Racial Justice* (Chapel Hill: University of North Carolina Press), chapter 2.
6. The term "Jim Crow" emerged from minstrelsy. Jim Crow was a popular song and dance originated in the 1820s. By the 1830s, White minstrel performer, Thomas "Daddy" Rice, had developed "Jim Crow" into a character using blackface. Thomas' antics, which interpreted and misinterpreted Black behavior eventually became synonymous with African American laziness, stupidity, and trickery. In time, "Jim Crow" came to embody what Whites thought of Blacks—the term Jim Crow became shorthand for Black people. Southerners eventually referred to these racial laws as "Jim Crow." On Jim Crow, see, Henry Louis Gates, Jr., *Stony the Road: Reconstruction, White Supremacy, and the Rise of Jim Crow* (New York: Penguin, 2019).
7. For interactive portrayal of the Jim Crow system, see https://americanhistory.si.edu/brown/history/1-segregated/jim-crow.html.
8. Julian Maxwell Hayter, "Vulnerability and a Truer Democracy," *On Monument Avenue*, May 12, 2018. https://onmonumentave.com/blog/2018/5/11/vulnerability-and-a-truer-democracy.
9. V. O. Key, *Southern Politics in State and Nation*, (New York: Knopf, 1949) and *Vote Here! Virginia's History of Voting and Elections* at https://henrico.us/pr/hctv-programs/?subject=history.
10. Julian Maxwell Hayter, "Revising Revisionism: Beyond the Lost Cause," *Voices: The Cheats Movement*, https://thecheatsmovement.com/voices-revising-revisionism-beyond-the-lost-cause-by-julian-hayter-ph-d/.

11. Kevin M. Levin, "Richmond's Confederate Monuments Were Used to Sell a Segregated Neighborhood," *The Atlantic*, June 11, 2020. https://www.theatlantic.com/ideas/archive/2020/06/its-not-just-the-monuments/612940/.
12. June Manning Thomas and Marsha Ritzdorf (eds.), *Urban Planning and the African American Community: In the Shadows*, (Thousand Oaks, CA: Sage Publications, 1997), chapter 2.
13. Hayter, *The Dream Is Lost*, 15.
14. Gary Gallagher and Alan T. Nolan, eds., *The Myth of the Lost Cause and Civil War History* (Bloomington: Indiana University Press, 2010).
15. Mildred Lewis Rutherford, *A Measuring Rod to Test Textbooks, and Reference Books in Schools, Colleges and Libraries* (New York: Forgotten Books, 2018).
16. Rutherford, *A Measuring Rod*.
17. Virginius Dabney, *Richmond: The Story of a City* (Charlottesville: University of Virginia Press, 1990).
18. Rex Springston, "Happy Slaves? The Peculiar Story of Three Virginia School Textbooks." *Richmond Times-Dispatch*, April 18, 2018.
19. https://www.people-press.org/2011/04/08/civil-war-at-150-still-relevant-still-divisive/.
20. Ed Grimsley, *Richmond Times-Dispatch*, March 17, 1959, 1–2.
21. Tracy Epp, *Dreams4RPS Goal 2: Graduation: Update for the Richmond City School Board*, Richmond City School Board Meeting, November 16, 2020, https://www.wric.com/wp-content/uploads/sites/74/2020/11/Goal-2-Graduation-Update-for-11-16-20-Board-Meeting.pdf.
22. Tyler Layne, "Richmond has no plan to reimagine the future of Monument Avenue," WTVR Richmond, April 17, 2024.
23. Ellie Alcorn, "Toppled Jefferson Davis Statue on Display at The Valentine," *VPM*, June 22, 2022. Editors' note: We left the reporter's quote intact, but it makes the common mistake of humanizing an inanimate object.

APPENDIX A

Contents of the Stonewall Jackson Monument Cornerstone Box

As published in the *Richmond Times-Dispatch* on June 4, 1915:

The box deposited yesterday afternoon in the corner-stone of the Stonewall Jackson equestrian statue at the intersection of Monument Avenue and the Boulevard contains articles suggestive of the historic occasion, redolent of the glorious past of the South and reflective of the current life of the former capital of the Confederacy. The list of contents of the box follows:

Badge of the twenty-fifth annual reunion of the United Confederate Veterans;
Badge of the R. E. Lee Camp, No. 1, Confederate Veterans;
Cross of honor;
Constitution of the Stonewall Camp, Portsmouth, with list of officers;
Program of the twenty-fifth annual reunion of the United Confederate Veterans;
Proceedings of the twenty-fifth, twenty-sixth, and twenty-seventh annual meetings of Grand Camp, Confederate Veterans of Virginia
Catalog of portrait gallery and library R. E. Lee Camp, No. 1, UCV
Uniform and dress of the army of the Confederate States
Package of Confederate money
Roster of the R. E. Lee Camp, No. 1, Confederate Veterans
"Stonewall Jackson at Chancellorsville," by James Power Smith, a member of his staff
A description of seal and flag of Virginia
Membership Chamber of Commerce, Richmond, 1915
Work of the (Virginia) State Board of Charities and Correction, 1914

The fiftieth anniversary of the First National Bank, Richmond, by Colonel John B. Purcell, president
Second annual report of the Administrative Board
Parade program for June 2, 1915
Richmond magazine for April 1915
Memory medal of the unveiling of the R. E. Lee Monument on May 29, 1890
One $1,000 7 percent Confederate States bond, No. 8387, bearing date February 20, 1863 with the picture of Lieutenant General Jackson on its face;
Ceremony laying corner-stone;
Book Grand Lodge of Virginia, 1915
Virginia textbook, Masonic
Dalcho consistory[1]
Steel engravings of prominent Masons, George Washington, John Blair, first grand master of Mason or Virginia and John Dove, grand secretary
Souvenir pictorial of beautiful Richmond
Photograph of General Jackson at Winchester, October 1862
Photograph and memoir of Julia Jackson, by her mother, Mrs. T. J. Jackson;
Scrapbook containing clippings related to General and Mrs. T. J. Jackson with an autograph letter from Mrs. Jackson, contributed by Mrs. G. T. W. Kern
Scrapbook of Confederate items, contributed by Mrs. Lizzie Cary Daniel

NOTE

1. Dalcho Consistory, No. 1 was established in 1890 in Richmond as a body within Scottish Rite Freemasonry. The group must have added some publication to the Davis cornerstone box. "Orient History," Orient of Virginia, https://www.vascottishrite.org/orient-history.

APPENDIX B

Contents of the Jefferson Davis Monument Cornerstone Box

As published in the *Times* on July 3, 1896:

The Grand-Treasurer read the inscription as follows: "Presented to the Davis monument by James E. Phillips, July 2, 1896."

Articles in the Box

"Guide to Richmond, Va., and the Battle-fields," and "Soldier Life in the Army of Northern Virginia, 1861–1865," by Carlton McCarthy, from the J. W. Randolph Company.

Souvenir Richmond Fire Department, 1894

Paperweight, Old Dominion Building and Loan Association, made from bronze used in casting Confederate Soldiers' and Sailors' monument, on Libby Hill, Richmond, Va., from J. Taylor Ellyson, president Jefferson Davis Monument Association.

One-hundred-dollar Confederate note, dated February 17, 1864, from J. L. Acree, Albany, Ga.

Newspaper, "The Day-Book," Norfolk, Va., dated April 19, 1862.

Warrock's Almanac, Virginia and North Carolina for the year 1864.

Four per cent, registered bond, Confederate States of American, $1,000

Six per cent, non-taxable certificate, Confederate States of America, $5,000.

Order of the Secretary of War G. W. Randolph for release of prison, dated 1862.

Autograph of D. B. Hill, major-general, 1865.

Two-thousand-dollar Confederate Government bond, 4 per cent.

Report of Commissioner Thompson Allen, August, 1864. Commissioner of Taxes for Confederate Government.

Masonic card, John F. Mayer, thirty-third degree, from John F. Mayer, agent Old Dominion Steamship Company.

One $50 and one $5 Confederate note, from Miss Cora Harrison.

Notice for meeting Executive and Advisory Committee for Entertainment of Veterans for the Sixth Annual Confederate Reunion.

Speech on Cuba, by Hon. Tazewell Ellet, in the House of Representatives, April 4, 1896.

Constitution and By-Laws of the Confederate Memorial Literary Society.

Thirteenth Annual Report of the Exchange for Woman's Work.

Handbook Association for the Preservation of Virginia Antiquities.

Programme Twenty-second Annual Commencement of the Richmond High School.

Programme Third Annual Music Festival of the Wednesday Club, Richmond, Va.

Picture of Baptist Cot, the Retreat for the Sick, Richmond, Va.

Circular for Ladies of the Hollywood Memorial Association, in reference to Organizing the Confederate Museum in the old Davis Mansion.

Register of the Second Baptist church, Richmond, Va., all presented by Mrs. J. Taylor Ellyson.

A Sketch of the origin of Decoration Day, founded April 26, 1865, Jackson, Miss., from Sue Landon Vaughan, "The Olives," Cuba.

Address of Hon. J. A. P. Campbell, on the Life and Character of Jefferson Davis, delivered before the Legislature of the State of Mississippi, January 22, 1890, from W. D. Holder, Jackson, Miss.

Photograph of Confederate Monument on Capitol Grounds, Jackson, Miss., from J. L. Power, Secretary of State, Miss.

Biographical Sketch of Jefferson Davis from Lour & McCardle's History of Mississippi, from J. L. Power, Secretary of State, Miss.

Constitution of rules for the Government of the Old Dominion Press Club, Richmond, Va.

Report of the Democratic National Committee meeting, Washington, DC, January 16, 1896.

Richmond Masonic Directory for 1893.

A valuable and interesting collection of Confederate notes, sent by Daniel S. Levy, Memphis, Tenn.

"The Golden City," a sermon by W.V. Tudor, D.D. from Alfred J. Gary.

Constitution and By-Laws of the Methodist Laymen's Union of Richmond, and Manchester, adopted May 20, 1890 from Alfred J. Gary.

An acrostic on Jefferson Davis, by Capers Dickson, Oxford, Ga.

Inside inscription, stamped in copper, “Presented to the Davis Monument by James E. Phillips, July 2, 1896.”

Reunion editions of Daily Dispatch, June 30, 1896; Richmond Times, State, Star, Richmond Progress, “The Jewish South.”

An official reunion badge, Sixth Annual Reunion United Confederate Veterans; laying corner-stone Jefferson Davis monument, June 30th, July 1st and 2d, 1896.

Mason programme of ceremony of laying the corner-stone

Badge of the R. T. W. Duke Camp, C. V. No. 1, from the Grand Senior Warden.

A $10 Confederate note, dated February 17, 1864, and a fifty-cent Confederate note of same date, from John F. Mayer.

Badge R. T. W. Duke Camp, No. 1, and badge of sixth annual reunion from Grand Senior Warden R. T. W. Duke, Jr.

Metal souvenir badge, Confederate army reunion.

Board proceedings of the 118th grand annual communication of the Most Worshipful Grand Lodge of Virginia from Grand Master J.P. Fitzgerald.

A polished chip of marble from the front step of the Jefferson Davis mansion, Richmond, from J.L. Bannon.

Prayer at laying of corner-stone, by Rev. George H. Ray, D.D., Grand Chaplain.

As published in the *Richmond Times-Dispatch* on April 12, 1907:

To the original contents of the box, which were found to be in excellent order, considering their damp location, a history of the present Davis Monument Association, written by Mrs. George S. Holmes, of Charleston, SC, president of the association was added. There was also placed in the collection a report of the Confederate Association of New Orleans, and plans of the monument, drawn by Noland & Baskervill. Among other relics deposited were the first and last ten-cent pieces taken in at the bazaar given for the benefit of the monument fund in the Masonic Temple several years ago.

APPENDIX C

Contents of Robert E. Lee Copper Cornerstone Box

Artifact Number	*Conservation Lab Number*	*Item name as it appears in the Richmond Dispatch 1887 inventory*	*Additional Items not in Historic Inventory*	*Notes, including titles as they appear on the object, which may differ from how it was listed in the Richmond Dispatch 1887 inventory*	*Associated Items*
	6878	Copper box containing items below			All other items on this list
CC023.01	6673	From George D. Fisher, compiled history of the Monumental church		Title reads: *History of the Monumental Church*, book, paper cover, wrapped in paper and twine; paper dust jacket over cover	Wrapped in paper and twine (CC023.02 & CC023.03)
CC023.02	6673		Paper wrapping, *History of the Monumental Church*	Handwritten note on paper	Covering *History of the Monumental Church* (CC023.01) bound with twine (CC023.03)
CC023.03	6673		Twine, *History of the Monumental Church*	Twine	Covering *History of the Monumental Church* (CC023.01) and envelope (CC023.02)
CC019.01	6669		Envelope	Fragment; contains muster roll and note	Roll of Company B, Twelfth Virginia Infantry (CC019.02) and paper reading "T. A. Brander" (CC019.03)
CC019.02	6669	T. A. Brander, Roll of Company B, Twelfth Virginia Infantry		Handwritten details, much of which has faded	Envelope fragment (CC019.01) and paper reading "T. A. Brander" (CC019.03)

Artifact Number	*Conservation Lab Number*	*Item name as it appears in the Richmond Dispatch 1887 inventory*	*Additional Items not in Historic Inventory*	*Notes, including titles as they appear on the object, which may differ from how it was listed in the Richmond Dispatch 1887 inventory*	*Associated Items*
CC019.03	6669		Note	"T. A. Brander" handwritten	Roll of Company B, Twelfth Virginia Infantry (CC019.02) and envelope (CC019.01)
CC011.01	6661		Envelope	Contains books, programme of banquet, and calling card	Constitution and by-laws of Lee Camp, Confederate Veterans (CC011.02), programme of banquet (CC011.03), and P. J. White calling card (CC011.04)
CC011.02	6661	P. J. White, constitution and by-laws of Lee Camp, Confederate Veterans		Title reads "By-Laws, rules of order and list of officers and members of R. E. Lee Camp, No.01, Confederate veterans, April 4th 1885", J. W. Fergusson & Sons, Printers; image of Lee on reverse; in envelope with reception menu (metal and paper) & calling card for P. J. White	Envelope (CC011.01), programme of banquet (CC011.03), P. J. White calling card (CC011.04)
CC011.03	6661		Programme of banquet for R. E. Lee Camp, No. 1	It is possible that the *Richmond Dispatch* had an error in the name of the programme and this is item listed as "programme of banquet to Lynn Post, No. 5"	Envelope (CC011.01), constitution and by-laws of Lee Camp, and P. J. White calling card (CC011.04)
CC011.04	6661		P. J. White calling card	In envelope with reception menu and "By-Laws, rules of order and list of officers and members of R. E. Lee Camp, No.01, Confederate veterans, April 4th 1885"	Envelope (CC011.01), constitution and by-laws of Lee Camp, Confederate Veterans (CC011.02), and programme of banquet (CC011.03)
CC007	6657	George T. Mattern, muster-roll of Richmond Sharpshooters, Twenty-first Virginia regiment			

Artifact Number	Conservation Lab Number	Item name as it appears in the Richmond Dispatch 1887 inventory	Additional Items not in Historic Inventory	Notes, including titles as they appear on the object, which may differ from how it was listed in the Richmond Dispatch 1887 inventory	Associated Items
CC077	6727	M. Staples & Co., copy of *Emigrants' Friend*		Title reads: *The Immigrant' Friend*, Published by Manning C. Staples & Co., handwritten note on back, red dye transfer on front, gild transfer on front	
CC018	6668	Mrs. H. A. Marshall, geneaelogical tree of the Lee family		By Mrs. H. A. Marshall, 1886	
CC006.01	6656		Envelope	Contains Confederate treasury notes	Confederate treasury notes (CC006.02–CC006.13)
CC006.02–CC006.13	6656	F. W. Jones, Confederate treasury notes		Twelve notes in envelope; one of the twelve notes recovered was donated from Master Nolting (see below)	Envelope (CC006.01)
CC013.01	6663		Envelope	Contains Confederate bond, photograph, and wax seal	$1,000,000 Confederate bond (CC013.02), photograph of Confederate cent (CC013.03), and wax seal (CC013.04)
CC013.02	6663	John F. Mayer, $100,000 Confederate bond, registered			Envelope (CC013.01), photograph of Confederate cent (CC013.03), and wax seal (CC013.04)
CC013.03	6663	John F. Mayer, photography-copy of Confederate cent		In envelope with wax seal and note with calling card. This is with wax seal, bond	Envelope (CC013.01), $1000,000 Confederate bond (CC013.02), and wax seal (CC013.04)
CC016.01	6666	J. H. Capers, roll of officers and members of Richmond Commandery, No. 2			J. H. Capers calling card (CC016.02)
CC016.02	6666		J. H. Capers calling card		Roll of officers and members of Richmond Commander, No.02 (CC016.01)
CC012.01	6662		Envelope	Contains English penny and Edward W. Price calling card	English penny 1812 (CC012.02), Edward W. Price calling card (CC012.03)

Artifact Number	*Conservation Lab Number*	*Item name as it appears in the Richmond Dispatch 1887 inventory*	*Additional Items not in Historic Inventory*	*Notes, including titles as they appear on the object, which may differ from how it was listed in the Richmond Dispatch 1887 inventory*	*Associated Items*
CC012.03	6662	J. H. Capers, individual card of Edward W. Price, General Commander, New Jersey			Envelope (CC012.01), English penny 1812 (CC012.02), Edward W. Price calling card (CC012.03)
CC015.01	6665	J. H. Capers, programme of the Ancient Order of Nobles of the Mystic Shrine on the occasion of the laying of the cornerstone		With Blair Meanley calling card and letter	Letter from Blair Meanley (CC015.02), Blaire Meanley calling card (CC015.03)
CC015.02	6665		Letter from Blair Meanley dated October 22, 1887		Programme of the Ancient Order of Nobles (CC015.01), Blair Meanley calling card (CC015.03)
CC015.03	6665	Blair Meanley calling card			Programme of the Ancient Order of Nobles (CC015.01), letter from Blair Meanley (CC015.02)
1886: CC0781887: CC079	1886: 67281887: 6729	George A. Ainslie, reports of the Chamber of Commerce for 1886 and 1887		*Reports of Chamber of Commerce., Richmond, VA*, two copies, 1886 & 1887	
CC064	6714	George A. Ainslie, constitution and by-laws of the Virginia Mechanics' Institute		1887, handwritten note on cover, unidentified letter adhered to reverse, "Lee Monument Box"	Unidentified letter (CC065)
CC069	6719	James E. Goode, Warrock-Richardson Virginia Almanac for 1887		Title reads: *The Warrock-Richardson Maryland, Virginia, and North Carolina Almanack for the Year of our Lord 1887*, James E Goode; handwritten note on cover; red dye transfered on reverse	
CC082	6732	J. W. Randolph & English, Soldiers' Life Army of Northern Virginia (by McCarthy)		Title reads: *Minutiae of Soldier Life listed below but not yet matched with an historic record entry? Check video. Page 157 confirmed; "CMoC" on spine*	Laying of the cornerstone badge (CC009) found on page 157

Artifact Number	Conservation Lab Number	*Item name as it appears in the Richmond Dispatch 1887 inventory*	*Additional Items not in Historic Inventory*	*Notes, including titles as they appear on the object, which may differ from how it was listed in the Richmond Dispatch 1887 inventory*	*Associated Items*
CC084	6734	J. W. Randolph & English, memorial volume of the Army of Northern Virginia		Reads: *Army of Northern Virginia Memorial Volume*; marbled paper on cover, leather binding, gilded lettering on spine	
CC062	6712	J. W. Randolph & English, a Guide to Richmond with maps of Richmond and Virginia		Reads: *Richmond, VA. A Guide to and Description of Its Principal Places and Objects of Interest.* Daniel Murphy 1881	
CC063	6713	J. W. Randolph & English, history of the First Battle of Manassas		Title reads: *Battle of Young's Branch or Manassas Plain, Fought July 21, 1861*, an account of the battle, T. B. Warder & Jas, M. Catlett; has small black card adhered to front	
CC070	6720	J. W. Randolph & English, Grantham's Historical Account of Some Memorable Actions in Virginia, 1716		*An Historical Account of Some Memorable Actions, Particularly in Virginia, Sir Thomas Grantham, Kt.; Sticker of bookseller adhered to front, "Randolph & English, Booksellers & Binders, Richmond, VA."; "x2" handwritten on front*	
CC072	6722	Emma R. Ball, report Mount Vernon Ladies' Association, 1887		Title reads: *Report of the Mt. Vernon Ladies' Association of the Union, 1887*	
CC005.01	6655	Miss Pattie Leake, picture of Lincoln lying in his coffin		Mended engraving by T. Nast in Harper's Weekly, possible reprint; mended	Mend (CC005.02)
CC005.02	6655		Mend for Lincoln engraving	Four fragments	Picture of Lincoln (CC005.01)
CC021.01	6671	W. H. Sands, programme Ancient Order Nobles of Mystic Shrine laying corner-stone of Lee Monument		With W. H. Sand lettercalling card associated?	Letter to W. B. Isaacs (CC021.02)

Artifact Number	Conservation Lab Number	Item name as it appears in the Richmond Dispatch 1887 inventory	Additional Items not in Historic Inventory	Notes, including titles as they appear on the object, which may differ from how it was listed in the Richmond Dispatch 1887 inventory	Associated Items
CC021.02	6671		W. H Sands letter to W. B. Isaacs		Programme Ancient Order of Nobles (CC021.01)
CC085	6671		W. B. Isaacs calling card with "H. L. Turner" / "Past Master Atlantic Lodge No. 2" name written on reverse		
CC025	6675	James Alfred Jones, *Weekly Dispatch* October 21, 1887, containing letter of Hon. W. W. Corcoran on General Lee			
CC073.01	6723	Miss Nettie Lee Brown, W. Gordon McCabe's address at the reunion of Pegram's battalion		Reads: *"Annual Reunion Pegram Battalion Association, Hal of the House of Delegates, Richmond, Va. May 21st, 1886."; Adhered to Grand Officers and Their Addresses*, 1886	
CC073.02	6723	Miss Nettie Lee Brown, W. Gordon McCabe's address at the reunion of Pegram's Battalion		Notice Pegram Battalion Association	
CC002	6652	Miss Nettie Lee Brown, picture of memorial window of Pegram's battalion at Soldiers' Home		Photograph, reproduction; mounted on card	
CC020.01-CC020.03	6670	C. S. DeVilliers, programme of three exhibitions by Bremond Institute for benefit of Lee monument fund		Three paper announcements for fundraising at the Norfolk Opera House, two dated June 22, 1876, one dated January 19, 1876.	
CC076	6726	William B. Isaacs, Richmond Directory		*Chataigne's Richmond Directory 1885*, W.E. Simons & Bro. Vol 24	

Artifact Number	*Conservation Lab Number*	*Item name as it appears in the Richmond Dispatch 1887 inventory*	*Additional Items not in Historic Inventory*	*Notes, including titles as they appear on the object, which may differ from how it was listed in the Richmond Dispatch 1887 inventory*	*Associated Items*
CC014.01			Envelope (wrapping)	Contains newspapers	Twine (CC014.02), rubber band (CC014.03), *Daily Dispatch Jan. 2, 1883 (CC014.04), Daily Dispactch* Dec. 2, 1868 (CC014.05), *The State* Apr. 2, 1887 (CC014.06), *Richmond Times* Oct. 23, 1887 (CC014.07)
CC014.04	6664		*Daily Dispatch*, January 2, 1883		Envelope (CC014.01), twine (CC014.02), rubber band (CC014.03), *Daily Dispactch* Dec. 2, 1868 (CC014.05), *The State* Apr. 2, 1887 (CC014.06), *Richmond Times* Oct. 23, 1887 (CC014.07)
CC014.05	6664		*Daily Dispatch*, December 2, 1886 Confirmed this is 1868		Envelope (CC014.01), twine (CC014.02), rubber band (CC014.03), *Daily Dispatch* Jan. 2, 1883 (CC014.04), *The State* Apr. 2, 1887 (CC014.06), *Richmond Times* Oct. 23, 1887 (CC014.07)
CC014.06	6664		*The State*, second edition, April 2, 1887,		Envelope (CC014.01), twine (CC014.02), rubber band (CC014.03), *Daily Dispatch* Jan. 2, 1883 (CC014.04), *Daily Dispactch* Dec. 2, 1868 (CC014.05), *Richmond Times* Oct. 23, 1887 (CC014.07)
CC014.07	6664	Richmond *Times*, copy of paper of 23rd October, 1887		*The Daily Times,* October 23, 1887	Envelope (CC014.01), twine (CC014.02), rubber band (CC014.03), *Daily Dispatch* Jan. 2, 1883 (CC014.04), *Daily Dispactch* Dec. 2, 1868 (CC014.05), *The State* Apr. 2, 1887 (CC014.06)

Artifact Number	*Conservation Lab Number*	*Item name as it appears in the Richmond Dispatch 1887 inventory*	*Additional Items not in Historic Inventory*	*Notes, including titles as they appear on the object, which may differ from how it was listed in the Richmond Dispatch 1887 inventory*	*Associated Items*
CC067	6617	Thomas J. Starke, one Holy Bible		Likely leather bound; descendents have been in contact by email—KCR confirmed bound in embossed leather; page edges gilded	
CC003 & CC004	6653 & 6654	W. B. Isaacs, copies of charters issued by Grand Lodge, Grand Chapter, and Grand Commandery of Virginia to its subordinates (on parchment)		On parchment, 2 copies, no date	
CC024.01	6674	Grand Lodge of Virginia, copy Grand Constitution of Grand Encampment United States Knights Templars and proceeding 1886		Bound; reads: *Grand Encampment of U.S. 1886*; cloth with gilded lettering; bound in paper and twine	Paper wrapping (CC024.02), twine (CC024.03)
CC024.02	6674		Paper wrapping *Grand Encampment of U.S. 1886*	Bound with twine	*Grand Encampment of U.S. 1886* (CC024.01), twine (CC024.03)
CC024.03	6674		Twine *Grand Encampment of U.S. 1886*	Around paper wrapping	*Grand Encampment of U.S. 1886* (CC024.01), twine (CC024.02)
CC071	6721	Programme of exercises observed on occasion of laying of Lee-monument cornerstone		Reads: *Programme of Exercises Grand Lodge of Va. A. F. & A. M. Laying of the Cornerstone of Lee Monument Thursday October 27th, 1887*, Published by William Ellis Jones, book and job printer 1887; Pam	
CC022.01	6672		Cover sheet		Letter from Mr. George A. Notting (CC022.02), $10 Confederate note (CC022.03)
CC022.02	6672		Letter from Mr. George A. Notting regarding son's contribution		Cover sheet (CC022.01), $10 Confederate note (CC022.03)

Artifact Number	Conservation Lab Number	Item name as it appears in the Richmond Dispatch 1887 inventory	Additional Items not in Historic Inventory	Notes, including titles as they appear on the object, which may differ from how it was listed in the Richmond Dispatch 1887 inventory	Associated Items
CC022.03	6672		$10 confederate notes with letter from Mr. Georege A. Notting (father) to son		Cover sheet (CC022.01), letter from Mr. George A. Notting (CC022.02)
CC068	6718		Unidentified textbook	This could be either "Grand Lodge of Virginia, fourth edition of Grand Lodge Text-Book" or "Grand Lodge of Virginia, copy of Text-Book Grand Chapter of Virginia and Digest" "RO . . ." / "AR . . ." / "TEXTBOOK"; cloth cover	
CC066	6716		Unidentified Masonic booklet	"Richmond Commandary" / "ENTOTT . . . I" / "NIKA"; PAPER SHEET PARTIALLY EXPOSED FROM BOTTOM OF BOOK	
			Army of the Northern Virginia Memorial Volume	Leather bound	
CC083.01	6733		*Proceedings of the Grand Lodge of Virginia, 1886*	This could be the "Copy of Proceedings, 1886. Grand Lodge, Grand Chapter, and Grand Commandery of Virginia"; bound in paper and twine	Paper wrap (CC083.02), twine (CC083.03)
CC083.02	6733		Paper wrapping *Proceedings of the Grand Lodge of Virginia 1886*	Bound in twine	*Proceedings of the Grand Lodge of Virginia 1886* (CC083.01), twine (CC083.03)
CC083.03	6733		Twine *Proceedings of the Grand Lodge of Virginia 1886*	Bound around paper wrapping	*Proceedings of the Grand Lodge of Virginia 1886 (CC083.01), twine (CC083.02)*
CC080	6730		*1886 Annual Convocation of the Grand Chapter of the State of Virginia*	*1886–7 Grand Officers and their Addresses.* Printed on reverse	

Artifact Number	Conservation Lab Number	Item name as it appears in the Richmond Dispatch 1887 inventory	Additional Items not in Historic Inventory	Notes, including titles as they appear on the object, which may differ from how it was listed in the Richmond Dispatch 1887 inventory	Associated Items
CC074	6724			"1886–7 / Grand Officers and their Addresses."; adhered to "Annual Reunion Pegram Battalion Hall of the House of Delegates" (CC073)	
CC075	6725		*Virginia Text-book*, Dove, Fourth Edition	This could be "Grand Lodge of Virginia, fourth edition of Grand Lodge Text-Book"	
CC081	6731		*Proceedings of the M. W. Grand Lodge of Ancient York Masons of the State of Virginia, from Its Organization, in 1778, to 1822, Prefaced by an Introduction Setting Forth the Origin and Progress of Masonry in Virginia, from 1733 to 1778*, by John Dove, G.S. / Volume I / Richmond; Printed by James E Goode. 1874		
CC008.01	6658		Envelope	Contains letter and badge corner-stone parade	Letter (CC008.02), badge corner-stone parade (CC008.03)
CC008.02	6658		Letter		Envelope (CC008.01), badge corner-stone parade (CC008.03)
CC055.01	6705		Paper wrapped around two mini-balls		Two whole mini-balls (CC055.02 & CC055.03)
CC054	6704	Cyrus Bossieux, Virginia Confederate buttons		One button	
CC017.01	6667		Envelope for battle flag and compass		Square and compass (CC017.02), battle flag (CC017.03)
CC017.02	6667	J. W. Talley, square and compass made from the tree over Stonewall Jackson's grave		Wood	Envelope (CC017.01), battle flag (CC017.03)

Artifact Number	Conservation Lab Number	*Item name as it appears in the Richmond Dispatch 1887 inventory*	*Additional Items not in Historic Inventory*	*Notes, including titles as they appear on the object, which may differ from how it was listed in the Richmond Dispatch 1887 inventory*	*Associated Items*
CC017.03	6667	J. W. Talley, battle flag made from the tree over Stonewall Jackson's grave		Wood	Envelope (CC017.01), square and compass (CC017.02)
CC029–CC041	6679–6691	Charles E. and Walter B. Harwood, twelve copper coins		Individually wrapped in paper, bound in twine	Paper wrapping (CC029.01), note (CC029.02), twine (CC029.03), coins (CC030–CC041)
CC029.01	6679		Outer wrapping of 12 coins		Note (CC029.02), twine (CC029.03), coins (CC030—CC041)
CC029.02	6679		Note		Paper wrapping (CC029.01), twine (CC029.03), coins (CC030—CC041)
CC029.03	6679		Twine wrapped around paper, note, and 12 copper coins from Charles E. and Walter B.		Paper wrapping (CC029.01), note (CC029.02), , coins (CC030—CC041)
CC009	6659	Carlton McCarthy, badge of the Association of Army Northern Virginia	Laying the Corner Stone Lee Monument Richmond, VA October 27, 1887	Found in *Minutiae of a Soldier's Life*, page 157 (CC082)	
CC012.02	6662	W. T. Mosely, English penny of 1812		In envelope with calling card of Edward W. Price	
CC059	6709	Master Frank Brown, piece of a stone wall, Fredericksburg, VA		One rock was in the box, it is not yet determined if this is the piece of stone wall listed	
CC027	6677		Rock		
CC055.02–CC055.03	6705		Two whole mini balls	Wrapped in paper	Paper wrapping (CC055.01)
CC056	6706		Whole miniball		
CC057	6707		Partially flattened miniball		
CC058	6708		Flattened miniball		

Artifact Number	Conservation Lab Number	Item name as it appears in the Richmond Dispatch 1887 inventory	Additional Items not in Historic Inventory	Notes, including titles as they appear on the object, which may differ from how it was listed in the Richmond Dispatch 1887 inventory	Associated Items
CC028	6678	Master Frank Brown, one piece of shell from Fredericksburg		Iron	
CC026	6676	Master Frank Brown, one piece of wood with minie-ball in it from battlefield of Fredericksburg		Wood and lead	
		Master Frank Brown, a cut from a tree at the Bloody Angle, Spotsylvania			
CC053	6703	C. S. DeVilliers, a button from coat of Captain Bremond			
CC049–CC052	6699–6702	William B. Isaacs, assortment of United States silver and copper coins			
CC013.04	6663	John F. Mayer, copy of seal of the Adjutant-General of the Confederate States			Envelope (CC013.01), $1000,000 Confederate bond (CC013.02), photograph of Confederate cent (CC013.03), and wax seal (CC013.04)
CC042	6692	Carlton McCarthy, one United States silver dollar, 1886			
CC043–CC048	6693–6698	J. Thompson Brown, assortment of United States fractional coins			Includes paper wrapped around coins
CC060	6710	Mortar			
CC061	6711	Wood fragment		Two mendable pieces	
CC023.03	6673		Twine wrapping *History of Monumental Church*		*History of the Monumental Church* (CC023.01) and paper wrapping (CC023.02)

Artifact Number	Conservation Lab Number	*Item name as it appears in the Richmond Dispatch 1887 inventory*	*Additional Items not in Historic Inventory*	*Notes, including titles as they appear on the object, which may differ from how it was listed in the Richmond Dispatch 1887 inventory*	*Associated Items*
CC014.02	6664		Twine wrapped around newspapers		Envelope (CC014.01), rubber band (CC014.03), *Daily Dispatch* Jan. 2, 1883 (CC014.04), *Daily Dispactch* Dec. 2, 1868 (CC014.05), *The State* Apr. 2, 1887 (CC014.06), *Richmond Times* Oct. 23, 1887 (CC014.07)
CC014.03	6664		Rubber band found with newspapers		Envelope (CC014.01), twine (CC014.02), *Daily Dispatch* Jan. 2, 1883 (CC014.04), *Daily Dispactch* Dec. 2, 1868 (CC014.05), *The State* Apr. 2, 1887 (CC014.06), *Richmond Times* Oct. 23, 1887 (CC014.07)
CC024.03	6674		Twine wrapped around *Grand Encampment of U.S. 1886*		*Grand Encampment of U.S. 1886* (CC024.01), paper wrapping (CC024.02)
CC083.03	6733		Twine *Proceedings of the Grand Lodge of Virginia 1886*		*Proceedings of the Grand Lodge of Virginia* 1886 (CC083.01), paper wrap (CC083.02)
CC008.03	6658	Carlton McCarthy, badge of the Association of Army Northern Virginia		With paper badge in envelope	Envelope (CC008.01), letter (CC008.02), badge corner-stone parade (CC008.03)
CC010	6660	Miss Nettie Lee Brown, Gray and Blue badge		California regiment 71 PA dedication of Monument and Reception of Pickett's division Gettysburg PA July, 2–4, 1887	
CC009	6659	J. W. Randolph & English, badge corner-stone parade			Found in *Minutiae of Soldier Life* on page 157 (CC0082)

CONTRIBUTORS

Patrick J. Boyle is currently a PhD student in Texas A&M University's nautical archaeology program and is the former assistant underwater archaeologist at Virginia Department of Historic Resources. He received an MPhil in 2017 from the University of Bristol and an MA from East Carolina University's Program in maritime studies in 2022.

Brendan Burke is the underwater archaeologist for the Virginia Department of Historic Resources (VDHR). He holds a BA in history and anthropology from Longwood College and an MA in anthropology from William & Mary. Prior to VDHR, Burke was the assistant director of research at the Lighthouse Archaeology Maritime Program in St. Augustine, Florida. His maritime research includes inland navigations of Virginia, vernacular Chesapeake watercraft, and the development of historic fisheries. In 2013 he coauthored *Shrimp Boat City* with Ed Long, which documented the construction of the largest wooden fishing fleet in the United States.

Maggie Creech received her BA in history and archaeology from the George Washington University and an MA in archaeology from the University College of London. She currently serves as director of education at the Virginia Museum of History & Culture, overseeing a talented staff focused on in-person and virtual learning experiences, community-based public programming, and teacher outreach. She has more than a decade of experience in public history, archaeology, and education and is passionate about the power of place and objects to create past-present connections and build empathy.

Adam H. Domby is associate professor of history at Auburn University and the author of *The False Cause: Fraud, Fabrication, and White Supremacy in Confederate Memory*.

Sue Donovan is the conservator for special collections at the University of Virginia Library. She earned her master's in the Conservation Restauration des Biens Culturels (Conservation of Cultural Heritage) at the Université de Paris Panthéon-Sorbonne specializing in Book and Paper.

Sam Florer is the manager of public programs with the Virginia Museum of History and Culture. With more than ten years of experience working in museum settings, focusing on education and public engagement, Sam also works as a historical researcher and writer, specializing in eighteenth- and nineteenth-century American history.

Laura Galke has thirty-five years of experience doing archaeology in the Middle Atlantic region in various roles including field director for a number CRM firms, chief curator at the Department of Historic Resources, field director/artifact analyst at The George Washington Foundation, anthropology instructor at Washington and Lee University, and assistant regional archaeologist for the Maryland Department of Housing and Community Development. They have published a number of peer-reviewed articles, and they currently work at the Washington Heritage Museums in Fredericksburg, Virginia. They possess a master's degree from Arizona State University and a bachelor's degree from George Mason University.

Erik Goldstein, senior curator of mechanical arts, metals, and numismatics at the Colonial Williamsburg Foundation, with a BA in fine arts/illustration from Parsons School of Design, is a lifelong student of the numismatics, arms, militaria, and material culture of the seventeenth and eighteenth centuries and a regular speaker at conferences across the United States. He has written more than three dozen articles in both specialties and six books relating to antique weaponry and military history.

Christopher A. Graham, curator of the American Revolution at the South Carolina State Museum. He is the author of *Faith, Race, and the Lost Cause: Confessions of a Southern Church*.

Julian Maxwell Hayter, a historian and associate professor in the Jepson School of Leadership Studies at the University of Richmond, is the author of *The Dream Is Lost: Voting Rights and the Politics of Race in Richmond, Virginia* and *The Making of Modern Richmond*.

Caroline E. Janney, John L. Nau III Professor in History of the American Civil War and director for the John L. Nau III Center for Civil War History at the University of Virginia, is the author of *Burying the Dead but Not the Past: Ladies' Memorial Associations and the Lost Cause* (2008), *Remembering the Civil War: Reunion and the Limits of Reconciliation* (2013), and *Ends of War: The Fight of Lee's Army After Appomattox* (2021).

Robert L. Jolley is the archaeologist for the Northern Regional Preservation office at the Virginia Department of Historic Resources.

Ervin L. Jordan Jr. is associate professor and research archivist at the University of Virginia's Albert and Shirley Small Special Collections Library and specializes in Civil War, African American, and Virginia history. He is the author of three books including *Black Confederates and Afro-Yankees in Civil War Virginia* (University Press of Virginia, 1995) and has published articles, blogs, book chapters, essays, playbills, and reviews for a variety of publications including the *Encyclopedia Virginia*. The subject of a *Wikipedia* entry, Professor Jordan serves on the Virginia American Revolution 250 Commission (VA250)'s African American Advisory Council and Virginia's State Historical Records Advisory Board.

Lea Lane (UVA BA 2012) is the curator of the Museum of Early Southern Decorative Arts (MESDA) and director of the MESDA Summer Institute.

Laura Lavernia is a former project review architectural historian at the Virginia Department of Historic Resources. Currently, she is a historic preservation program manager for US Customs and Border Protection.

Elizabeth A. Moore is the state archaeologist for the Virginia Department of Historic Resources. She holds an MA and PhD in anthropology from the American University. From 1996 to 2019, she was a curator at the Virginia Museum of Natural History where she established the archaeology program.

Katherine Ridgway is the state archaeological conservator for the Virginia Department of Historic Resources. She has her BA from The College of William and Mary in anthropology and classical studies and her MA in conservation of historic objects from the University of Durham in the United Kingdom. Prior to her current position she worked at Colonial Williamsburg, the National Museums of Scotland, The Field Museum, and George Washington's Mount Vernon. She works with professionals and the public around the Commonwealth to promote the preservation of the state's rich cultural heritage and led the team that opened the containers found under the Robert E. Lee Monument on Monument Avenue.

John S. Salmon (UVA BA 1970; W&M MA 1976), historian, was an archivist at the Library of Virginia (1973–1987), historian at the Virginia Department of Historic Resources (1987–2001) and the Tredegar National Civil War Center (2001–2004). He wrote *The Official Virginia Civil War Battlefield Guide* (2001), *Historic Photos of the Siege of Petersburg* (2007), and *Historic Photos of Gettysburg* (2007). He also wrote and edited interpretive markers and brochure texts for Virginia Civil War Trails, Inc., a nonprofit educational corporation (1994–2021). He continues to coauthor National Register of Historic Places nominations with architectural historians.

Hannah Sanner is a former conservation intern at the Virginia Department of Historic Resources who is currently pursuing an MS in the conservation of archaeological and museum objects at Durham University.

Sir Knight Peter R. Spring, KCT, Right Eminent Past Grand Commander, The Grand Commandery Knights Templar of Virginia, was born in London, England, emigrated to the United States in 2003, and became a US Citizen in 2008. A Freemason for the past forty-nine years, Peter retired as a director of a $35 billion US company and now enjoys helping nonprofit organizations.

Christina Keyser Vida is the Elise H. Wright Curator of General Collections at the Valentine Museum in Richmond, Virginia. She has researched and curated exhibitions on a variety of Richmond history topics, including monuments, Edward Valentine, and the Lost Cause mythology.

INDEX

Italicized page numbers refer to illustrations.